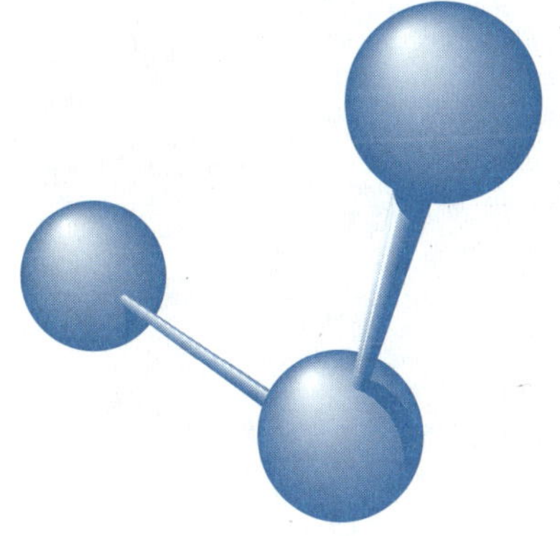

Word 2002

LEVEL 1

Word 2002

LEVEL 1

BRIAN FAVRO

RUSSEL STOLINS
Santa Fe Community College

Labyrinth Publications
3314 Morningside Drive
El Sobrante, California 94803
800.522.9746
labpub.com

Vice President of Marketing and Sales: David Gauny

Production Management, Design and Publishing Consultation: Seventeenth Street Studios

Composition: Seventeenth Street Studios

Printer: Courier, Kendallville

ISBN 1-59136-008-0

Manufactured in the United States of America.

10 9 8 7 6 5 4 3 2

Contents

Introduction to Labyrinth

Welcome to Labyrinth Publications, where you'll find your course to success. Our real world, project-based approach to education helps students grasp concepts—not just read about them—and prepares them for success in the workplace. Our books are written in straightforward, easy-to-follow language that is perfect for instructor-led classes and self-paced labs. At Labyrinth, we're dedicated to one purpose: delivering quality courseware that is comprehensive, effective, and affordable. It's no wonder that in just 10 years Labyrinth has become a recognized leader in Microsoft Office and operating systems courseware.

Labyrinth offers two primary courseware series for educational and professional training:

ProStart Series

Formerly our Off to Work Series, the full-length ProStart Series walks students through each application, from basics to advanced. These lessons are comprehensive and easy to read. The new ProStart Series offers many enhancements over previous versions, including streaming media videos for every lesson and a revised page design for increased clarity. New to this series is the Office XP Comprehensive Course. This book is ideal for introductory computer classes and also offers advanced topics, such as mail merge and projects with in-depth integration between applications.

Briefcase Series

A popular choice for schools and industry training programs, the Briefcase Series is designed for short-term classes and accelerated one-, two-, and three-day workshops. Each lesson is broken down into subtopics that provide quick access to key concepts. The result is a unique structure ideal for fast-paced lecturing. Briefcase books work well in 6- to 8-hour instructor-led workshops and self-paced courses lasting 25- to 35-hours. To ensure reinforcement of skills, the Briefcase Series now includes all of the end-of-lesson exercises found in the ProStart Series.

Labyrinth and the Microsoft Office User Specialist Program

Labyrinth teaches what the experts are using, and features the Microsoft Office User Specialist (MOUS) seal on each application textbook to guarantee it. Three Office XP certification levels are available: Core, Expert, and the new Comprehensive certification for PowerPoint. For easy reference, the exam objectives covered in each lesson are summarized at the beginning of each chapter.

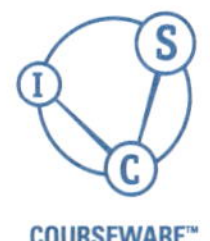

Integrated Courseware System (ICS)

Labyrinth's new Integrated Courseware System (ICS) provides a unique way for instructors to tailor their classes to MOUS exam objectives. Instructors can match the ProStart Office XP Comprehensive Course to advanced Briefcase titles without skipping or duplicating lessons. Level 1 and 2 Briefcase books now cover all exam objectives required for Core-level MOUS certification, while Level 3 books cover the Expert-level objectives.

New Features for Word 2002 Courseware

Streaming Video Demonstrations

Labyrinth now offers on-screen video demonstrations to supplement key exercises. These provide another layer of instruction that is particularly beneficial to audiovisual learners. Videos are immediately available from the Labyrinth website at **labpub.com** (under Student Resources) in streaming and downloadable formats. These videos are also available to schools on CD-ROM, though not to students directly. See your Labyrinth sales representative for details.

WebSim Multimedia Content

WebSim

No-cost multimedia supplements for classrooms are also available. From art and photography to entire web-based simulations that supplement the text, WebSims offer multiple benefits to both students and instructors:

- Content is always available, eliminating confusion caused by web pages that have been changed or removed.
- Simulations offer better classroom control, preventing students from wandering to unrelated sites.
- Network firewalls and restrictions on student email accounts can be circumvented, minimizing security issues while providing a full learning experience.

WebSims are immediately available from the Labyrinth website at **labpub.com** (under Student Resources). They're also available to schools on CD-ROM, though not to students directly. See your sales representative for details.

Enhanced Instructor Resources

To back your success, Labyrinth has improved the instructor support package for the ProStart and Briefcase Series texts. For example, the new instructor support CD-ROM features a graphic user-interface for easier navigation to a host of available support materials. Features include:

- Printer-friendly solutions guides, additional project-based Assessment exercises, and comprehensive course outlines and lecture notes.
- TestComposer™ software that allows convenient Microsoft Word editing. New test bank questions can now be sorted by lesson and topic, rather than by question type. Each lesson includes dozens of true/false and multiple choice questions, all of which can be modified using the TestComposer™ software.
- Complete PowerPoint presentations for every ProStart and Briefcase title to bring lectures to life.

Instructors can also visit the new Labyrinth website at **labpub.com** for additional resources, including online discussion boards for sharing ideas and the new Projects Page for downloading or posting projects created for classroom use. Look under the Educators Resource section.

Concept discussions are concise and use illustrations for added clarity.

Important information is highlighted with icons placed in the margin. Reference items and tips are presented without cluttering the page.

Quick Reference tables provide summaries of the steps needed to complete key tasks. A list of these tables appears at the beginning of the book, providing excellent at-a-glance reference.

Hands-On exercises immediately follow concept discussions to reinforce learning. As a result, students spend less time reading and more time in the applications.

Tightly integrated text and screen captures clearly demonstrate topics—perfect for instructor-led and self-paced classes.

AutoSum

The power of Excel becomes apparent when you begin using formulas and functions. The most common type of calculation is when a column or row of numbers is summed. In fact, this type of calculation is so common that Excel provides the AutoSum function specifically for this purpose.

FROM THE KEYBOARD
ALT+= for AutoSum

The AutoSum Σ button on the Standard toolbar automatically sums a column or row of numbers. When you click AutoSum, Excel proposes a range of numbers. You can accept the proposed range or drag in the worksheet to select a different range. When you complete the entry, Excel inserts a SUM function in the worksheet, which adds the numbers in the range.

QR

QUICK REFERENCE: EXPLODING PIE CHARTS	
Explode one slice.	■ Click once to select the entire pie. ■ Click the slice you wish to explode.
Explode all slices.	■ Click once to select the pie. ■ Drag any slice (without clicking first), and all slices will separate.

Hands-On 1.9 Use AutoSum

In this exercise, you will use AutoSum to calculate several totals. Keep in mind that this section provides an introduction to formulas. You will learn more about formulas as you progress through this course.

Calculate One Column Total

1. Click Cell C8.
2. Click the AutoSum Σ button.
3. Follow these steps to review the formula and complete the entry.

SIN ▾ ✕ ✓ fx =SUM(C5:C7)

	A	B	C	D
1	Computer Depot Weekly Sales Data			
2			Wednesday	Thursday
3				
4	PCs		3	10
5		Compaq	4	8
6		IBM	6	13
7		Acer		
8		Total	=SUM(C5:C7)	

A Notice that Excel proposes the formula =SUM(C5:C7) in Cell 8 and in the Formula bar. All formulas begin with an equal (=) sign. SUM is a built-in function that adds the numbers in a range (in this example the range is C5:C7).

B Notice the flashing marquee surrounding the range C5:C7. AutoSum assumes you want to add together all cells above C8 until the first empty cell is reached. The marquee identifies this range of cells.

C Click the Enter ✓ button on the Formula bar to complete the entry. The total should be 13.

(Continued on the next page)

Lessons end with brief true/false and multiple choice sections, but the teaching goes much further. Project-based Skill Builder exercises present hands-on projects with only moderate assistance, while project-based Assessment exercises offer less assistance and require even more independent thought. Finally, Critical Thinking exercises provide complex word problems to thoroughly test skill mastery.

Skill Builders

Skill Builder 6.1 Create a Column Chart

In this exercise, you will create a column chart to display student enrollments at a university.

Expand a Series

1. Open the workbook named Skill Builder 6.1.
   Notice that the enrollment data has been completed in Column B, but the years have not been completed in Column A. Notice the first two years (1985 and 1986) form the beginning of the series 1985–2001. The best way to expand this series is with the fill handle.
2. Select Cells A4 and A5.
3. Drag the fill handle down to Row 20 to expand the series.
4. Left align the years in Column A.

Distance Learning Courses

Labyrinth offers quality distance learning courses for WebCT and Blackboard platforms that leverage the strengths of both online and print-based content to deliver a rich learning experience. These platforms provide everything instructors need to get their classes up and running, including a customization guide so that instructors can modify courses to meet their specific curriculum requirements and teaching styles.

WebCT and Blackboard Courseware Features

Instructors and students can experience the promise of the Internet for online teaching and learning, campus communities, and integration of web-enabled student services. Labyrinth's distance learning courses run on Blackboard and WebCT Standard and Campus editions and are available for various Off to Work and ProStart titles, including the Office XP Comprehensive Course, Office XP Essentials Course, Word 2002, and Excel 2002 texts. Each lesson contains multimedia resources and online Concepts Review and Assessment tests that can be used as-is or customized to meet individual teaching styles. Production tasks for testing are also included—complete with instructions on how to deliver assignments as email attachments and with drop-box features. Another feature of Labyrinth's distance learning courses is online multimedia, including highly compressed streaming videos that are easily delivered over modem-based Internet connections.

To find out more about implementing a Blackboard or WebCT distance-learning program at your campus, please contact your Labyrinth sales representative.

Company Contact Information

To learn more about Labyrinth products and resources, or to find a sales representative in your area, please visit our website at labpub.com.

Labyrinth's dedicated customer service staff is available to assist you with ordering, billing, and any other issue between 7:30 AM and 5:00 PM [PST].

Labyrinth Publications, Inc.
3314 Morningside Dr.
El Sobrante, CA 94803
(800) 522-9746
(510) 222-7925 Fax
custserv@labpub.com

Word 2002 Keyboard Summary Sheet

NAVIGATION

Beginning of document	CTRL+HOME
Beginning of line	HOME
Browse object menu (displaying)	ALT+CTRL+HOME
End of document	CTRL+END
End of line	END
Go To	CTRL+G
Next paragraph	CTRL+↓
Next word	CTRL+←
Previous paragraph	CTRL+↑
Previous word	CTRL+→

SELECTING

Beginning of line	SHIFT+HOME
Document	CTRL + A
End of line	SHIFT+END
Text	SHIFT while tapping arrow keys

EDITING

Copy while dragging	CTRL
Copy	CTRL+C
Cut	CTRL+X
Delete to beginning of word	CTRL+BACKSPACE
Delete to end of word	CTRL+DELETE
Find	CTRL+F
Paste	CTRL+V
Redo	CTRL+Y
Repeat	CTRL+Y
Replace	CTRL+H
Show/hide nonprinting characters	CTRL+SHIFT+8
Spell check	F7
Spike (cutting to)	CTRL+F3
Spike (pasting contents)	CTRL+SHIFT+F3
Thesaurus	SHIFT+F7
Undo	CTRL+Z

FORMATTING

Bold	CTRL+B
Decrease font size one point	CTRL+[
Increase font size one point	CTRL+]
Indent (hanging)	CTRL+T
Indent (left)	CTRL+M
Indent (removing hanging)	CTRL+SHIFT+T
Indent (removing left)	CTRL+SHIFT+M
Italics	CTRL+I
Line spacing (1.5)	CTRL+5
Line spacing (double)	CTRL+2
Line spacing (single)	CTRL+1
Outline-style numbered list (demote)	TAB
Outline-style numbered list (promote)	SHIFT+TAB
Underline	CTRL+U

Word 2002 Keyboard Summary Sheet (continued)

DIALOG BOXES

Hyperlink	CTRL+K
Office Assistant (displaying)	F1
Office Assistant (hiding speech balloon)	ESC
Open	CTRL+O
Print	CTRL+P
Save As	CTRL+S
VBA editor window	ALT+F11

INSERTING AND UPDATING

Date (inserting)	ALT+SHIFT+D
Endnote (inserting)	ALT+CTRL+D
Footnote (inserting)	ALT+CTRL+F
Index entries (marking)	ALT+SHIFT+X
Nonbreaking hyphens (inserting)	CTRL+SHIFT
Nonbreaking spaces (inserting)	CTRL+SHIFT+SPACE BAR
Style list (displaying full list)	SHIFT while clicking style list button
Table of contents (updating)	F9
Time (inserting)	ALT+SHIFT+T

MAIL MERGE

Data form (displaying)	ALT+SHIFT+E
Insert Merge Fields box (displaying)	ALT+SHIFT+F
Merge to new document	ALT+SHIFT+N
Merge to printer	ALT+SHIFT+M

TABLES AND COLUMNS

Column break	CTRL+SHIFT+ENTER
Display column measurements	ALT while dragging column boundaries
Move back one cell	SHIFT+TAB
Move forward one cell	TAB
Use tabs within tables	CTRL+TAB

DRAWING OBJECTS

Draw circle	SHIFT while drawing new oval
Draw lines at 15-degree increments while drawing new line	SHIFT
Draw square while drawing new rectangle	SHIFT
Maintain proportions of existing oval while sizing existing oval	SHIFT
Maintain proportions of existing rectangle	SHIFT while sizing existing rectangle
Nudge object	CTRL while tapping arrow keys
Prevent object from snapping to grid	ALT while dragging object
Size object while maintaining proportions	SHIFT while sizing object

Quick Reference Index

Quick Reference tables contain generic instructions for performing tasks. They can be useful if you forget how to perform a particular task. You can use Quick Reference instructions to perform tasks long after your course is complete. The following index lists all Quick Reference tables in the *Word 2002 Briefcase Sequence.*

Quick Reference Index (continued)

MOUS Program

What Does This Logo Mean?

It means this courseware has been approved by the Microsoft Office User Specialist Program to be among the finest available for learning Word 2002. It also means that upon completion of this courseware, you may be prepared to become a Microsoft Office User Specialist.

What is a Microsoft Office User Specialist?

A Microsoft Office User Specialist is an individual who has certified skills in one or more Microsoft Office desktop applications such as Microsoft Word, Microsoft Excel, Microsoft PowerPoint, Microsoft Outlook, Microsoft Powerpoint, or Microsoft Project. The Microsoft Office User Specialist Program typically offers certification exams at the "Core" and "Expert" skill levels.* The Microsoft Office User Specialist Program is the only Microsoft-approved program in the world for certifying proficiency in Microsoft Office desktop applications and Microsoft Project. This certification can be a valuable asset in any job search or career advancement.

Which Exam(s) Will This Publication Prepare You To Take?

Word 2002: Level 1, Word 2002: Level 2, and *Word 2002: Level 3* used in combination have been approved by Microsoft as courseware for the Microsoft Office User Specialist program. After completing a two-course sequence, students will be prepared to take the Core level Word 2002 MOUS exam. After completing a three-course sequence, students will be prepared to take both the Core and Expert level Word 2002 MOUS exams.

More Information:

To learn more about becoming a Microsoft Office User Specialist, visit www.microsoft.com/mous

To purchase a Microsoft Office User Specialist certification exam, visit www.DesktopIQ.com

To learn about other Microsoft Office User Specialist approved courseware from Labyrinth Publications, visit labpub.com/mous.

* The availability of Microsoft Office User Specialist certification exams varies by application, application version, and language. Visit www.microsoft.com/mous for exam availability.

Word 2002
MOUS Exam Objectives Map

Core Level

MOUS Objective Number	MOUS Objective Description	Briefcase Level	Concept Page References	Exercise Page References
W2002-1	**Inserting and Modifying Text**			
W2002-1-1	Insert, modify and move text and symbols	1	15, 55, 85	15, 56–57, 85–87
W2002-1-1	Insert, modify and move text and symbols	2	18, 141–142	19–20, 142–144
W2002-1-2	Apply and modify text formats	1	53	53–54
W2002-1-3	Correct spelling and grammar usage	1	80–82, 84	81–84
W2002-1-4	Apply font and text effects	1	167–168	168–169
W2002-1-4	Apply font and text effects	2	138	139–140
W2002-1-5	Enter and format Date and Time	1	44	44–45
W2002-1-6	Apply character styles	2	70	109
W2002-2	**Creating and Modifying Paragraphs**			
W2002-2-1	Modify paragraph formats	1	50, 107–108	51, 107–109
W2002-2-1	Modify paragraph formats	2	8	8
W2002-2-2	Set and modify tabs	2	4, 6	5–7
W2002-2-3	Apply bullet, outline, and numbering format to paragraphs	1	128–131	128–133
W2002-2-3	Apply bullet, outline, and numbering format to paragraphs	2	83	84–86
W2002-2-4	Apply paragraph styles	2	70–71, 74	71–76
W2002-3	**Formatting Documents**			
W2002-3-1	Create and modify a header and footer	2	92–95	93–95
W2002-3-2	Apply and modify column settings	2	46–47	47–48
W2002-3-3	Modify document layout and Page Setup options	1	49, 122, 148	49–50, 122–123, 149–150
W2002-3-3	Modify document layout and Page Setup options	2	90–91	91–92
W2002-3-4	Create and modify tables	1	190, 193, 196–202, 205	191, 194–202, 210
W2002-3-4	Create and modify tables	2	49	49
W2002-3-5	Preview and Print documents, envelopes, and labels	1	26–27	26–27
W2002-3-5	Preview and Print documents, envelopes, and labels	2	21–22	21–24

MOUS Objective Number	MOUS Objective Description	Briefcase Level	Concept Page References	Exercise Page References
W2002-4	**Managing Documents**			
W2002-4-1	Manage files and folders for documents	2	164	165
W2002-4-2	Create documents using templates	2	9–11	12–13
W2002-4-3	Save documents using different names and file formats	1	12	13
W2002-4-3	Save documents using different names and file formats	2	164	165
W2002-5	**Working with Graphics**			
W2002-5-1	Insert images and graphics	1	154–157	157–159
W2002-5-2	Create and modify diagrams and charts	2	50, 54	51–52, 54–55
W2002-6	**Workgroup Collaboration**			
W2002-6-1	Compare and Merge documents	2	136–137	137–138
W2002-6-2	Insert, view and edit comments	2	125–131	128–132
W2002-6-3	Convert documents into Web pages	2	171	172–173

Expert Level

MOUS Objective Number	MOUS Objective Description	Briefcase Level	Concept Page References	Exercise Page References
W2002e-1	**Customizing Paragraphs**			
W2002e-1-1	Control Pagination	1	49	49–50
W2002e-1-1	Control Pagination	3	74	81–82
W2002e-1-2	Sort paragraphs in lists and tables	3	8	8-9
W2002e-2	**Formatting documents**			
W2002e-2-1	Create and format document sections	2	44, 81–82	63–64, 82–83
W2002e-2-2	Create and apply character and paragraph styles	2	70–78	71–80, 109
W2002e-2-3	Create and update document indexes and tables of contents, figures, and authorities	2	87–89, 96–99	88–90, 97–100
W2002e-2-4	Create cross-references	2	101–102	102–103
W2002e-2-5	Add and revise endnotes and footnotes	3	69–73	70–74
W2002e-2-6	Create and manage master documents and subdocuments	2	103–105	105–106
W2002e-2-7	Move within documents	2	86	87
W2002e-2-7	Move within documents	3	75	76
W2002e-2-8	Create and modify forms using various form controls	3	100–104	101–105
W2002e-2-9	Create forms and prepare forms for distribution	3	106	107

Word 2002 MOUS Exam Objectives Map (continued)

MOUS Objective Number	MOUS Objective Description	Briefcase Level	Concept Page References	Exercise Page References
W2002e-3	**Customizing Tables**			
W2002e-3-1	Use Excel data in tables	3	14–15	15–16
W2002e-3-1	Perform calculations in Word tables	3	4, 9–10	4–5, 11–12
W2002e-4	**Creating and Modifying Graphics**			
W2002e-4-1	Create, modify, and position graphics	3	37–42	38–44
W2002e-4-2	Create and modify charts using data from other applications	3	16	17
W2002e-4-3	Align text and graphics	3	39	40
W2002e-5	**Customizing Word**			
W2002e-5-1	Create, edit, and run, macros	3	88–93	89–94
W2002e-5-2	Customize menus and toolbars	3	94–97	96–98
W2002e-6	**Workgroup Collaboration**			
W2002e-6-1	Track, accept, and reject changes to documents	3	122–130	123–132
W2002e-6-2	Merge input from several reviewers	3	128–130	128–132
W2002e-6-3	Insert and modify hyperlinks to other documents and web pages	2	174–175	175–177
W2002e-6-4	Create and edit Web documents in Word	2	171–173	172–174
W2002e-6-5	Create document versions	3	138–139	139
W2002e-6-6	Protect documents	3	133	134–135
W2002e-6-7	Define and modify default file locations for workgroup templates	2	173	174
W2002e-6-8	Attach digital signatures to documents	3	135–136	137
W2002e-7	**Using Mail Merge**			
W2002e-7-1	Merge letters with a Word, Excel, or Access data source	2	200–215, 218	202–215, 219–220
W2002e-7-3	Use Outlook data as mail merge data source	2	220–221	222–223

Visual Conventions

This book uses many visual and typographic cues to guide you through the lessons. These pages provide examples and describe the function of each cue.

`Type this text` Anything you should type at the keyboard is printed in this typeface.

Tips, Notes, and Warnings are used throughout the text to draw attention to certain topics.

Command→Command Indicates multiple selections to be made from a menu bar. For example: File→Save means you should click the File command in the menu bar, then click the Save command on the menu.

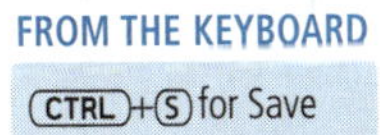

These margin notes indicate shortcut keys for executing a task described in the text. For example, CTRL+S to save your work.

Quick Reference tables provide generic instructions on how to perform tasks. You should not perform instructions in Quick Reference tables unless you are told to do so in a Hands-On exercise.

Multimedia videos for various topics in the text are on the labpub.com Web site. The video icons specify topics for which multimedia support is available.

This icon indicates the availability of a Web-based simulation for a Hands-On exercise. You may need to use Web-based exercises if your computer lab is not set up to support particular exercises.

Hands-On exercises are introduced immediately after concept discussions. They provide detailed step-by-step tutorials, allowing you to master the skills introduced in the concept discussions.

Concepts Review questions are true/false and multiple choice questions designed to gauge your understanding of concepts.

Skill Builder exercises provide additional hands-on practice and may introduce variations on techniques.

Assessment exercises are designed to assess your skills. They describe the results you should achieve, without providing specific instructions.

Critical Thinking exercises are the most challenging. They provide general instructions, allowing you to use your skills and creativity to achieve the result you envision.

Additional Learning Resources

This book has a Web site designed to support the lessons and to provide additional learning resources. The URL for the main Web page is labpub.com/learn/bc/word1. Some of the items you will find on the Web pages of both the ProStart and Briefcase series titles are described below.

Student Exercise Diskette Files If the text contains an exercise diskette, then the files on the original diskette are available for download on the Web page.

Downloads Required course files can be downloaded on the lesson pages.

Links to Multimedia Videos Each lesson page contains links to multimedia videos. The videos can be accessed in streaming media format or downloaded to a hard drive.

Web Based Simulations Some books in the series contain topics that have Web-based simulations. These simulations can be accessed through the lesson pages.

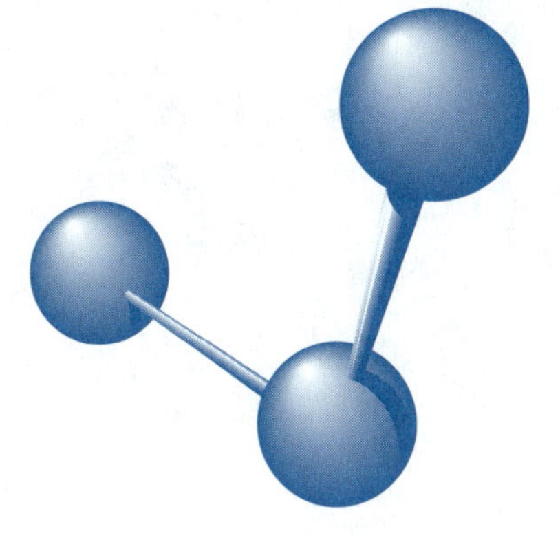

Word 2002

LEVEL 1

LESSON 1

Creating and Editing Business Letters

In this lesson, you will learn the basics of word processing using Microsoft Word 2002. You will create a variety of business letters while learning proper business document formatting. You will also learn fundamental techniques of entering and editing text, saving documents, and using Word 2002 commands.

IN THIS LESSON

Word 2002 Core MOUS Objectives Covered in this Lesson

MOUS Objective Number	MOUS Objective Description	Concept Page References	Exercise Page References
W2002-1-1	Insert, modify and move text and symbols	15	15
W2002-3-5	Preview and Print documents, envelopes, and labels	26, 27	26, 27
W2002-4-3	Save documents using different names and file formats	12	13

See the Lesson 1 Web Page at: labpub.com/learn/bc/word1/lesson1

Case Study

Susan Adams is the top sales representative for Western Office Supplies. Western Office Supplies distributes office equipment, including copy machines, laser printers, fax machines, and digital scanners to customers throughout the Western United States. Susan and her manager Richard Jones have just delivered a dynamic presentation to Sandra Evans, Vice President of Integrated Office Solutions. Like all top-notch sales representatives, Susan provides excellent follow-through and customer support. As a follow-up to her sales presentation, Susan writes a formal business letter to Sandra Evans thanking her for her time and preparing the next step in the sales process. Susan uses Word 2002 to create and edit her business letter.

June 26, 2001

Ms. Sandra Evans
Vice President
Integrated Office Solutions
2756 Industrial Lane
Los Angeles, CA 90024

Dear Ms. Evans:

It was a pleasure meeting with you and the rest of your staff yesterday. Both Richard Jones and I were quite impressed with your facilities and the quality of your team. You certainly have a group of hard working and creative people.

Our presentation was designed to give you an overview of our high-performance copiers, laser printers, fax machines, and digital scanners. We would like to follow up our presentation with a live demonstration. You must see our products in action to truly appreciate their benefits.

I will contact you early next week to arrange a demonstration. In the meantime, feel free to contact me if I can be of further assistance.

Sincerely,

Susan Adams
Sales Representative

xx

What Is Microsoft Word 2002?

Microsoft Word 2002 is a program that makes word processing a pleasure instead of a chore. Word's powerful suite of tools lets you easily create and modify a variety of documents. Word provides tools to assist you in virtually every aspect of document creation. From desktop publishing to Web publishing, Word has the right tool for the job. For these and many other reasons, Word is the most widely used word processing program in both homes and businesses.

Why Use Word?

Word provides a number of important features and benefits that make it a smart choice to use.

- **GUI—**Word's Graphical User Interface is so easy to use that even beginning computer users find it simple. The interface reduces the need to memorize commands, and it will make you more productive.
- **Writing Tools—**Word has powerful writing tools, including automatic grammar checking and spell checking, as you type. These and other tools will help you improve your writing skills.
- **Widely Used—**Word is the most widely used word processing software. Word is the right choice if you are trying to develop marketable skills and find employment.
- **Integration with Other Office Programs—**Word 2002 is part of the Microsoft Office XP suite of programs, which also includes Excel, Access, PowerPoint, and Outlook. The ability to exchange data with these programs is one of the most powerful and attractive features of Word.
- **Web Integration—**Word 2002 lets you easily publish your documents to Web sites on the World Wide Web or to your company Intranet.

It's Time to Master Word!

It's time to put your fears behind and master this wonderful program. You will be amazed at the power and simplicity of Word and how easy it is to learn. The knowledge you are about to gain will give you a marketable skill and make you a master of Word.

Starting Word 2002

The method you use to start Word and other Office programs depends in large part upon whether you intend to create a new document or open an existing document. If you intend to create a new document, then use one of the following methods to start Word. Once the Word program has started, you can begin working in the new document window that appears.

- Click the Start button, and choose Microsoft Word from the Programs menu.
- Click the Microsoft Word button on the Quick Launch toolbar (located near the Taskbar).
- Click the Start button, choose New Office Document, choose the General tab, and double-click the Blank Document icon.

Use one of the following methods if you intend to open an existing Word document. Once the Word program has started, the desired document will open in a Word window.

- Navigate to the desired document using Windows Explorer or My Computer, and double-click the document.
- Click the Start button and point to Documents. You can choose the desired document from the Documents list. The Documents list displays the most recently used documents.

Hands-On 1.1 Start Word

1. If necessary, start your computer, and the Windows Desktop will be displayed.
2. Click the Start button, and choose Programs.
3. Choose Microsoft Word from the Programs menu.
The Word program will load, and the document window shown below will appear. Don't be concerned if your document window appears different from this example.

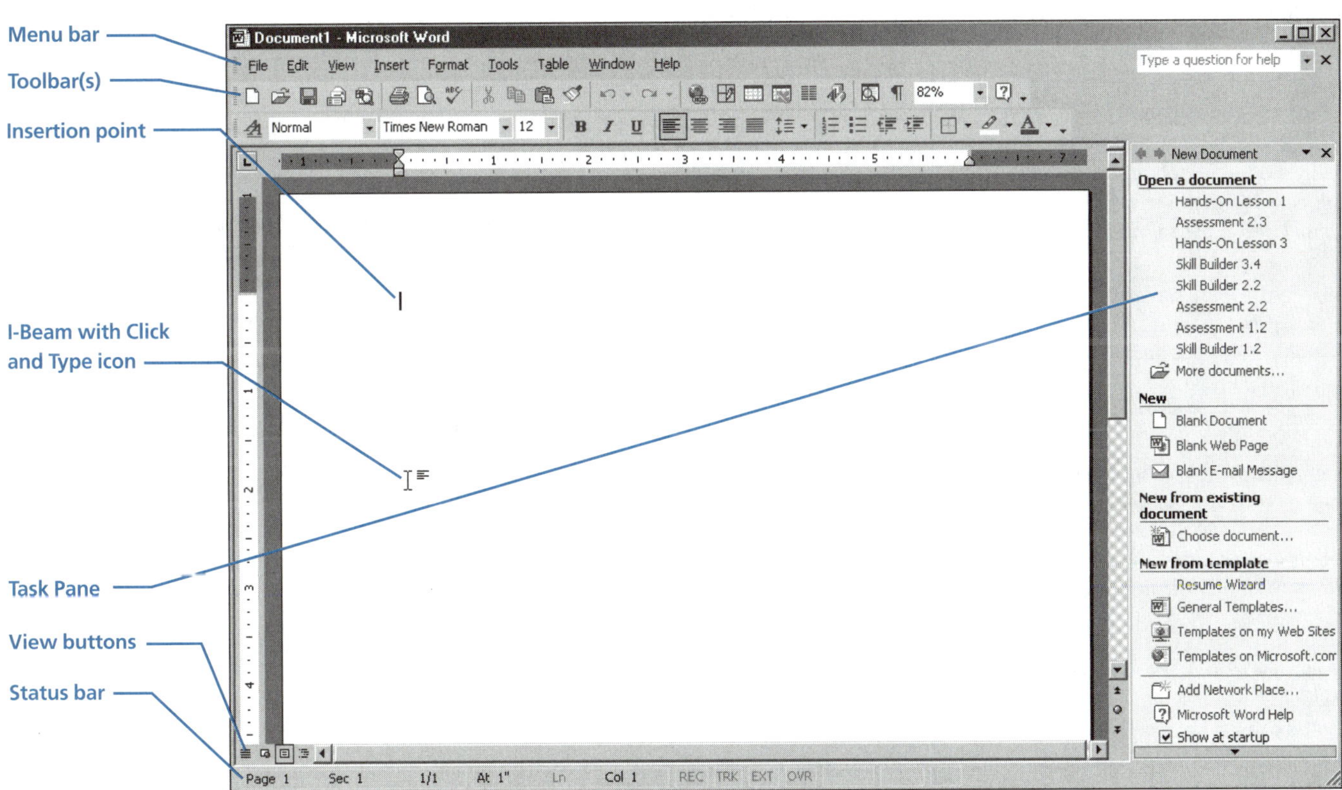

The document window is where you type information into Word. The document window allows you to access Word commands, and it can be customized to suit your particular needs. You will learn how to modify the document window at a later time.

Business Letter Styles

There are several acceptable styles of business letters. The styles discussed in this text include block, modified block, and personal. All business letters contain the same, or similar, elements but with varied formatting.

Block Style Letter

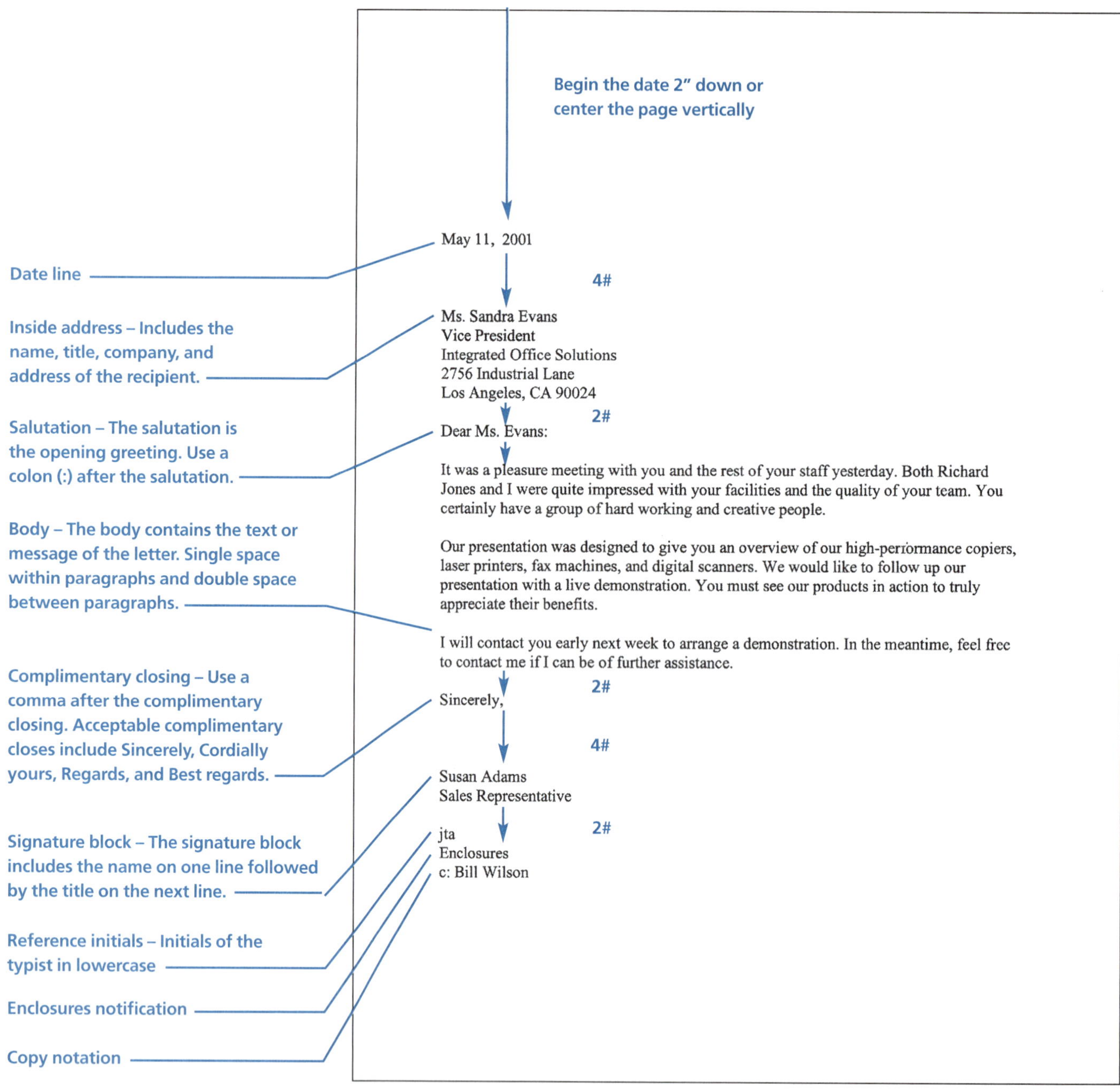

May 11, 2001

Ms. Sandra Evans
Vice President
Integrated Office Solutions
2756 Industrial Lane
Los Angeles, CA 90024

Dear Ms. Evans:

It was a pleasure meeting with you and the rest of your staff yesterday. Both Richard Jones and I were quite impressed with your facilities and the quality of your team. You certainly have a group of hard working and creative people.

Our presentation was designed to give you an overview of our high-performance copiers, laser printers, fax machines, and digital scanners. We would like to follow up our presentation with a live demonstration. You must see our products in action to truly appreciate their benefits.

I will contact you early next week to arrange a demonstration. In the meantime, feel free to contact me if I can be of further assistance.

Sincerely,

Susan Adams
Sales Representative

jta
Enclosures
c: Bill Wilson

Modified Block Style Letter

The modified block style has the same elements and spacing between paragraphs as the block style. However, the date line, complimentary closing, and signature block begin near the center of the lines as shown below.

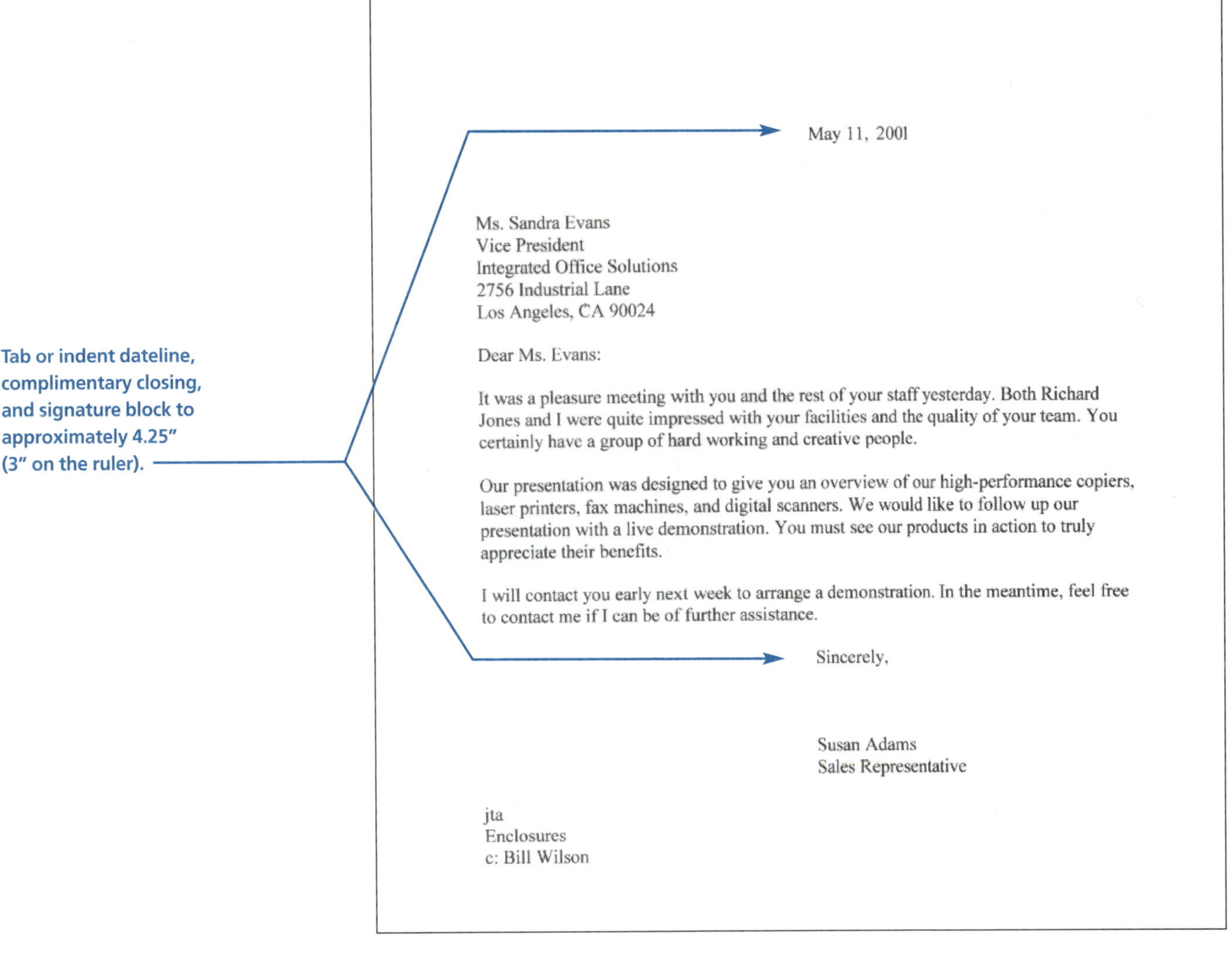

May 11, 2001

Ms. Sandra Evans
Vice President
Integrated Office Solutions
2756 Industrial Lane
Los Angeles, CA 90024

Dear Ms. Evans:

It was a pleasure meeting with you and the rest of your staff yesterday. Both Richard Jones and I were quite impressed with your facilities and the quality of your team. You certainly have a group of hard working and creative people.

Our presentation was designed to give you an overview of our high-performance copiers, laser printers, fax machines, and digital scanners. We would like to follow up our presentation with a live demonstration. You must see our products in action to truly appreciate their benefits.

I will contact you early next week to arrange a demonstration. In the meantime, feel free to contact me if I can be of further assistance.

Sincerely,

Susan Adams
Sales Representative

jta
Enclosures
c: Bill Wilson

Personal Business Letter (Block Style)

Personal business letters are used when an individual representing himself or herself sends a letter to a recipient in a business. Personal business letters can be composed using either the block or modified block style.

Today's Date

Mr. Jake Wilson
Rebate Manager
Sierra Snowboards
4200 University Avenue
Berkeley, CA 94702

Dear Mr. Wilson:

Thank you for your excellent advice on the snowboarding equipment I recently purchased. Sierra Snowboards certainly has the best equipment in the business.

I would like to know when I can expect the rebate on the board I purchased. I mailed in my rebate coupon last month and I have yet to hear from the company. Do rebates normally take this long? Please contact me as soon as possible at (510) 223-3344. Thank you for your assistance.

Sincerely,

Melissa Jackson
1223 Appian Way
El Sobrante, CA 94803

In a personal business letter, the signature block includes the sender's address.

Inserting Text

Text is always inserted into a Word document at the flashing insertion point. For this reason, it is important to position the insertion point at the desired location before inserting text. You will learn how to position the insertion point later in this lesson.

Other Ways to Insert Text

Most users insert text using the keyboard. In fact, keyboarding is arguably the most important skill an office user can possess. However, all Office XP programs now include Microsoft's speech recognition technology so you can enter text by dictating into a microphone connected to your computer. You can also activate buttons, menu commands, and other commands by speaking the desired commands. Speech recognition technology can be especially useful if you have a physical disability or suffer from an ailment such as carpal tunnel syndrome.

Word Wrap

If you continue typing after the insertion point reaches the end of a line, Word automatically wraps the insertion point to the beginning of the next line. This feature is known as word wrap. If you are creating a paragraph with two or more lines, then you should let word wrap do its job. Just keep typing until the entire paragraph is complete. Word wrap will format the paragraph by wrapping the lines at the appropriate location. If you let word wrap format the paragraph initially, then the paragraph will also be reformatted as you insert or delete text.

Taking Control With the (ENTER) Key

You use the (ENTER) key to begin a new paragraph or to insert blank lines in a document. (ENTER) inserts a hard carriage return that can only be removed by the user.

AutoComplete

Word 2002 includes numerous features to assist you in entering text and creating documents. AutoComplete recognizes certain phrases, such as dates and company names, and offers to complete them for you. You accept a phrase that AutoComplete proposes by tapping (ENTER). You can increase the number of phrases that AutoComplete recognizes by adding new AutoText entries into the system. In the next exercise, you will use AutoComplete to enter the current date into a business letter.

Smart Tags

Word marks certain types of text with purple dotted lines. When you point to text marked with a purple dotted line, a smart tag button appears. Clicking a smart tag button displays a menu of available actions. The available actions depend on the type of text marked. For example, if the text is a date then you can choose the Schedule a Meeting action to schedule a meeting in your Microsoft Outlook calendar. You will encounter smart tags from time-to-time as you work with Word and other Office XP programs.

Hands-On 1.2 Begin Typing a Business Letter

Use AutoComplete

1. Tap (ENTER) six times.
   Each time you tap (ENTER), the insertion point moves down one line. (ENTER) is used to insert blank lines in documents.
2. Notice the vertical position indicator on the status bar as shown below.

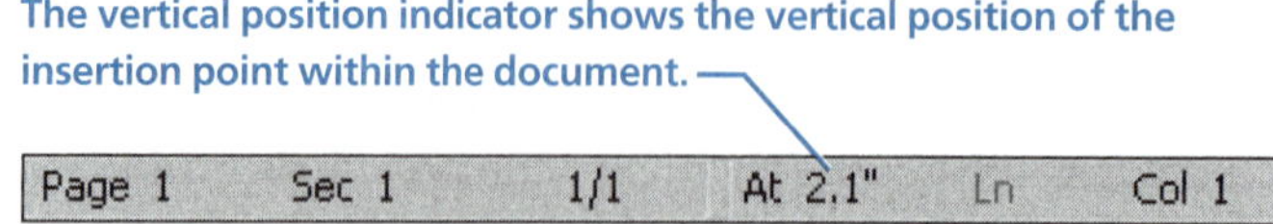

3. Type today's date, but stop typing when AutoComplete displays a yellow date tip as shown at the right.
   The example at the right uses the date June 26, 2001, but you should type today's date. Also, AutoComplete may not display the date tip. This is because AutoComplete may not be set up to automatically display tips.

   June 26, 2001 (Press ENTER to Insert)
   June

4. If AutoComplete displays the date tip, then tap (ENTER) to complete the date. Otherwise, complete today's date by typing it.
   You can always accept an item that AutoComplete proposes by tapping (ENTER).

Complete the Inside Address

5. Tap (ENTER) four times.
   Business letters require four returns after the date. Word will most likely underline the date with a purple dotted line. This indicates that a smart tag is associated with the date.
6. Position the mouse pointer over the date to display the Smart Tag button.
7. Click the Smart Tag button to display the list of available actions.
8. Choose Remove This Smart Tag to remove the tag.
   This example showed you how to remove a smart tag. However, it isn't necessary to remove smart tags unless you find them distracting.
9. Now complete the inside address and salutation as shown to the right.
   Only tap (ENTER) in the locations indicated. The Office Assistant may appear when you tap (ENTER) after typing the salutation.

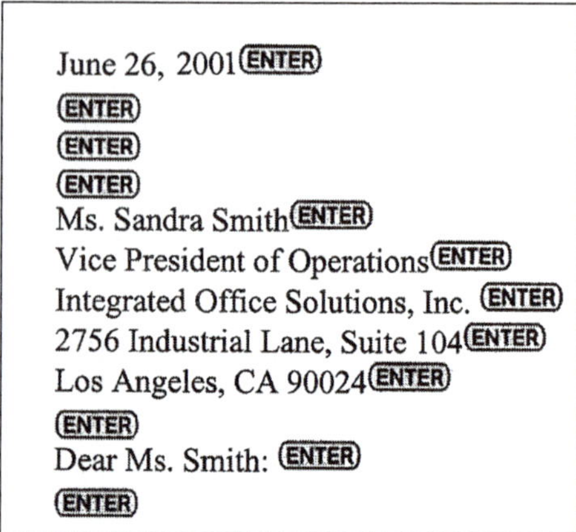
June 26, 2001(ENTER)
(ENTER)
(ENTER)
(ENTER)
Ms. Sandra Smith(ENTER)
Vice President of Operations(ENTER)
Integrated Office Solutions, Inc. (ENTER)
2756 Industrial Lane, Suite 104(ENTER)
Los Angeles, CA 90024(ENTER)
(ENTER)
Dear Ms. Smith: (ENTER)
(ENTER)

The Office Assistant

You can click anywhere in the document window to close the Office Assistant balloon.

The Office Assistant is an interactive Help tool that monitors your activities and provides suggestions whenever it assumes you need assistance. The Office Assistant has a balloon window that pops up, allowing you to ask questions and get assistance.

10. If the Office Assistant balloon pops up as shown here, then choose the Just Type the Letter Without Help option to close it.
11. Now complete the letter as shown below. Only tap (ENTER) in the indicated locations. Use (BACKSPACE) to correct any typing mistakes. Word automatically checks spelling and grammar as you type. Word underlines misspelled words with wavy red underlines and grammar errors with wavy green underlines. For now, ignore any red or green underlining that may appear.

Dear Ms. Smith:

It was a pleasure meeting with you yesterday. Both Richard Brown and I were quite impressed with your facilities and the quality of your team. You certainly have a group of hard working people.(ENTER)
(ENTER)
Our meeting was designed to give you an overview of our copiers, laser printers, fax machines, and digital scanners. We would like to follow up our presentation with a live demonstration. You must see our products in action to truly appreciate their benefits. I will contact you early next week to arrange a demonstration.(ENTER)
(ENTER)
In the meantime, please feel free to contact us if we can be of further assistance.(ENTER)
(ENTER)
Sincerely,(ENTER)
(ENTER)
(ENTER)
(ENTER)
Susan Adams(ENTER)
Sales Representative

Save Concepts

One important lesson to learn is to save your documents frequently! Power outages and careless accidents can result in lost data. The best protection is to save your documents every 10 or 15 minutes, or after making significant changes. Documents are saved to storage locations such as floppy disks, hard disks, or to Web sites on the World Wide Web.

Save Command

The Save button on the Standard toolbar and the File→Save command initiate the Save command. If the document had previously been saved, then Word replaces the previous version with the new edited version. If the document had never been saved, then Word displays the Save As dialog box. The Save As dialog box lets you specify the name and storage location of the document. You can also use the Save As dialog box to make a copy of a document by saving it under a new name or to a different location. You can use filenames containing as many as 255 characters. The following illustration describes the Save As dialog box.

FROM THE KEYBOARD

CTRL+S for save

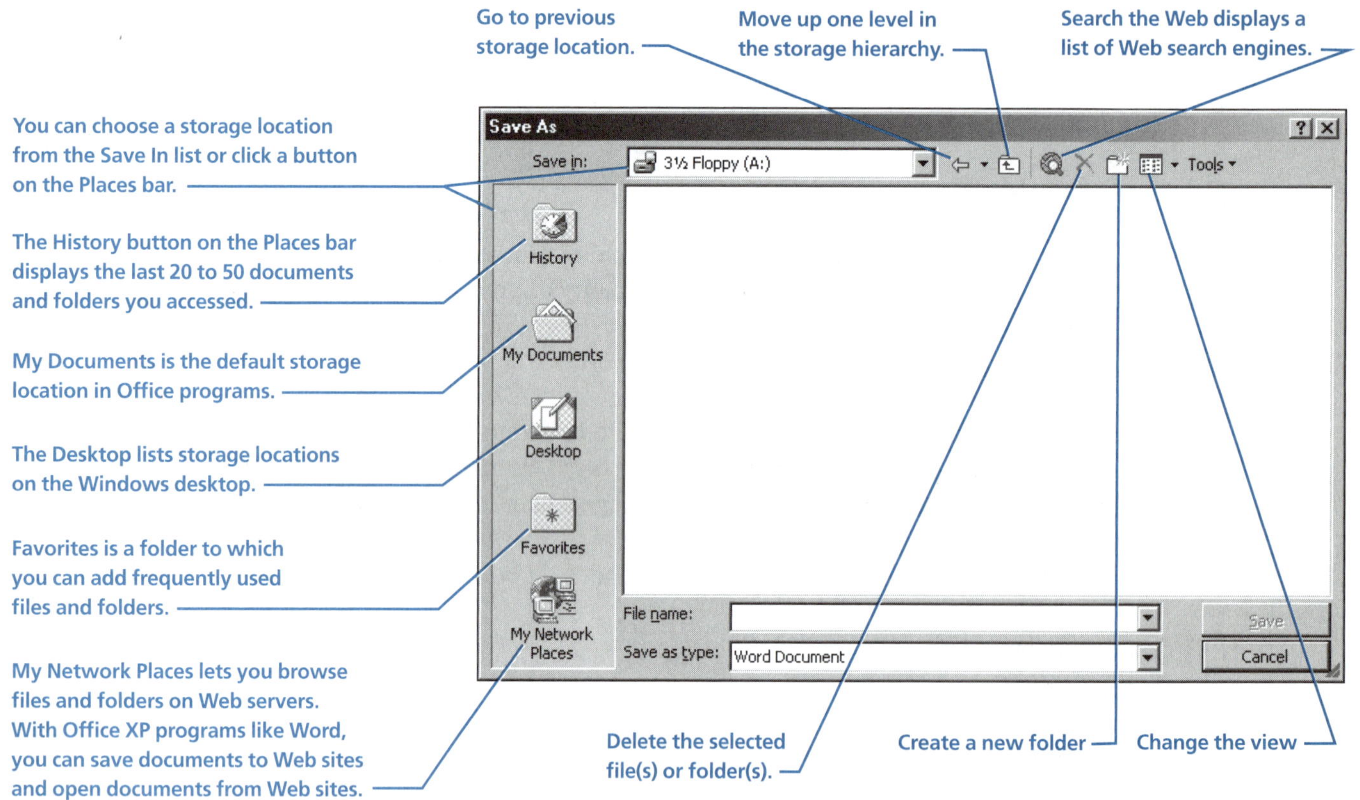

Hands-On 1.3 Save the Letter

In this exercise, you will save the letter that was created in the previous exercise. Your instructor will most likely want you to save your documents onto the exercise diskettes that are provided with this course. You will most likely be saving documents onto the A: disk drive.

1. Click the Save button and the Save As dialog box will appear.
2. Follow these steps to save the letter.
   Keep in mind that your dialog box will contain more files than shown here.

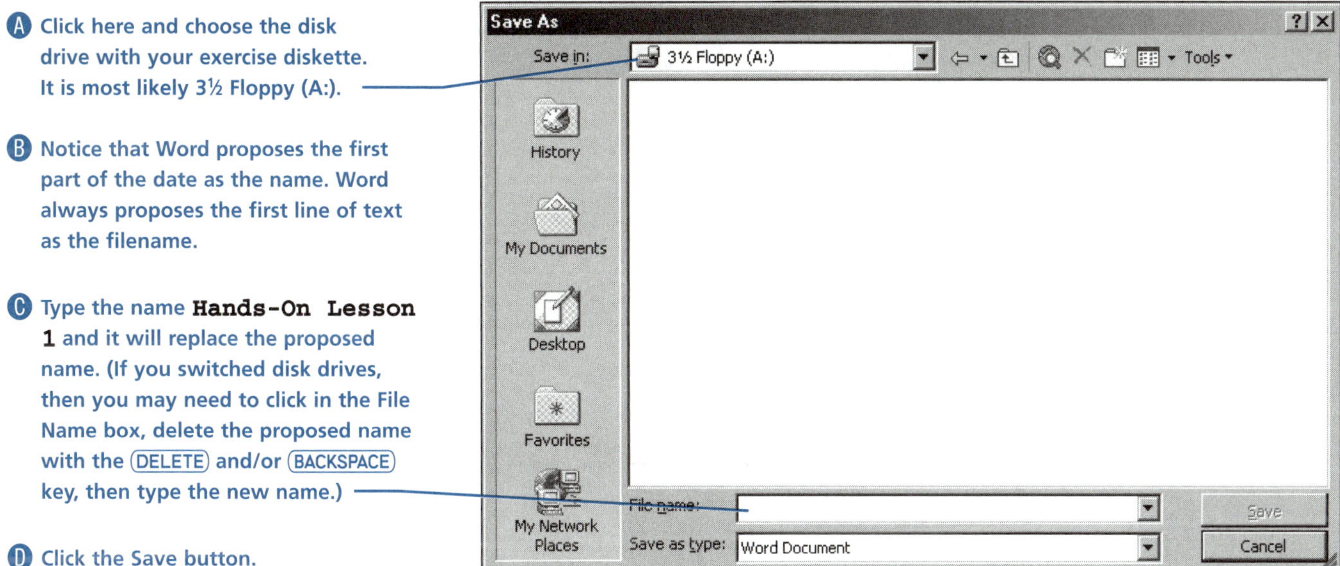

Notice that the letter was saved and remains on the screen. You will continue to use the letter throughout this lesson.

Scrolling Documents and Repositioning the Insertion Point

The vertical and horizontal scroll bars let you browse through documents. However, scrolling does not move the insertion point. You must click in the document to reposition the insertion point. The vertical scroll bar is on the right side of the document window and the horizontal scroll bar is at the bottom of the document window. Scroll bars also appear in many dialog boxes. The following illustration shows the scroll bars and their components.

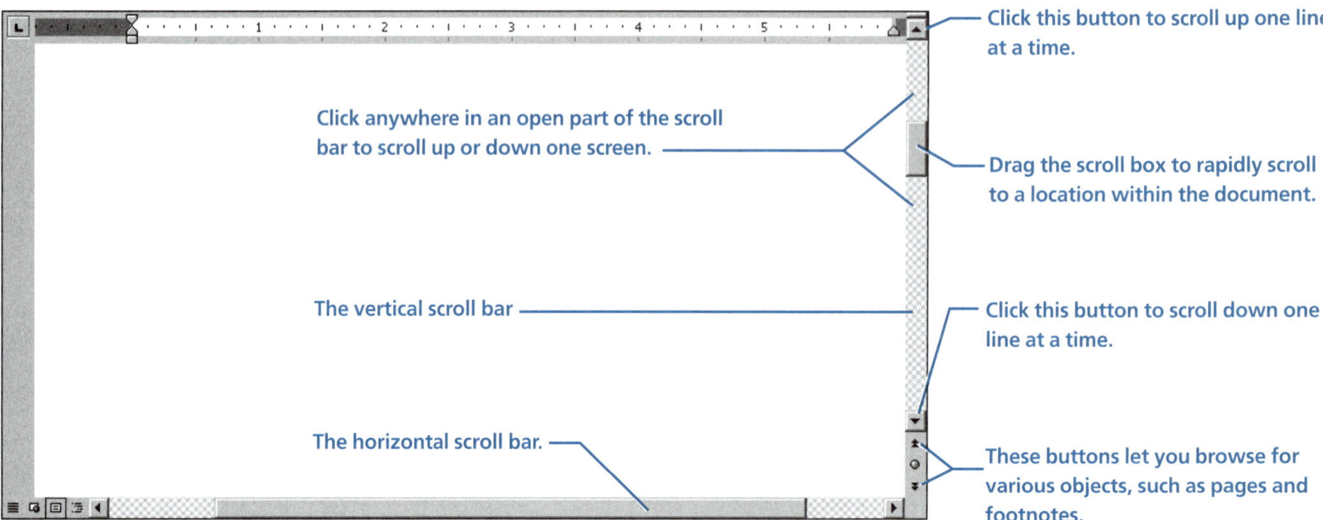

Hands-On 1.4 Practice Scrolling

1. Click the Scroll Down button five times.
   Notice that the document scrolls down, but the insertion point does not move.
2. Click the Scroll Up button until the date is visible at the top of the letter.
3. Slide the mouse; the pointer will have an I-Beam shape when it is in the typing area.
   The pointer must have this I-Beam shape before the insertion point can be repositioned.
4. Click the I-Beam anywhere on the date, and the blinking insertion point will be positioned there.
5. Move the I-Beam into the left margin area, and it will become an arrow.
   This arrow should not be present if you are trying to reposition the insertion point.
6. Position the I-Beam on the first line of the inside address just in front of Ms., and click the left mouse button.
   The insertion point should be positioned just in front of Ms. If a black background appears behind the text, then you have accidentally selected it. Selecting is discussed later in this lesson. If you accidentally selected the text, then deselect it by clicking the mouse pointer outside of it.
7. Take a few minutes to practice scrolling and repositioning the insertion point.

Inserting and Overtyping Text

You will almost always work in Insert mode.

Insert mode is the default editing mode in Word. In insert mode, existing text moves to the right as new text is typed. The new text is thus inserted into the document. Thus far, you have been working in insert mode. In overtype mode, existing text is replaced as new text is typed. You switch between insert mode and overtype mode by double-clicking the OVR (overtype) indicator on the status bar as shown in the following illustration.

Double-clicking the OVR (overtype) indicator switches between insert mode and overtype mode. The mode is set to overtype when the OVR indicator is bold as shown here.

Page 1 Sec 1 1/1 At 1" Ln Col 1 REC TRK EXT OVR

Hands-On 1.5 Inserting and Overtyping Text

Insert Text

1. Click just in front of the word *yesterday* in the first body paragraph as shown below.

Click here

It was a pleasure meeting with you yesterday.

2. Type the phrase **and the rest of your staff**, and tap the (SPACE BAR) once.
3. Use the technique in Steps 1 and 2 to insert the phrase **and creative** in front of the word *people* at the end of the paragraph. The completed paragraph is shown below.

It was a pleasure meeting with you and the rest of your staff yesterday. Both Richard Brown and I were quite impressed with your facilities and the quality of your team. You certainly have a group of hard working and creative people.

Overtype Text

4. Position the insertion point in the inside address in front of the *S* in *Smith*.
5. Double-click the OVR button on the status bar.
   The OVR button should now appear bold.
6. Type the word **Evans**, and *Smith* should be replaced by *Evans*.
   If insert mode had been active, the name Smith would have moved to the right, making room for Evans.
7. Now click in front of the name *Smith* in the salutation line, and type **Evans**.
8. Double-click the OVR button on the status bar when you have finished.
   The letters OVR will be dimmed on the status bar, indicating that insert mode is active.
9. Click the Save button to save the changes to your exercise diskette.

Selecting Text

You must select text if you wish to perform some action on that text. Suppose you want to delete an entire paragraph. You would select the paragraph first and then tap the DELETE key. Selected text is usually displayed in white on a black background. The illustration to the right shows a selected paragraph in the inside address of your letter.

Ms. Sandra Evans
Vice President of Operations
Integrated Office Solutions, Inc.

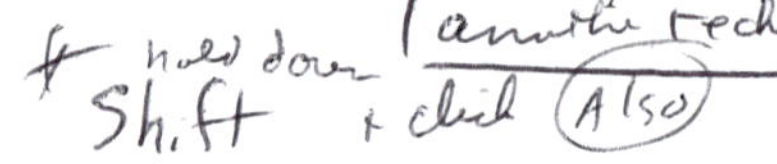

Selection Techniques

Word provides many selection techniques using both the mouse and keyboard. The mouse techniques are usually more intuitive; however, beginners may find it difficult to control the mouse. The keyboard techniques tend to provide greater control. You can use the keyboard techniques if you have difficulty controlling the mouse. The following quick reference table illustrates the available selection techniques.

QR

QUICK REFERENCE: SELECTION TECHNIQUES

Item to be Selected	Mouse Technique	Keyboard Technique
One word	Double-click the desired word.	Click at beginning of word, press and hold SHIFT and CTRL while tapping →.
A phrase or continuous section of text	Drag the I-beam in any direction over the desired text.	Click at beginning of phrase, press and hold SHIFT while tapping any arrow keys. You can also click at beginning of phrase, press and hold SHIFT, and then click at end of phrase.
A line	Position the mouse pointer to the left of the line, and click when the pointer has an arrow shape.	Press SHIFT+END to select from insertion point to end of line. Press SHIFT+HOME to select from insertion point to beginning of line.
One paragraph	Triple-click anywhere on the paragraph. You can also position the mouse pointer to the left of the paragraph in the margin and double-click when the pointer has an arrow shape.	
Multiple paragraphs	Drag the I-beam over the desired paragraphs. You can also position the mouse pointer to the left of the paragraphs and drag up or down when the pointer has an arrow shape.	
Entire document	Triple-click to the left of any paragraph, or press and hold CTRL and click to the left of any paragraph.	Press CTRL+A to execute Select All command, or press CTRL and click in left margin.
Noncontiguous Areas	Press and hold the CTRL key while dragging over the selected text.	

Hands-On 1.6 Practice Selecting Text

Select Using the Left Margin

1. Follow these steps to select text using the left margin.

Ⓐ Place the mouse pointer to the left of this line and it will have this shape. Click the mouse button to select the entire line.

Ⓑ Click here to select this line. Notice that the previously selected paragraph is no longer selected.

Ⓒ Select this paragraph by double-clicking in front of it.

Ms. Sandra Evans
Vice President of Operations
Integrated Office Solutions, Inc.
2756 Industrial Lane, Suite 104
Los Angeles, CA 90024

Dear Ms. Evans:

It was a pleasure meeting with you and the rest of your staff yesterday. Both Richard Brown and I were quite impressed with your facilities and the quality of your team. You certainly have a group of hard working and creative people.

2. Try dragging the mouse pointer down in the left margin.
Be sure to press and hold the left mouse button as you drag, and multiple lines will be selected.
3. Try triple-clicking the mouse pointer anywhere in the left margin.
The entire document will become selected. Triple clicking can be tricky, so you may need to try it several times. Also, you can select the entire document by pressing CTRL *and clicking in the left margin.*
4. Deselect the document by clicking anywhere on the selected text.

Select Words

5. Double-click the I-beam on any word.
The word should become selected.
6. Double-click a different word, and notice that the previous word has been deselected.
7. Select five different words one after another by double-clicking them.
8. Deselect the last word you selected by clicking the I-Beam anywhere outside of it.

Noncontiguous Selections

9. Select any word or paragraph.
10. Press and hold the CTRL key while you select another word or paragraph.
Both your first and your second selections will be in effect. You can select as many noncontiguous areas of a document as desired using this technique. This can be quite useful when formatting documents.

(Continued on the next page)

Drag Select

11. Follow these steps to drag select a phrase.

(A) Position the I-beam here just in front of *It was a pleasure . . .*

(B) Press and hold the left mouse button, then drag to the right until the phrase *It was a pleasure meeting with you* is selected.

Dear Ms. Evans:

It was a pleasure meeting with you and the rest of your staff
Brown and I were quite impressed with your facilities and th
certainly have a group of hard working and creative people.

(C) Release the mouse button and the text will remain selected.

TIP! *Use Undo if you accidentally move text.*

12. Practice drag selecting text in the second large paragraph. Try dragging the mouse in all directions.
Notice how the selection block expands and contracts as you move the mouse.
13. Deselect by clicking anywhere on the selected text.
14. Take two minutes to practice selecting text using the drag technique.
15. Take five minutes to practice selecting text using all of the techniques discussed in the table at the beginning of this topic. In particular, try using the keystroke techniques discussed in the table.

Editing Text

FROM THE KEYBOARD

CTRL+BACKSPACE to delete from insertion point to beginning of word.
CTRL+DELETE to delete from insertion point to end of word.

The DELETE and BACKSPACE keys are used to remove text from a document. DELETE removes the character to the right of the insertion point and BACKSPACE removes the character to the left of the insertion point. You can also remove an entire selection by tapping DELETE or BACKSPACE. If you are removing just a few characters, it is usually more efficient to click in front of the characters and tap DELETE one or more times. If you are removing a word, phrase, or paragraph, it is more efficient to select the desired text and then tap DELETE to remove the selection.

You can replace text by selecting the desired text and then typing the replacement text. Selected text is removed as you begin typing replacement text. The replacement text is then inserted in the document as you continue to type.

Undo and Redo

FROM THE KEYBOARD

CTRL+Z for undo
CTRL+Y for redo

Word's Undo button lets you reverse your last editing action(s). You can reverse simple actions such as accidental text deletions, or you can reverse more complex actions such as margin changes. Most actions can be undone. Actions that cannot be undone include commands such as printing documents and saving documents.

The Redo button reverses Undo. Use Redo when you Undo an action but decide to go through with that action after all.

Undoing and Redoing Multiple Actions

The arrows ▾ on the Undo and Redo buttons display lists of actions that can be undone or redone. You can undo or redo multiple actions by dragging the mouse over the desired actions. You can undo or redo an almost unlimited number of actions using this method. However, you must undo or redo actions in the order in which they appear on the drop-down list.

Repeat

The Edit→Repeat command lets you repeat your last action. For example, imagine you want to change the font size at several locations in a document. To accomplish this, you could change the font size at one location, reposition the insertion point, and then issue the Repeat command. The Repeat command would set the font size at the new location to the same size you set at the previous location. You can repeat an action as many times as desired. However, the Repeat command is only available when the Redo button is unavailable. The Edit→Repeat command changes to Edit→Redo as soon as you undo an action.

FROM THE KEYBOARD

CTRL+Y for repeat

Hands-On 1.7 Edit the Letter and Use Undo

Delete Several Words

1. Follow these steps to delete text from the inside address block.

Ms. Sandra Evans
Vice President of Operations
Integrated Office Solutions, Inc.
2756 Industrial Lane, Suite 104

A Drag the mouse pointer over the phrase *of Operations* as shown here.

B Tap DELETE to remove the phrase, then tap BACKSPACE to remove the space after the word President.

C Select the word *Inc* by double-clicking it, then tap DELETE to delete the word.

D Tap DELETE once to remove the period, then tap BACKSPACE once to remove the comma.

E Click in front of this comma, then tap DELETE repeatedly to remove the phrase, *Suite 104.*

Select and Replace Words

2. Follow these steps to select and replace several words and to insert a phrase.

It was a pleasure meeting with you and the rest of your staff yesterday. Brown and I were quite impressed with your facilities and the quality of certainly have a group of hard working and creative people.

Our meeting was designed to give you an overview of our copiers, laser machines, and digital scanners. We would like to follow up our present demonstration. You must see our products in action to truly appreciate will contact you early next week to arrange a demonstration.

In the meantime, please feel free to contact us if we can be of further as

A Double-click the last name *Brown* and type the replacement name **Jones**.

B Double-click the word *meeting* and type the replacement word **presentation**.

C Click in front of the word *copiers,* type the phrase **high-performance,** and tap SPACE BAR. The new phrase should be inserted in front of the word copiers.

D Select the word *us* and type the replacement word **me**.

E Replace *we* with **I**.

(Continued on the next page)

To turn off Auto capitalization, choose Tools→AutoCorrect Options and uncheck the Capitalize First Letter Of Sentences box.

Use Undo to Override AutoCorrect

AutoCorrect is a tool that automatically corrects many common spelling errors, and looks for other potential problems. One of these potential problems is the lack of capitalization at the start of a sentence. AutoCorrect will automatically capitalize the first letter of a sentence if you fail to capitalize it yourself. This is acceptable most of the time, but there are occasions when you may want to override AutoCorrect.

3. Scroll to the bottom of the document, and click to the right of the title Sales Representative in the signature block.
4. Tap (ENTER) twice.
5. Type your initials in lowercase, and then type a colon (**:**).
   AutoCorrect should spring into action, capitalizing your first initial. Unfortunately, typists initials should appear in lowercase in business correspondence.
6. Click Undo, and the capital letter should return to lowercase.
   You can always use Undo to override AutoCorrect.
7. Tap (SPACE BAR), and type the document name **Hands-On Lesson 1**.
   The completed signature block should be xx: Hands-On Lesson 1, where xx are your initials.
8. Click Save to save the changes to your document.

It is important to save now because you will experiment with Undo and Redo in the remainder of this exercise.

Practice Using Undo and Redo

9. Delete any word in the letter.
10. Click Undo and the word will be restored.
11. Select any paragraph, then tap (DELETE) to remove the paragraph.
12. Click Undo to restore the paragraph.
13. Click Redo and the paragraph will vanish again.
    Redo always reverses the most recent Undo.
14. Click Undo again to restore the paragraph.

Undo and Redo Multiple Actions

15. Follow these steps to explore the Undo actions list, and to delete three items.

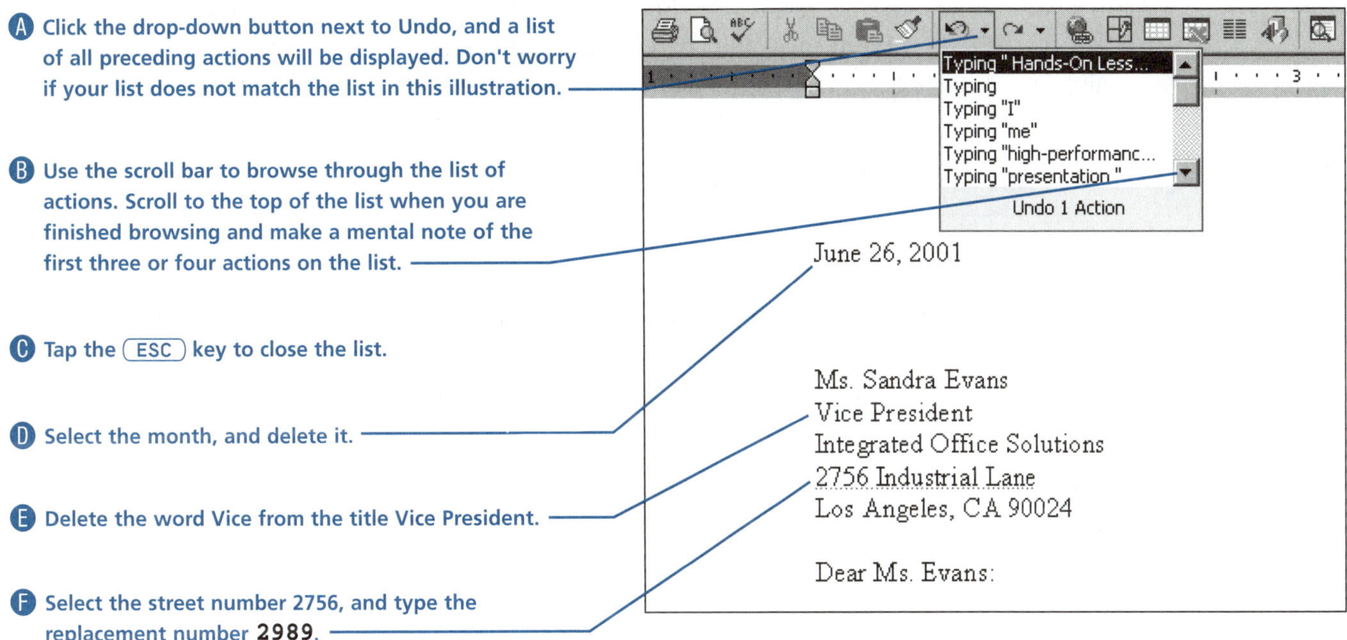

16. Follow these steps to undo the last three actions:

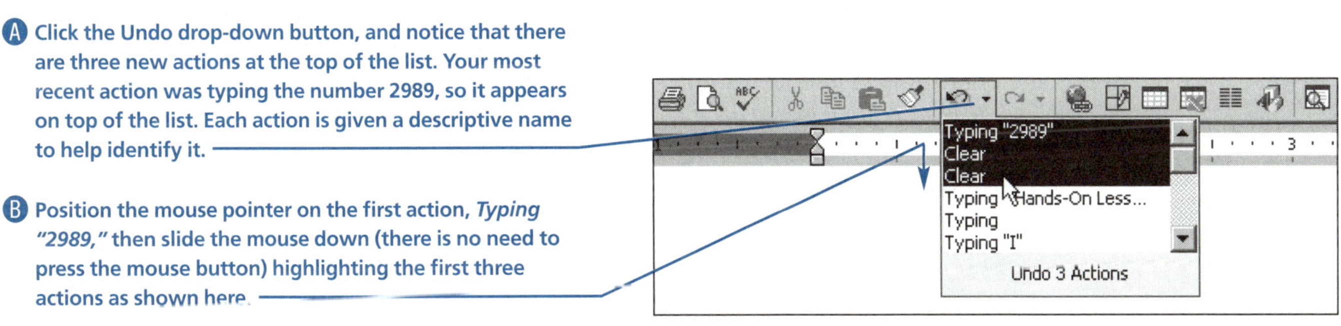

C Click when the actions are selected, and all three actions will be undone. Your document should be exactly as it was prior to making the changes.

17. Feel free to experiment with Undo and Redo.

Closing Documents

The File→Close command is used to close an open document. When you close a document, Word prompts you to save the changes. If you choose Yes at the prompt and the document had previously been saved, then Word saves the changes. If the document is new, Word displays the Save As dialog box, allowing you to assign a name and storage location to the document.

Hands-On 1.8 Close the Document

1. Choose File→Close from the menu bar.
2. Click the No button if Word asks you to save the changes.
   You can always close without saving to eliminate changes that have occurred since the last save. The next exercise will instruct you to open the letter. You will notice that the most recent changes have not been saved.
3. Finally, notice that there is no document in the document window.
   The document window always has this appearance when all documents have been closed.

Opening Documents

FROM THE KEYBOARD

CTRL+O to display open dialog box.

The Open button on the Standard toolbar and the File→Open command display the Open dialog box. The Open dialog box lets you navigate to any storage location and open previously saved documents. Once a document is open, you can browse it, print it, or even make editing changes. The organization and layout of the Open dialog box is similar to the Save dialog box discussed earlier in this lesson.

Hands-On 1.9 Open the Letter

1. Click Open on the Standard toolbar.
2. Follow these steps to open the Hands-On Lesson 1 document.
   Keep in mind that your dialog box will display files not shown here.

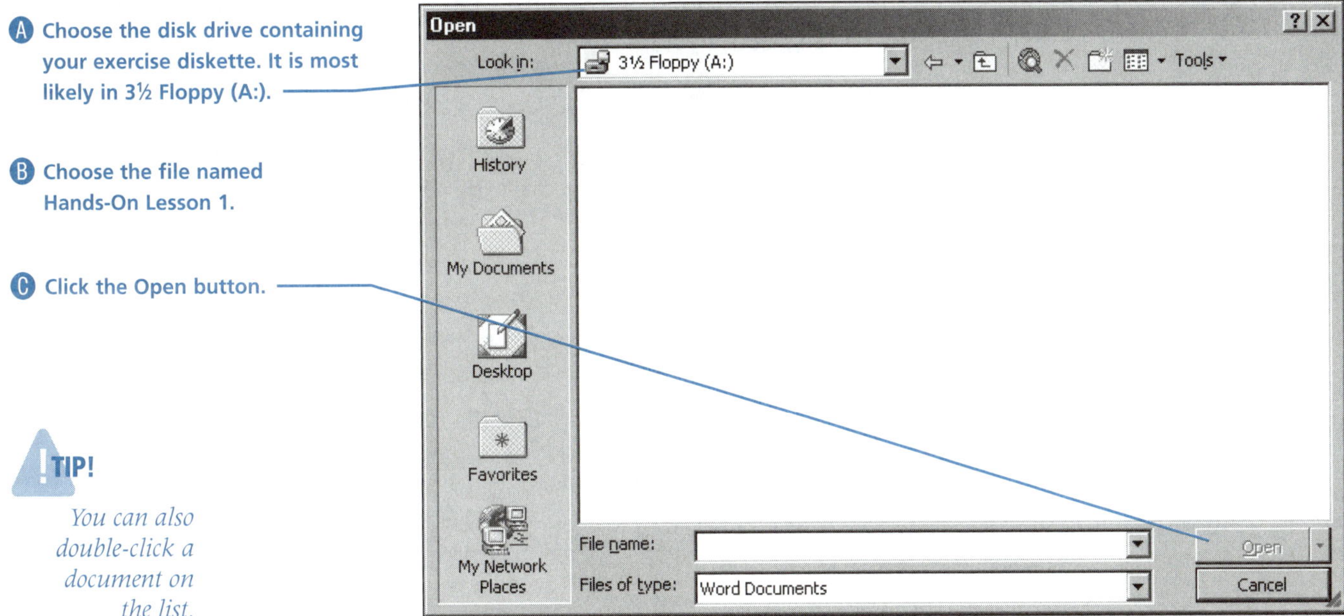

TIP!

You can also double-click a document on the list.

3. Take a few moments to scroll through the letter. Notice that the most recent changes were not saved (because you closed without saving).

Showing Nonprinting Characters

FROM THE KEYBOARD

CTRL+SHIFT+8 to show or hide characters

The Show All ¶ button on the Standard toolbar shows or hides all nonprinting characters in a document. Nonprinting characters include spaces, tab characters, and carriage returns that do not appear on the printed page. Showing these characters can be important, especially when editing a document. For example, you may need to display the nonprinting characters to determine whether the space between two words was created with SPACE BAR or TAB. The following illustration shows the location of the Show All button and the characters that are inserted whenever SPACE BAR and ENTER are tapped.

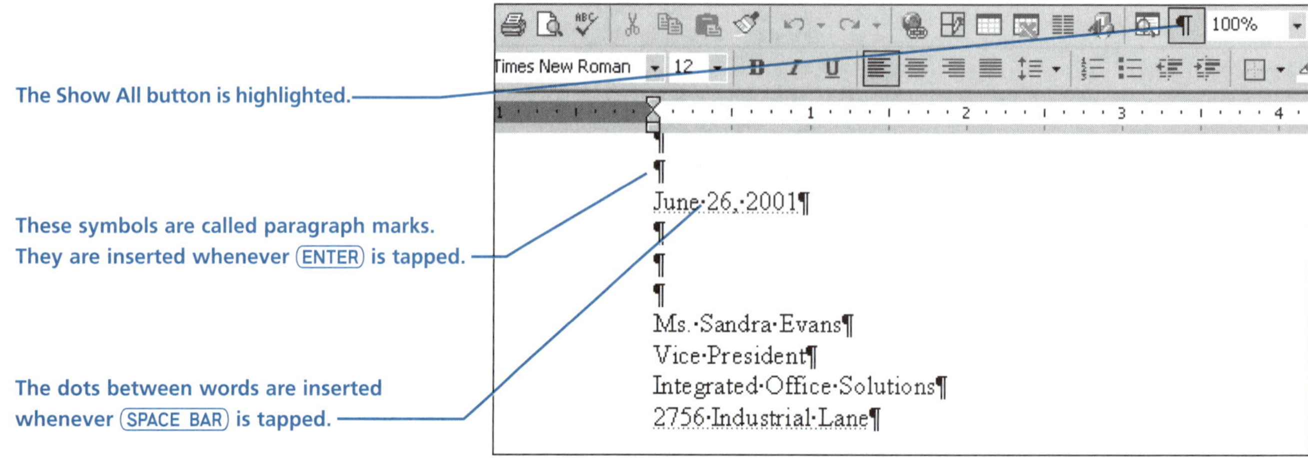

Inserting and Deleting Paragraph Marks

Paragraph marks ¶ (or carriage returns) play an important role in Word documents. Every paragraph ends with a paragraph mark. A paragraph mark is inserted whenever ENTER is tapped. Paragraph marks affect the appearance and format of documents. You may need to delete paragraph marks as you edit and format documents. For example, suppose you want to combine two paragraphs into one large paragraph. To accomplish this, you would delete the paragraph mark separating the paragraphs. It is usually best to display the nonprinting characters with the Show All button before deleting paragraph marks and other nonprinting characters. You can delete the paragraph mark to the right of the insertion point using DELETE. Likewise, the paragraph mark to the left of the insertion point can be removed with BACKSPACE.

Hands-On 1.10 Insert and Delete Paragraph Marks

In this exercise, you will restructure several paragraphs in the letter. Remember to use Undo if you make a mistake.

Combine Two Paragraphs

1. Click Show All ¶ to display the symbols.
2. Position the insertion point in front of the paragraph mark at the end of the second main paragraph as shown here.

presentation·with·a·live·demonstration.·You·must·see·our·products·in·action·to·truly·
appreciate·their·benefits.·I·will·contact·you·early·next·week·to·arrange·a·demonstration.¶
¶
In·the·meantime,·please·feel·free·to·contact·me·if·I·can·be·of·further·assistance.¶

Position insertion point here.

3. Tap DELETE once.
   The paragraph mark to the right of the insertion point will be deleted. The mark below the paragraph will immediately move up to take its place. Notice that the gap between the paragraphs is no longer a double space.
4. Tap DELETE again, and the paragraphs will be joined together.
5. Tap SPACE BAR once to create space between the two sentences in the combined paragraph.

Split the Combined Paragraph

6. Follow these steps to split the paragraph into two smaller paragraphs.

Our·presentation·was·designed·to·give·you·an·overview·of·our·high-performance·copiers,·
laser·printers,·fax·machines,·and·digital·scanners.·We·would·like·to·follow·up·our·
presentation·with·a·live·demonstration.·You·must·see·our·products·in·action·to·truly·
appreciate·their·benefits.·I·will·contact·you·early·next·week·to·arrange·a·demonstration.·In·
the·meantime,·please·feel·free·to·contact·me·if·I·can·be·of·further·assistance.¶

A Click here just in front of the word I.

B Tap ENTER twice to push the last two sentences down and to form a new paragraph.

7. Click Show All ¶ to hide the symbols.
   At this point, your letter should match the example shown in the case study at the start of this lesson (except for the date).

Print Preview

The Print Preview button and the File→Print Preview command display the Print Preview window, which shows how a document will look when it is printed. Print Preview can save time, paper, and wear-and-tear on your printer. Print Preview is especially useful when printing long documents, or with documents containing intricate graphics and formatting. It is always wise to preview a long or complex document before sending it to the printer.

When you display the Print Preview window, the standard toolbars are replaced by the Print Preview toolbar. The following illustration describes the important buttons on the Print Preview toolbar.

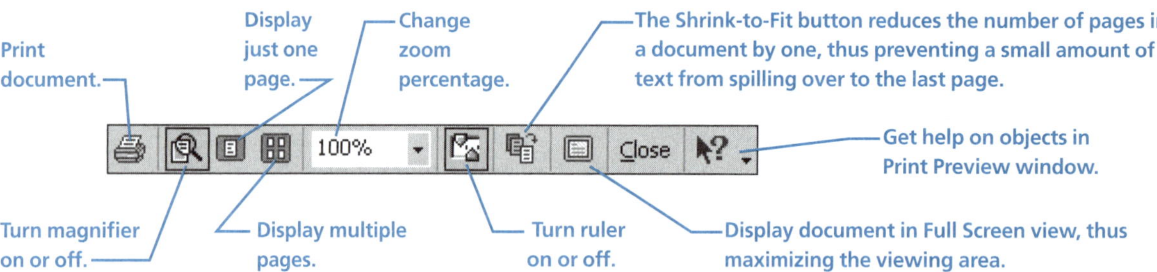

Hands-On 1.11 Use Print Preview

1. Click Print Preview on the Standard toolbar.
2. Make sure the Magnifier button is highlighted on the toolbar.
3. Position the mouse pointer over the document, and the pointer will look like a magnifying glass.
4. Zoom in by clicking anywhere on the document.
5. Zoom out by clicking anywhere on the document.
   You can zoom in and out whenever the magnifier is on. When the magnifier is off, the mouse pointer functions normally, allowing you to edit the document in Print Preview mode.
6. Feel free to experiment with the other buttons on the Print Preview toolbar.
7. When you have finished, click the Close button on the Print Preview toolbar to exit from Print Preview.

Print Preview has a Toolbar Shrink to Fit

Printing

The Print button on the Standard toolbar sends the entire document to the current printer. You must display the Print dialog box if you want to change printers, specify the number of copies to be printed, print selected pages, and to set other printing options. The Print dialog box is displayed with the File→Print command. When you print a document, a printer icon appears on the status bar. The Printer icon indicates that Word is processing the print job and is preparing to send the job to the printer. The following illustration explains the most important options available in the Print dialog box.

FROM THE KEYBOARD

CTRL+P to display Print dialog box

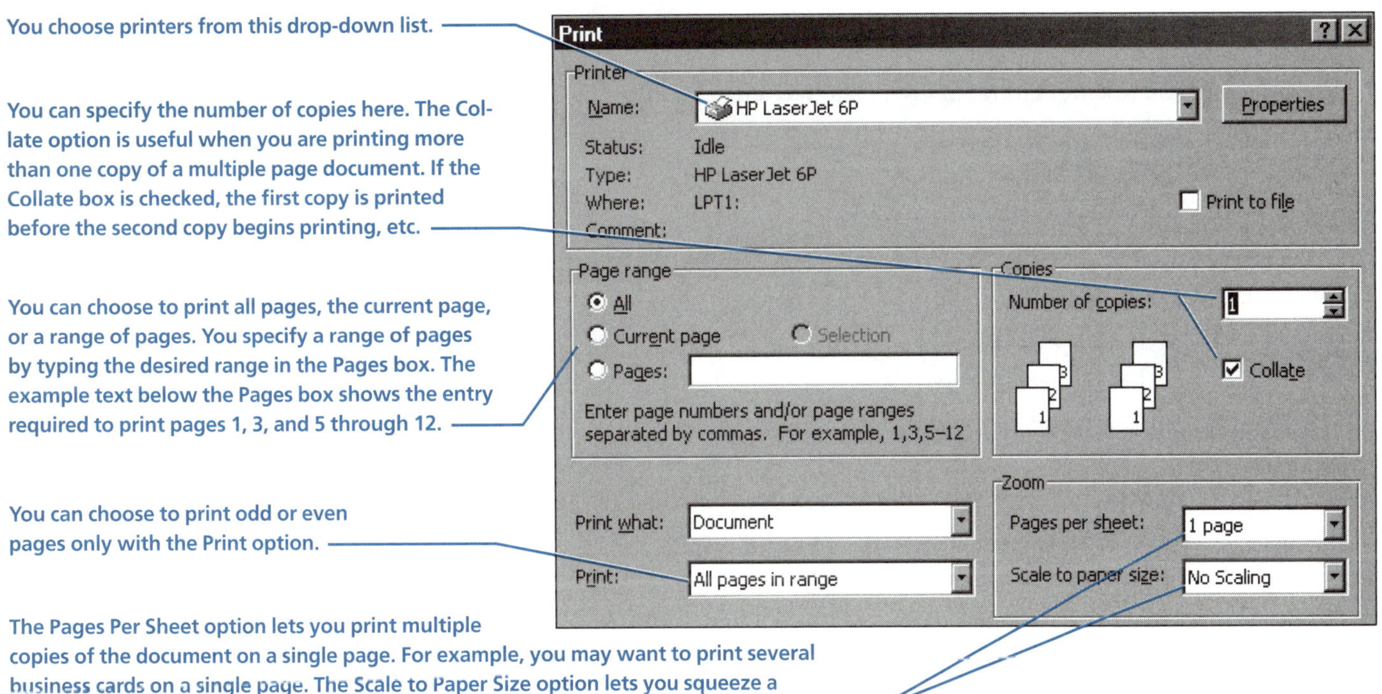

 Hands-On 1.12 Print the Document

1. Choose File→Print to display the Print dialog box.
2. Take a few moments to check out the dialog box options.
3. When you are ready to print, make sure the options are set as shown in the preceding illustration, and click the OK button.
   Keep in mind that your printer will probably be different than the printer shown in the Name box in the illustration.
4. Retrieve your document from the printer.

Canceling Print Jobs

Sometimes you will want to cancel a print job after issuing the Print command. When you print a document, Word processes the print job and sends it to the printer. Most modern printers contain memory where the Print job is stored while it is being printed. For this reason, it is not always possible to terminate a print job from Word or other Office programs. The difficult work of canceling the print job must often be done at the printer. This is especially true with newer computers. Newer computers are so fast that the print job is often sent to the printer before you have time to cancel it from within the application. The following quick reference steps can be used to effectively cancel print jobs. This sequence of steps is designed to save paper, prevent jamming of the printer, and effectively terminate the print job.

QUICK REFERENCE: CANCELLING PRINT JOBS

- Remove the paper stack from the printer, or remove the paper tray. You should be able to do this even if the printer is in the middle of printing a page.
- Double-click the Printer icon on the status bar. This will terminate further processing of the job by Word. The Printer icon won't be visible if Word has finished processing the job.
- If a page was being printed when you pulled out the paper tray, make sure it has finished printing.
- Switch off the power on the printer. This will clear the job out of the printer's memory.
- Pause 30 seconds and turn the printer back on.
- Reinsert the paper stack or the paper tray.

WARNING!

Turning off the printer may disrupt other users in a networked computer lab or office environment.

Exiting From Word

The File→Exit command is used to close the Word program. You should close Word and other programs if you are certain you won't be using them for some time. This will free up memory for other programs. When you close Word, you will be prompted to save any documents that have unsaved edits.

Hands-On 1.13 Exit from Word

1. Choose File→Exit from the menu bar.
2. Choose Yes when Word asks if you would like to save the changes.
   Word will close, and the Windows desktop will appear. Continue with the questions and exercises on the following pages.

Concepts Review

True/False Questions

1.	The insertion point is automatically repositioned when you scroll through a document.	TRUE	FALSE
2.	ENTER can be used to end one paragraph and begin another.	TRUE	FALSE
3.	The Show All button is used to display nonprinting characters, such as paragraph marks.	TRUE	FALSE
4.	The ENTER key should be tapped twice when creating space between the date and the inside address in a business letter.	TRUE	FALSE
5.	A single word can be selected by clicking once on the word.	TRUE	FALSE
6.	Paragraph marks cannot be deleted once they have been inserted in a document.	TRUE	FALSE
7.	BACKSPACE deletes the character to the right of the insertion point.	TRUE	FALSE
8.	The SHIFT key is used to select noncontiguous parts of a document.	TRUE	FALSE

Multiple-Choice Questions

1. Which shape does the mouse pointer have when it is in the text area?
   a. Right-pointing arrow
   b. I-beam
   c. Left-pointing arrow
   d. None of the above

2. Which of the following methods can be used to select a paragraph?
   a. Double-click anywhere in the paragraph.
   b. Triple-click anywhere in the paragraph.
   c. Triple-click anywhere in the left margin.
   d. None of the above

3. What is happening if your existing text is disappearing as you type new text?
   a. You are in overtype mode.
   b. You are in insert mode.
   c. You are tapping DELETE by accident.
   d. None of the above

4. Which of the following statements is true?
   a. Undo is only available if Redo has been used.
   b. Redo is only available if Undo has been used.
   c. Both a and b
   d. Neither a nor b

Skill Builder 1.1 Create a Block Style Letter

1. Start Word, and a new document window will appear. If you did not exit Word at the end of the last exercise, then click the New button on the Standard toolbar (first button on the toolbar). The New button is used to open a new document.
2. Type the following letter, tapping (ENTER) only as indicated. Notice the six hard returns shown at the top of the document. These hard returns position the date at approximately the 2" position.

(ENTER)
(ENTER)
(ENTER)
(ENTER)
(ENTER)
(ENTER)
June 26, 2001(ENTER)
(ENTER)
(ENTER)
(ENTER)
Ms. Melissa Thompson(ENTER)
Customer Service Representative(ENTER)
Urbana Software Services(ENTER)
810 Ivanhoe Way(ENTER)
Urbana, IL 61801(ENTER)
(ENTER)
Dear Ms. Thompson:(ENTER)
(ENTER)
I would like to take this opportunity to thank you for your excellent customer service. You were patient, courteous, and very helpful. The installation assistance you provided was invaluable.(ENTER)
(ENTER)
I have already put your program to good use. As you know, application programs can boost personal productivity. Your program has allowed me to manage my business much more effectively. I have enclosed the $45 fee you requested.(ENTER)
(ENTER)
Please send me a receipt and a catalog.(ENTER)
(ENTER)
Sincerely,(ENTER)
(ENTER)
(ENTER)
(ENTER)
Denise Smith(ENTER)
Administrative Assistant(ENTER)

3. Use Show All [¶] to display the hidden characters.
4. Position the insertion point just in front of the sentence *I have enclosed the $45 . . .* in the second paragraph, and tap (ENTER) twice to create a new paragraph.
5. Position the insertion point at the end of the new paragraph just in front of the paragraph mark.
6. Tap (DELETE) twice to remove the two paragraph marks separating the new paragraph from the following paragraph.
7. Tap (SPACE BAR) once to insert a space between the two sentences in the combined paragraph.
8. Position the insertion point just to the right of the sentence *The installation assistance . . .* at the end of the first paragraph. The insertion point should be just to the right of the period ending the sentence.
9. Tap (SPACE BAR), and then type the sentence **I also appreciate the overnight delivery.**
10. Type **The program is also a lot of fun.** at the end of the second paragraph.
11. Insert your initials, below the signature block.
12. Save the document to your exercise diskette with the name **Skill Builder 1.1**; then close the document.

Skill Builder 1.2 Edit a Document

1. Click Open on the Standard toolbar.
2. Navigate to your exercise diskette, and double-click the file named Skill Builder 1.2.
   You will edit this document during this exercise. Notice that this document contains formatting that you have not yet learned about. For example, the title is centered and bold, and the paragraphs are formatted with double line spacing. This document is formatted like this because it is a report.

(Continued on the next page)

3. Follow these guidelines to make the editing changes shown below.

- If only one or two characters require deletion, then position the insertion point in front of the character(s) and use (DELETE) to remove them.
- If one or more words require deletion, then select the text and use (DELETE) to remove the selected text.
- If a word or phrase needs to be replaced with another word or phrase, then select the desired text and type the replacement text.
- Use Undo if you make mistakes.

4. When you have finished, Save the changes, and Close the document.

MAINE – THE PINE TREE STATE

Maine is recognized as one of the most ~~healthy~~ healthful states in the nation with summer temperatures averaging 70°F and winter temperatures averaging 20°F. It has 3,~~7~~500 miles of coastline, is about 320 miles long and 210 miles wide, with a total area of 33,215 square miles or about as big as all of the other five New England States combined. It comprises 16 counties with 22 cities, 424 towns, 51 plantations, and 416 unorganized townships. Aroostook county is so large (6,453 square miles) that it covers an area greater than the combined size of Connecticut and Rhode Island.

Maine abounds in natural assets—542,629 acres of state and national parks, including the 92-mile Allagash Wilderness Waterway, Acadia National Park (second most visited national park in the United States), and Baxter State Park (location of Mt. Katahdin and the northern end of the Appalachian Trail). Maine has one mountain ~~which~~ that is approximately one mile high—Mt. Katahdin (5,268 ft. above sea level) and also claims America's first chartered city: York, 1641.

Maine's blueberry crop is the largest ~~blueberry crop~~ in the nation—98% of the low-bush blueberries in the United States. Potatoes rank third in acreage and third in production nationally. Maine is nationally famed for its shellfish; over 46 million pounds of ~~shellfish~~ lobster were harvested in 1997. The total of all shellfish and fin fish harvested was approximately 237 million pounds with a total value of $273 million ~~during the 1997 fishing season.~~ in 1997

Skill Builder 1.3 Create a Modified Block Style Letter

A modified block style letter has the same elements and similar formatting as a block style letter. However, the modified block style positions the date, complimentary close, and signature block near the center of the lines.

1. Click New [icon] to open a new document window.
2. Type the following modified block style letter. Start the letter approximately 2" down from the top of the page. Tap TAB seven times to begin the date, complimentary close, and signature block just past the center of the lines. Finally, use the correct number of hard returns between the various paragraphs so that you have a properly formatted business letter.
3. When you have finished, save the document with the name **`Skill Builder 1.3`**, and then close the document.

Today's Date

Ms. Jessica Simms
811 Fairview Drive
Kansas City, MO 64106

Dear Ms. Simms:

I am pleased to inform you that you had excellent scores on all of your placement tests. You scored 98% on the word processing test, 97% on the spreadsheet test, and 99% on the office procedures test. These scores were far above average and are a testament to the quality of the vocational training program you recently completed.

I am pleased to offer you employment with Wilkinson Legal Services. Sarah Adams is looking forward to working with you should you decide to accept our offer.

I know you have several other job offers, and I hope you will give Wilkinson serious consideration. Sarah has already expressed an interest in having you train our staff members due to your excellent knowledge in Word and Excel. You will certainly have a bright future at Wilkinson.

Ms. Simms, please contact me soon. We look forward to having you as part of the Wilkinson team.

Sincerely,

Cynthia Lentz
Director, Human Resources

xx

Skill Builder 1.4 Create a Personal Style Business Letter

Personal business letters are used when an individual representing himself or herself sends a letter to a recipient in a business. Personal business letters can be composed using either the block or modified block style. Notice below that the return address is included in the signature block.

1. Start a new document, space down 2", and type the letter shown below.
2. When you have finished, save the document with the name **Skill Builder 1.4**, and then close the document.

Today's Date

Mr. Richard Johnson
Customer Service Manager
Colonial Credit Corporation
1000 Sherwood Place
East Brunswick, NJ 08816

Dear Mr. Johnson:

I have been with Colonial Credit for three years, and I have always paid my bills promptly. My annual income has also increased 30% in the past three years. For these reasons, I would like my credit limit raised to $3,000. The increase is necessary because I am traveling on business quite often.

Please respond as soon as possible. I appreciate your assistance.

Sincerely,

Jill Simms
2010 Washington Way
Racine, WI 53403

Assessments

Assessment 1.1 Block Style Letter

1. Create the block style business letter shown below. Space down the proper distance from the top of the page, and use proper spacing between paragraphs.
2. Save the letter to your exercise diskette with the name **`Assessment 1.1`**.
3. Print the letter, and then close the document.

Today's Date

Mrs. Suzanne Lee
8445 South Princeton Street
Chicago, IL 60628

Dear Mrs. Lee:

Thank you for your interest in the Back Bay Users Group. We will be holding an orientation for new members on the first Thursday in April at our headquarters.

Please let us know if you can attend by calling the phone number on this letterhead. Or, if you prefer, you may respond in writing or via email.

Sincerely,

Jack Bell
Membership Chair

xx

Assessment 1.2 **Editing Skills**

1. Open the document on your exercise diskette named Assessment 1.2.
2. Make the editing changes shown in the following document.
3. Use (ENTER) to push the entire document down so that the date is positioned at approximately the 2″ position.
4. Use (TAB) to move the date, complimentary close, and signature block to approximately the 3″ position on the ruler. This will convert the letter from block style to modified block style.
5. When you have finished, save the changes, print the letter, and close the document.

Today's Date

~~Ms. Cynthia Wilson~~ Mr. Roosevelt Jackson
~~118 Upper Terrace~~ 8 Spring Street
~~Freehold, NJ 08845~~ Martinville, NJ 08836

Dear ~~Ms. Wilson~~ Mr. Jackson:

Thank you for your recent letter concerning back injuries in your office. Yes, back injuries are a common problem for office workers today. It was estimated by the U. S. Bureau of Labor Statistics that in one year over ~~490~~ 580,000 employees took time from work due to back injuries.

Encourage your office employees to make certain their work surface is at a ~~suitable~~ comfortable height. They should also be encouraged to take frequent breaks from their desks.

~~Feel free to~~ Please contact my office if you would like more information.

Sincerely,

Elaine Boudreau
Ergonomics Specialist

Assessment 1.3 Personal Style Business Letter

1. Create the personal style business letter shown below.
2. Save the letter to your exercise diskette with the name **Assessment 1.3**.
3. Print the letter, and then close the document.

Today's Date

Mr. Jake Wilson
Rebate Manager
Sierra Snowboards
4200 University Avenue
Berkeley, CA 94702

Dear Mr. Wilson:

Thank you for your excellent advice on the snowboarding equipment I recently purchased. Sierra Snowboards certainly has the best equipment in the business.

I would like to know when I can expect the rebate on the board I purchased. I mailed in my rebate coupon last month and I have yet to hear from the company. Do rebates normally take this long? Please contact me as soon as possible at (510) 223-3344. Thank you for your assistance.

Sincerely,

Melissa Jackson
1223 Appian Way
El Sobrante, CA 94803

Critical Thinking

Critical Thinking 1.1 On Your Own

Cathy Jacobson is an Administrative Assistant in the Marketing Department of Big Time Video Distributors. Big Time distributes videos to small video stores throughout the local area. Cathy works for Donald Livingston, the Director of Marketing. Donald and his marketing team have decided to offer promotional discounts to customers depending upon their sales volume in the previous quarter. The discounts are designed to encourage customers to order all of their videos from Big Time and to entice larger accounts to begin ordering from Big Time. Donald has instructed Cathy to prepare a letter to be sent to all Big Time customers.

Follow these guidelines to prepare a formal business letter announcing the promotional offer.

- Use the following generic text for the inside address.
  Name
  Company
  Address
  City, State Zip
- Let the customers know that the promotion will begin on the first day of the coming month. Use the date for the first day of the month following the preparation date of the letter.
- The discount schedule is shown below. You can describe the discount schedule in a paragraph, or you can lay it out as shown below using the TAB key to create a column effect.

Volume in Previous Quarter	Discount Percentage
$50,000	10%
$100,000	15%
$200,000	25%

- Inform the customers that in order to get the discount they must respond within 30 days by returning the enclosed card. Your letter should include an enclosure notation indicating that there is an enclosure.

Save your completed letter as **Critical Thinking 1.1**.

Critical Thinking 1.2 On Your Own

Compose a personal business letter to Donna Wilson, the Loan Manager of Citizen's Bank. The address of Citizen's bank is 12300 West Washington Avenue, Los Angeles, CA 90024. The purpose of the letter is to thank Donna for approving your $15,000 automobile loan. Donna worked hard to secure the best interest rate and terms for your loan, so you should let her know just how much you appreciate her excellent service. Save your completed letter as **Critical Thinking 1.2**, and then close it.

Critical Thinking 1.3 On Your Own

Open the Critical Thinking 1.2 letter that you composed in the previous exercise. Insert a new paragraph requesting that Donna send you information on Citizen Bank's new Small Business Credit Line program. Let Donna know that you are starting a new business venture (you choose the venture), and you are interested in obtaining financing from the bank. Save the completed letter as **Critical Thinking 1.3**.

Critical Thinking 1.4 Web Research

George Wilson is a certified financial planner and the owner of PlanRight Retirement Services. George sends correspondence to his clientele quite often and he usually includes one or more helpful hints on ways they can save money. Use Internet Explorer and a search engine of your choice to locate the Web site URLs of American Airlines, United Airlines, and Southwest Airlines. Compose a letter from George to his clientele letting them know that their 2002 tax packages are ready and available for pickup or mailing. In addition, include a paragraph describing the savings that can be realized by booking airline reservations through the Web sites of United, American, and Southwest airlines. Include the Web site URLs so that George's customers can visit the sites. Use the same generic text for the inside address that you used in Critical Thinking 1.1. Save your completed letter as **Critical Thinking 1.4**.

Critical Thinking 1.5 With a Group

Choose a classmate whom you will work with on the With a Group critical thinking exercises throughout this course. You and your classmate have started a new Web-based business named Health-e-Meals.com. Health-e-Meals.com delivers healthy, nutritious meals directly to homes, businesses, and school lunch programs. Together, compose a business letter to Donna Wilson at Citizen's Bank using the address information for Donna from Critical Thinking 1.2. Let Donna know that you are interested in establishing a $100,000 credit line with the bank and that you would like to schedule an appointment to meet with her. You compose a short paragraph describing the clientele and the product/service you are offering. Have your classmate compose a paragraph describing the current monthly sales, expenses, and growth rate of the company. Save your completed letter as **Critical Thinking 1.5**.

LESSON 2

Creating a Memorandum and Press Release

In this lesson, you will expand upon the basic skills you developed in the previous lesson. You will create a two-page document that uses a page break to separate the pages. Paragraph formatting is an important technique in Word. This lesson introduces paragraph formatting and paragraph alignment techniques. You will learn how to apply various text formats, and you will use Cut, Copy, and Paste to rearrange text and paragraphs. Finally, you will unleash the power of Word's Format Painter—a powerful tool that is used to rapidly format text and ensure formatting consistency throughout a document.

IN THIS LESSON

Word 2002 Core MOUS Objectives Covered in this Lesson

MOUS Objective Number	MOUS Objective Description	Concept Page References	Exercise Page References
W2002-1-1	Insert, modify and move text and symbols	46, 55	46, 56–57
W2002-1-2	Apply and modify text formats	53	53–54
W2002-1-5	Enter and format Date and Time	44	44–45
W2002-2-1	Modify paragraph formats	50	51–52
W2002-3-3	Modify document layout and Page Setup options	49	49–50

See the Lesson 2 Web Page at: labpub.com/learn/bc/word1/lesson2

Case Study

Lashanda Robertson is the Public Affairs Representative for Flexico, Inc., a fabrics manufacturer specializing in materials for active wear. Image and public perception are important determinants of success in the high-profile world of fashion design. Flexico is a progressive company that understands the importance of image. As the Public Affairs Representative for Flexico, Lashanda's responsibilities include issuing press releases to inform clothing manufacturers and other potential customers of forthcoming fabrics and materials. Lashanda creates a memorandum to which she attaches her latest press release announcing the new FlexMax line of fabrics for active wear. Memorandums are used for internal communication within a company or organization, whereas business letters are used for external communication. A sample of the memorandum and press release are shown below.

MEMO TO: Bill Watson

FROM: Lashanda Robertson

DATE: April 25, 2001

SUBJECT: Flexico® Press Release

I have attached a press release to announce the launch of our new FlexMax™ line of fabrics. Please review the press release and let me know if you have comments or suggestions. I will submit this press release to the media organizations next week.

xx
Attachment

Flexico®, Inc.

Press Release

Flexico Announces FlexMax™ Fabric

Announcement
San Francisco, Ca.—July 10, 2001—Flexico, Inc. today announced the FlexMax fabric for active wear. This revolutionary fabric is designed by Flexico and allows for maximum range of motion while providing support, comfort, and moisture protection. Flexmax fabric is ideally suited for active wear such as biking, hiking, and aerobics attire.

Delivery and Availability
FlexMax products are expected to reach retailers shelves by the third quarter of this year. Look for the distinctive Flexico logo and the FlexMax trademark. FlexMax products will be available at most quality sporting goods stores.

FlexMax Styles
Initially, FlexMax fabric will be available in two weights and a variety of colors. Contact Flexico or your distributor for information and samples.

About Flexico
Founded in 1988, Flexico is a leading manufacturer of fabrics for active wear and outdoor activities. Flexico fabrics are used in fine active wear products worldwide.

Memorandum Styles

There are a variety of acceptable memorandum styles in use today. All memorandum styles contain the same elements but with varied formatting. Many new formats have emerged since the widespread use of computer and word processing technology. The style illustrated below is a traditional memorandum style with minimal formatting.

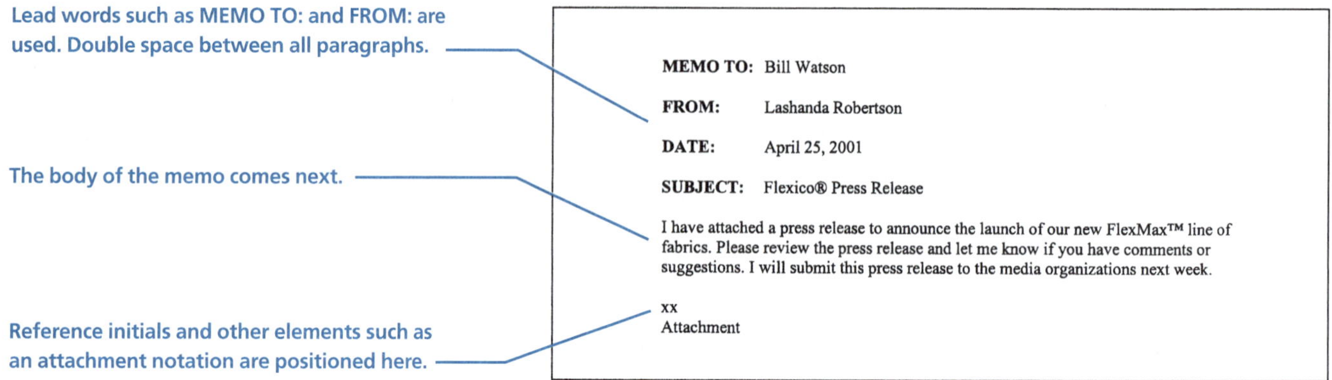

MEMO TO: Bill Watson

FROM: Lashanda Robertson

DATE: April 25, 2001

SUBJECT: Flexico® Press Release

I have attached a press release to announce the launch of our new FlexMax™ line of fabrics. Please review the press release and let me know if you have comments or suggestions. I will submit this press release to the media organizations next week.

xx
Attachment

Managing Toolbars

Word 2002 includes more than 20 toolbars to assist you in creating and formatting documents. The Standard and Formatting toolbars contain the most frequently used buttons, so they are located at the top of the Word window just below the menu bar.

Displaying and Hiding Toolbars

You can display or hide toolbars by first displaying the Toolbars list and then choosing the desired toolbar(s) from the list. The Toolbars list is displayed using the View→Toolbars command or by right-clicking any displayed toolbar. A checkmark appears on the Toolbar list next to each toolbar that is currently displayed.

Moving Toolbars

You can move toolbars to any screen location. For example, many users like to position toolbars as floating pallets over the worksheet area. You can move a toolbar by dragging the Move handle located on the left end of the toolbar.

The Move pointer appears when you point to a Move handle. You can move a toolbar to any screen location by dragging the Move handle.

Displaying the Standard and Formatting Toolbars on Separate Rows

In Word 2002, the Standard and Formatting toolbars are placed side-by-side on a single row, just below the menu bar. This arrangement was introduced in Word 2000. In earlier versions of Word, the Standard and Formatting toolbars were displayed on separate rows. The following illustration outlines the various toolbar options.

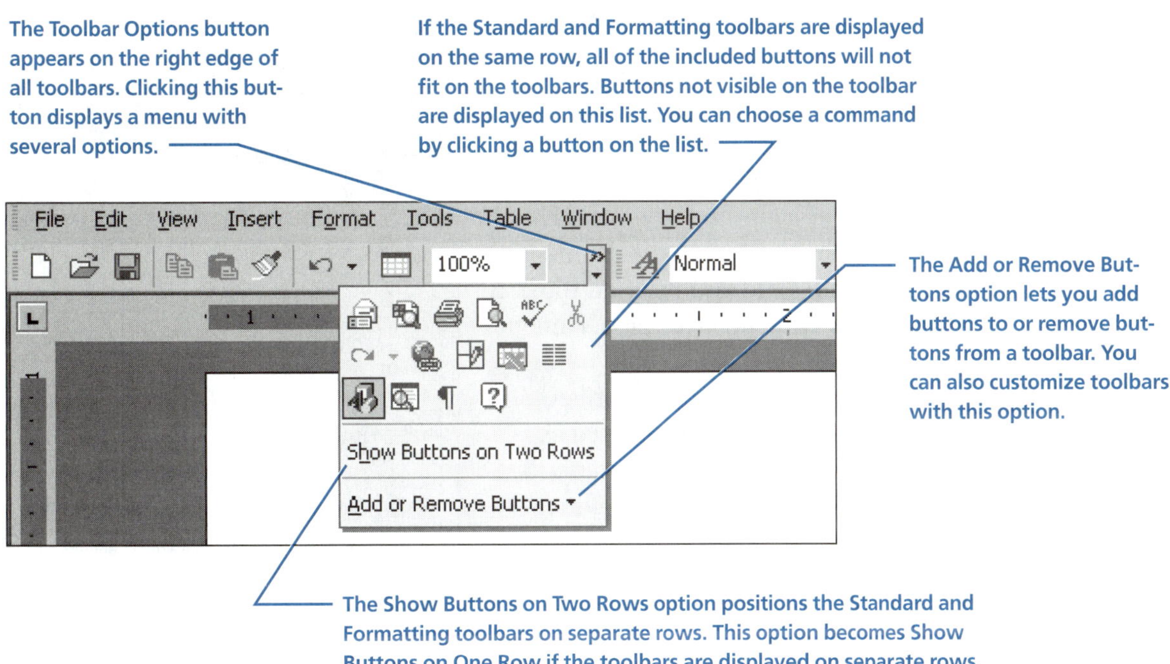

Hands-On 2.1 Display the Formatting Toolbar on a Separate Row

1. Start Word, and follow these steps to display the Standard and Formatting toolbars on separate rows:

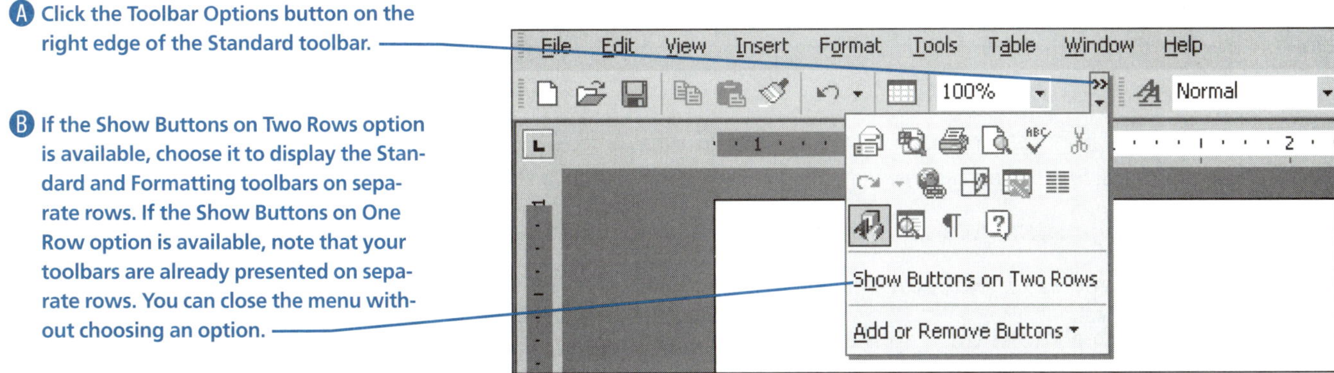

IMPORTANT! *From this point forward, the instructions in this text will assume that the Standard and Formatting toolbars are displayed on two rows. This will make it easier for you to locate buttons when instructed to do so.*

Inserting and Formatting the Date and Time

FROM THE KEYBOARD

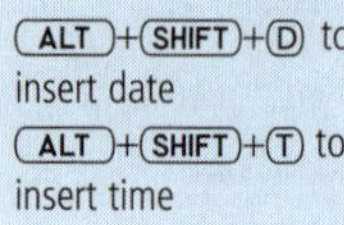

Word lets you insert the current date and time using a variety of formats. For example, the date could be inserted as 4/25/01, April 25, 2001 or 25 April 2001. The Date and Time box is displayed with the Insert→Date and Time command. The desired date and/or time format can then be chosen and inserted.

The Update Automatically Option

You can insert the date and time as text or as a field. Inserting the date as text has the same effect as typing the date into a document. Fields, however, are updated whenever a document is opened or printed. For example, imagine you created a document on April 25, 2001, and you inserted the date as a field. If you had opened the document the next day, then the date would have automatically been updated to April 26, 2001. The date and time are inserted as fields whenever the Update Automatically box is checked, as shown to the right.

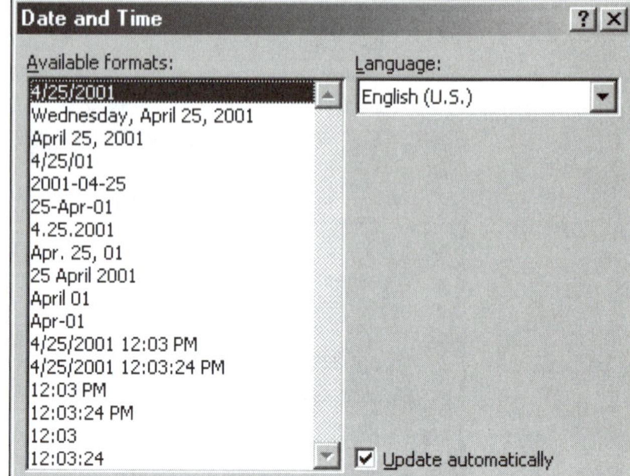

When to Use the Update Automatically Option

Maintaining the original date in a document may be important. For example, the date is important in documents such as business letters and legal agreements. If you insert the date in such documents using the Update Automatically option, then you will lose the original date the next time you open the document.

To find the original date that a document was created, right-click the document in My Computer or Windows Explorer, choose Properties, and click the General tab.

Hands-On 2.2 Set Up the Memo and Insert the Date

Set Up the Memo

1. Use ENTER to space down to approximately the 2" position.
   Memorandums generally begin 2" down from the top of the page.
2. Type **MEMO TO:** and tap the TAB key.
3. Type **Bill Watson**, and tap ENTER twice.
4. Type **FROM:** and tap the TAB key.

5. Type **Lashanda Robertson**, and tap ENTER twice.

6. Type **DATE:** and tap the TAB key twice.
It was necessary to tap TAB twice to align the date with the names. The first tab aligned the insertion point with the ½" mark on the ruler (located just above the document). The second tab aligned the insertion point with the 1" position on the ruler.

Choose a Date Format and Insert the Date

TIP!

If the date and time are not accurate on your computer, double-click the clock on the right end of the Taskbar, set the correct date and time, and click OK.

7. Choose Insert→Date and Time from the menu bar.

8. Make sure the Update Automatically box is checked at the bottom of the dialog box.
This option instructs Word to insert the date as a field. Once again, be careful when using this option. It is being used in this memorandum for instructional purposes only. You may want to avoid using this feature in business correspondence.

9. Choose the third date format on the list, and click OK.
Notice that the date appears to be in a shaded box. The shaded box indicates that the date has been inserted as a field.

10. Complete the remainder of the memorandum as shown in the following illustration.
Make sure you double-space after the date line, the subject line, and after the main paragraph. Also, use TAB to line up the phrase Flexico Press Release after the SUBJECT: lead word.

MEMO TO: Bill Watson

FROM: Lashanda Robertson

DATE: April 25, 2001

SUBJECT: Flexico Press Release

I have attached a press release to announce the launch of our new FlexMax line of fabrics. Please review the press release and let me know if you have comments or suggestions. I will submit this press release to the media organizations next week.

xx
Attachment

11. Click the Save button, and save the memorandum as **Hands-On Lesson 2**.
You will continue to enhance the memorandum throughout this lesson.

Inserting Symbols

Word lets you insert a variety of symbols, typographic characters, and international characters not found on the keyboard. Most symbols are inserted by using the Insert→Symbol command and choosing the desired symbols from the Symbol dialog box. You can also use keystrokes to insert common typographic symbols such as the Registered ® symbol and some international characters. The following illustration shows the organization of the Symbol dialog box.

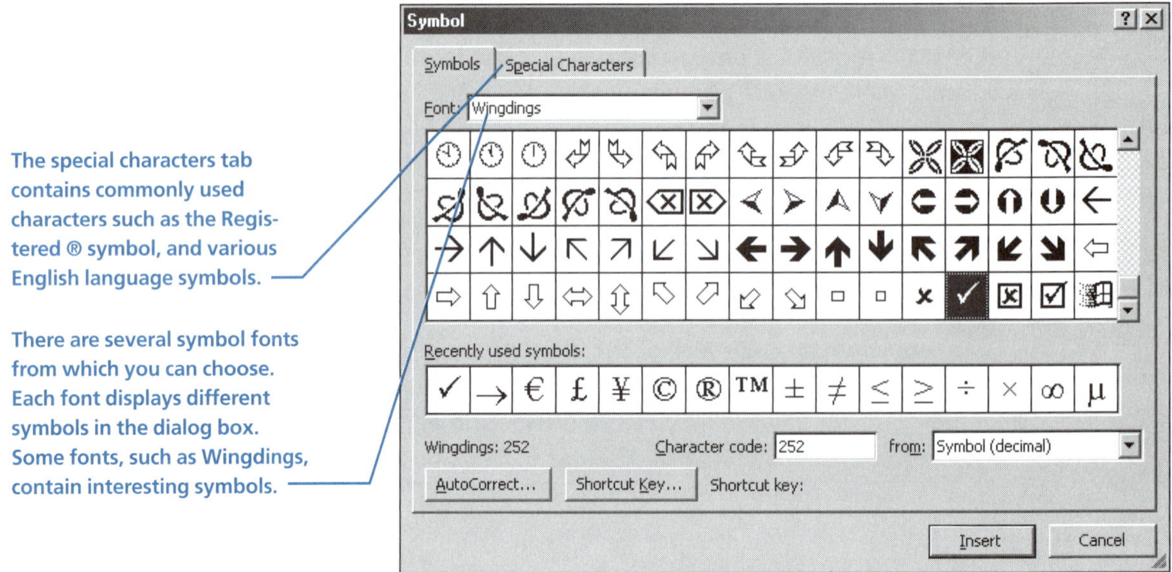

Hands-On 2.3 Insert Symbols

1. Position the insertion point to the right of the word Flexico on the SUBJECT: line.
   You will insert a Registered Trademark ® symbol in the next few steps. A registered trademark gives a company the exclusive right to use a trademark (Flexico in this case) nationwide.
2. Choose Insert→Symbol from the menu bar.
3. Click the Special Characters tab.
4. Choose the Registered ® symbol, and click the Insert button.
   The Registered ® symbol is inserted in the document, and the Symbol dialog box remains open. Word leaves the dialog box open in case you wish to insert additional symbols.
5. Click the insertion point to the right of the word FlexMax in the main paragraph (you may need to drag the dialog box out of the way in order to see the word).
6. Insert the Trademark ™ symbol.
   The Trademark symbol indicates that a company claims a phrase or icon as their trademark, but they have not received federal protection (indicated by the Registered ® symbol).
7. Click the Symbols tab on the Symbol dialog box.
8. Try choosing a different font from the Font list, and you will see a new set of symbols.
9. When you have finished experimenting, click the Close button to close the dialog box.
10. Click the Save button to save the changes.

Views

Word lets you view documents in several ways. Each view is optimized for specific types of work, thus allowing you to work efficiently. The views change the way documents appear onscreen but have no impact on the appearance of printed documents. You can choose the desired view from the View menu or from the View bar at the left end of the horizontal scroll bar as shown to the right. The following table outlines the views available in Word 2002.

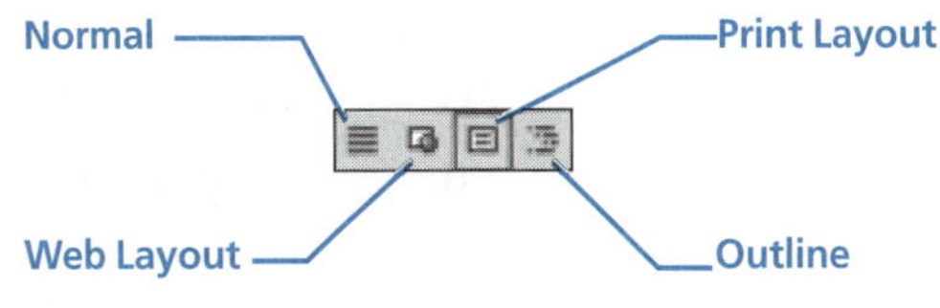

QUICK REFERENCE: VIEWS

View	Description
Print Layout	Print Layout is the default view in Word 2002. In Print Layout, documents look almost exactly as they will when printed. Print Layout is the most versatile view, allowing you to see text, graphics, headers and footers, and other types of objects. You will probably use Print Layout view most of the time.
Normal	Normal view simplifies page layout by eliminating page numbers, page breaks, and a few other elements from the view. Normal view can be useful if you want to concentrate on the text in your document. Normal view may also speed up scrolling and other tasks, especially if you have an older computer or large documents with many graphics.
Web Layout	Web Layout displays your document, as it would look on a Web page. Text, graphics, and background patterns are visible. The document is displayed on one long page without page breaks.
Outline	Outline view is useful for organizing documents.

Hands-On 2.4 Experiment with Views

1. Locate the Views bar on the left end of the horizontal scroll bar.
2. Position the insertion point over each button, and a descriptive ScreenTip will pop up.
3. Click each button to see how the appearance of the document changes.
   You may not notice much of a difference because your document lacks graphics and other more advanced elements.
4. Switch to Print Layout view when you have finished experimenting.

Zooming

The Zoom Control lets you "zoom in" to get a close-up view of a document or "zoom out" to see the "big picture." Zooming changes the size of onscreen text and graphics but has no affect on printed text and graphics. You can zoom from 10% to 500%.

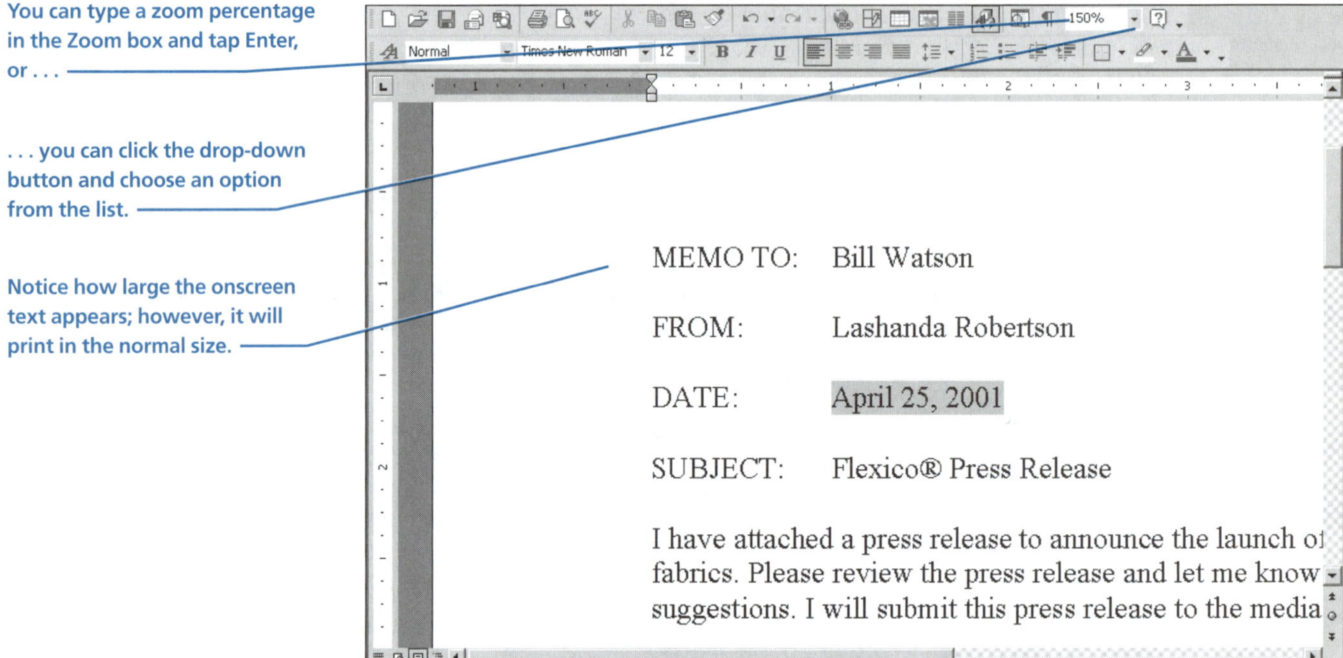

Hands-On 2.5 Use the Zoom Control

1. Follow these steps to experiment with the zoom control.

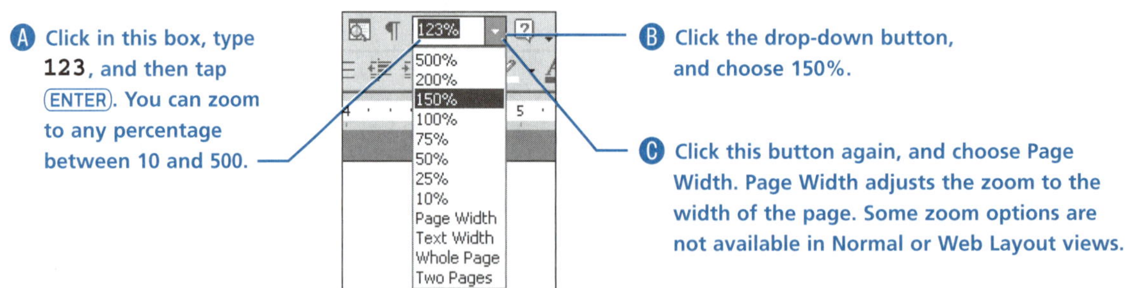

2. Use the zoom control to select the following three zoom settings: Whole Page, 75%, and Page Width. Feel free to experiment with the zoom control.

Page Breaks

If you are typing text and the insertion point reaches the bottom of a page, Word automatically breaks the page and begins a new page. This is known as an automatic page break. The location of automatic page breaks may change as text is added to or deleted from a document. Automatic page breaks are convenient when working with long documents that have continuously flowing text. For example, imagine you were writing a novel, and you decided to insert a new paragraph in the middle of a chapter. With automatic page breaks, you could insert the paragraph, and Word would automatically repaginate the entire chapter.

FROM THE KEYBOARD

CTRL+ENTER to insert page break

You can force a page break to occur at any location in a document by inserting a manual page break. A manual page break remains in place unless you remove the break. You insert manual page breaks whenever you want to control the starting point of a new page. You can insert a manual page break with the Insert→Break command.

Removing Manual Page Breaks

In Normal view, manual page breaks appear as a horizontal line with the phrase Page Break appearing on the line. The page break line also appears in Print Layout view if you click the Show All button. You can remove a manual page break by positioning the insertion point on the page break line and tapping DELETE, as shown in the following illustration.

You can remove a manual page break by showing the nonprinting characters, clicking on the Page Break line, and tapping DELETE.

I have attached a press release to announce the launch of our new FlexMax™ line of fabrics. Please review the press release and let me know if you have comments or suggestions. I will submit this press release to the media organizations next week.

xx

Attachment

Page Break

Hands-On 2.6 Page Breaks

Insert a Page Break

1. Make sure you are in Print Layout view.
2. Position the insertion point to the right of the word Attachment on the attachment line.
3. Choose Insert→Break from the menu bar.
   Notice that several types of breaks are listed on the Breaks menu. This lesson only introduces page breaks.
4. Make sure Page Break is chosen, and click OK.
   You should be able to see the bottom portion of page 1 and the top of page 2.
5. Look at the Status bar at the bottom of the screen; it will show the insertion point is on Page 2.

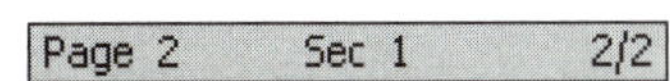

(Continued on the next page)

TIP!

You can remove a break without showing the nonprinting characters. However, this takes a little practice.

Remove the Page Break

6. Scroll up until the attachment line is visible.
7. Click the Show/Hide ¶ button, and a Page Break line will appear.
8. Click on the Page Break line, and tap DELETE.
9. Try scrolling down to the second page, and you will see that it has been removed.

Reinsert the Break

10. Scroll up, and the insertion point should be just below the attachment line.
11. Press CTRL+ENTER to reinsert the page break.
    This shortcut keystroke is useful to remember because page breaks are inserted often.
12. Click Show/Hide ¶ to hide the nonprinting characters.
    The insertion point should be positioned at the top of the second page.

Formatting Paragraphs

The word paragraph has a special meaning in Word. A paragraph includes any text or objects followed by a paragraph mark. Word lets you format paragraphs in a variety of ways. For example, you can change paragraph alignment, add bullets and numbering to paragraphs, indent paragraphs, and apply paragraph styles.

¶

A paragraph mark

You can click anywhere in a paragraph and apply the desired formats. When you tap ENTER, the formats from the current paragraph are applied to the new paragraph. For example, if a heading is centered and you tap ENTER, then the new paragraph will also be centered. You can format several paragraphs by first selecting the desired paragraphs and then applying the formats.

Aligning Text

FROM THE KEYBOARD

CTRL+L Align Left
CTRL+E for Center
CTRL+R for Align Right
CTRL+J for Justify

The alignment buttons on the Formatting toolbar allow you to align paragraphs horizontally. Text can be left or right-aligned, centered, or justified. The alignment commands affect all text in a paragraph. To mix alignments within a line, you must use customized tab stops or tables.

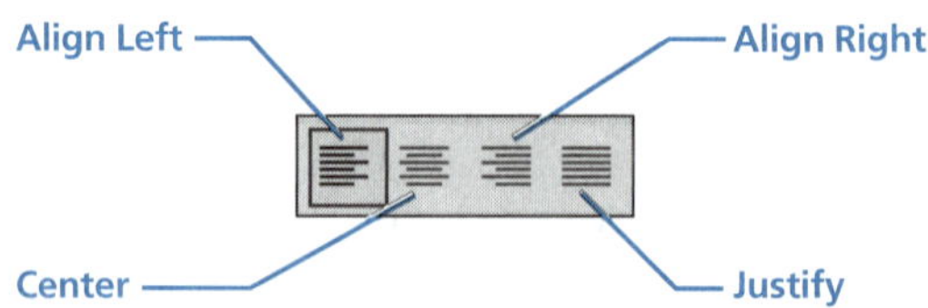

Hands-On 2.7 Set Up a Press Release

In this exercise, you will set up a press release. A press release is a type of announcement, so you will begin the first line 2″ down from the top of the page.

Set Up the Title Lines

1. Make sure the insertion point is at the top of the new page, and tap ENTER several times to space down to approximately the 2″ position.
2. Locate the alignment buttons on the Formatting toolbar, and notice that the Align Left button is pushed in.
   Left alignment is the default setting in Word.
3. Click the Center button.
   The insertion point moves to the center of the line.
4. Type the title **Flexico Announces FlexMax™ Fabric**, inserting the Trademark symbol as shown.
5. Tap ENTER twice, and notice that the center alignment is still in effect.
   Paragraph formats (including alignments) are copied to the next paragraph when ENTER is tapped.
6. Type **Press Release**, and tap ENTER twice.
7. Type **Flexico®, Inc.** inserting the Registered symbol as shown.
8. Tap ENTER twice; then click Align Left to restore left alignment.
   You are now ready to set up the body of the press release.

Set Up the Body

9. Type the heading **Announcement**, and tap ENTER.
10. Type the phrase **San Francisco, Ca**.
    In the next step, you will insert an em dash. Em dashes are used as connectors within sentences and are available on the Symbols dialog box.

FROM THE KEYBOARD

Type two hyphens with no spaces before or after hyphens. Word will convert hyphens to em dash when SPACE BAR is tapped after typing second connector word.

11. Display the Symbols dialog box, choose Em Dash from the Special Characters tab, and click Insert.
12. If necessary, move the Symbol dialog box out of the way, and click in the document to the right of the em dash.
13. Type the current date, and insert another em dash.

(Continued on the next page)

14. Close the Symbol dialog box, and complete the press release as shown below.

Flexico Announces FlexMax™ Fabric

Press Release

Flexico®, Inc.

Announcement
San Francisco, Ca.—July 10, 2001—Flexico, Inc. today announced the FlexMax fabric for active wear. FlexMax fabric is ideally suited for active wear such as biking, hiking, and aerobics attire. This revolutionary fabric is designed by Flexico and allows for maximum range of motion while providing support, comfort, and moisture protection.

About Flexico
Founded in 1988, Flexico is a leading manufacturer of fabrics for active wear and outdoor activities. Flexico fabrics are used in fine active wear products worldwide.

FlexMax Styles
Initially, FlexMax fabric will be available in two weights and a variety of colors. Contact Flexico or your distributor for information and samples.

Delivery and Availability
FlexMax products are expected to reach retailers shelves by the third quarter of this year. Look for the distinctive Flexico logo and the FlexMax trademark. FlexMax products will be available at most quality sporting goods stores.

15. Save the changes, and continue with the next topic.

Formatting Text

In Word and other Office programs, you can format text by changing the font, font size, and color. You can also apply various font formats including bold, italics, and underline. If no text is selected, the format settings take effect from that point forward or until you change them again. If you wish to format existing text, you must select the text and then apply the desired formats. Text can be formatted using options in the font box. The font box is displayed with the Format→Font command. In addition, you can format text with buttons on the Formatting toolbar, as shown in the following illustration.

FROM THE KEYBOARD

CTRL+B for Bold
CTRL+U for Underline
CTRL+I for Italics
CTRL+] to increase size one point
CTRL+[to decrease size one point

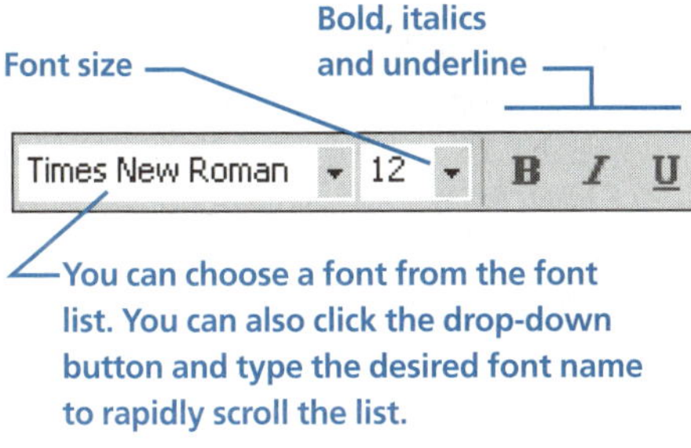

The Font Color button is on the right end of the Formatting toolbar. The color palette appears when you click the drop-down button. Once you choose a color, the color is displayed on the button. From that point forward, you can rapidly apply the color by clicking the button.

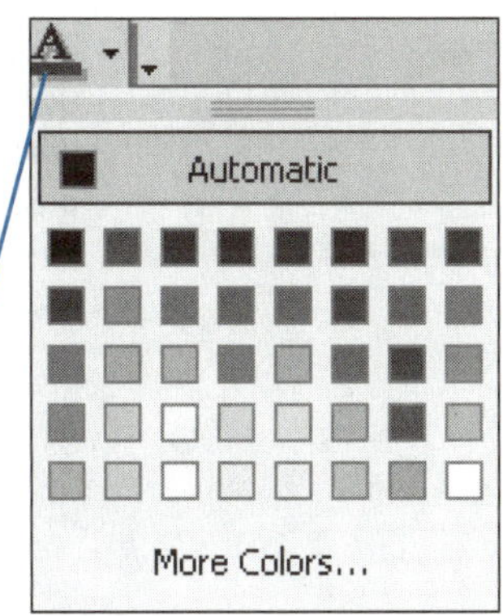

Hands-On 2.8 Format Text

Format the Press Release Title Lines

1. Follow this step to select the press release title lines.

2. Follow these steps to format the title lines.

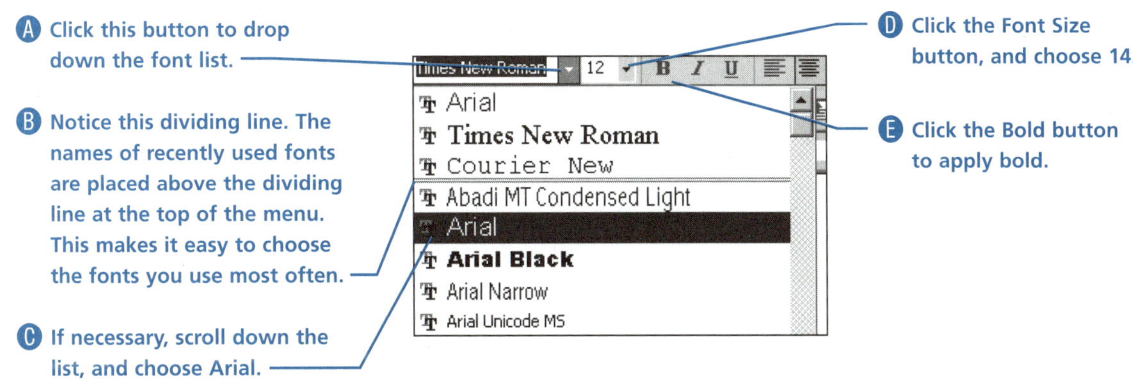

(Continued on the next page)

3. Click the drop-down button on the Font Color button (on the right end of the Formatting toolbar), and choose your favorite color.

Use Keystrokes to Select and Format

The following steps show you how to select using the keyboard. In some situations, keyboard selecting can give you greater precision and control.

4. Scroll up to the first page of the document to view the memorandum.
5. Follow these steps to select the phrase MEMO TO:

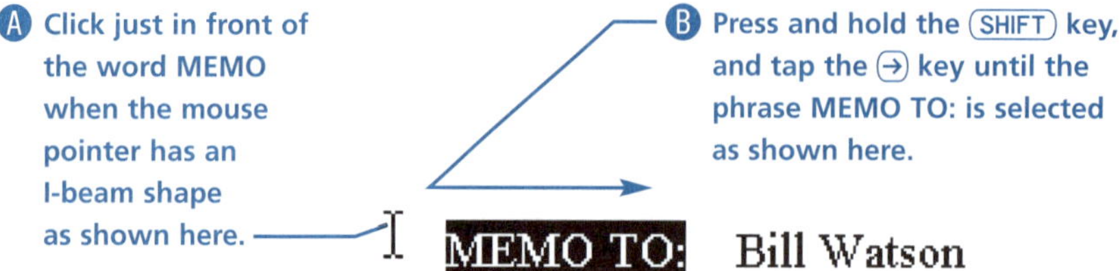

6. Press CTRL+B to apply bold to the phrase.
7. Use the techniques in the previous two steps to apply bold to the next lead word, FROM:.
8. Now apply bold to the lead word DATE:. You should see the date move one tab stop to the right, thus throwing off the alignment.
   This occurred because the bold format increased the size of the lead word DATE:. The increased size pushed the lead word past the tab stop at the ½" position on the ruler. This in turn pushed the date past the tab stop at the 1" position. In the next few steps, you will solve this dilemma by removing a tab stop.

Remove a Tab Stop

9. Click the Show/Hide ¶ button to display the nonprinting characters.
10. Notice the tab → symbols between DATE: and the date.
    The tab symbols show each location where the TAB key was tapped.
11. Click between the tab → symbols, and tap DELETE to remove the second symbol.
    The date will move to the left, restoring proper alignment.
12. Click Show/Hide ¶ to hide the nonprinting characters.
13. Now apply bold to the SUBJECT: heading.
14. Save the changes, and continue with the next topic.

Cut, Copy, and Paste

Cut, Copy, and Paste are available in all Office XP applications. With Cut, Copy, and Paste you can move or copy text within a document, between documents, or between different Office applications. For example, you could use the Copy command to copy an important paragraph from one document, and the Paste command to paste the paragraph to another document. Cut, Copy, and Paste are most efficient for moving or copying text a long distance within a document or between documents. Cut, Copy, and Paste are easy to use if you remember the following concepts:

- You must select text before issuing a Cut or Copy command.
- You must position the insertion point at the desired location before issuing the Paste command. Otherwise, you will paste at the wrong location.

QUICK REFERENCE: USING CUT, COPY, AND PASTE

Command	Description	How to Issue the Command
Cut	The Cut command removes selected text from its original location and places it on the Office Clipboard.	Click the Cut button, or press CTRL+X.
Copy	The Copy command also places selected text on the Office Clipboard, but it leaves a copy of the text in the original location.	Click the Copy button, or press CTRL+C.
Paste	The Paste command pastes the most recently cut or copied text into the document at the insertion point location.	Click the Paste button, or press CTRL+V.

The Office Clipboard

The Office Clipboard lets you collect items from any Office document or program and paste them into any other Office document. For example, you can collect a paragraph from a Word document, data from an Excel worksheet, and a graphic from a PowerPoint slide and then paste them all into a Word document. The Office Clipboard can also be used within an application like Word to collect several items and then paste them as desired. The Office Clipboard can hold up to 24 items.

How it Works

You can place multiple items on the Office Clipboard using the standard Cut and Copy commands; however, the Office Clipboard must first be displayed in the Task Pane. The Office Clipboard is displayed with the Edit→Office Clipboard command. Once the Office Clipboard is displayed, you can choose an item and paste it into your document.

Hands-On 2.9 Use Cut and Paste

In this exercise, you will use Cut and Paste to rearrange the title lines in the press release.

1. Scroll down to the press release page.
2. Follow these steps to Cut and Paste a title line.

The Press Release title and the paragraph mark below it should have pushed the Flexico Announces heading down, maintaining the double-spacing of the title lines. This occurred because of the way you selected the text prior to issuing the Cut command. By dragging in the margin to the left of the text, you selected both the text and the paragraph marks. The paragraph marks were pasted along with the text. The paragraph marks pushed the Flexico Announces paragraph down, maintaining the double-spacing. This was, by the way, the intended result.

3. Now select the third title line, Flexico®, Inc., and the empty paragraph below it by dragging in the left margin.
4. Click the Cut button.
5. Position the insertion point just in front of the first heading, Press Release.
6. Click the Paste button.
Your headings should now have the arrangement shown to the right.

Use the Office Clipboard

7. Click the drop-down button on the Undo button.
If you performed the preceding steps correctly, the first four items on the Undo list should be Paste, Cut, Paste, Cut.
8. Slide the mouse pointer over the first four items to select them, and click the mouse button.
The press release headings should be in the same order they were in prior to cutting and pasting.

9. Choose Edit→Office Clipboard from the menu bar.
The Clipboard task pane will appear, displaying the Office Clipboard. Notice that the Office Clipboard displays a Paste All button that allows you to paste all items currently on the clipboard and a Clear All button that allows you to clear the clipboard. Individual items on the clipboard can be pasted by clicking them or by pointing at them and choosing Paste from the pop-up menu.
10. Click the Clear All button to clear the clipboard.
11. Select the Press Release heading and the empty paragraph below it.
12. Click the Cut button.
Notice that the item appears on the clipboard.
13. Select the Flexico®, Inc. heading and the empty paragraph below it.
14. Click the Cut button.
The clipboard should now display two items.
15. Position the insertion point just in front of the Flexico Announces title line.
16. Follow these steps to paste the Press Release item:

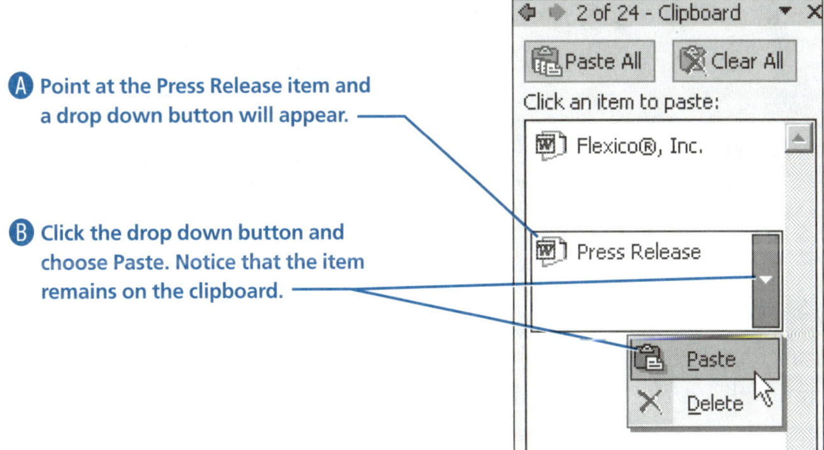

17. Position the insertion point just in front of the Press Release title line.
18. Now paste the Flexico®, Inc. item by simply clicking it on the clipboard.
As you can see, the Office Clipboard can be useful if you are collecting items from several places in a document. Keep in mind, however, that Cut, Copy, and Paste can be used without the Office Clipboard.
19. Click the Clear All button to clear the clipboard contents.
20. Close the Clipboard task pane by clicking its Close button.

Drag and Drop

Drag and drop produces the same result as Cut, Copy, and Paste. However, Drag and Drop is usually more efficient if you are moving or copying text a short distance within the same document. If the original location and destination are both visible in the current window, then it is usually easier to use Drag and Drop. With Drag and Drop, you select the text you wish to move or copy and release the mouse button. Then you drag the text to the desired destination. If you press the CTRL key while releasing the mouse button, the text is copied to the destination.

Right Dragging

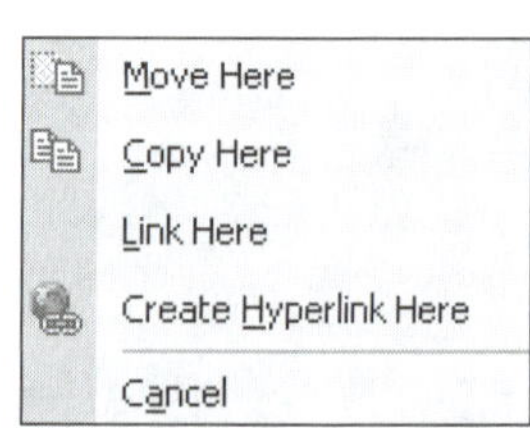

Right-Drag Pop-Up Menu

Right dragging is a variation of the drag-and-drop technique. Many beginners find Drag and Drop difficult to use because they have difficulty controlling the mouse. This difficulty is compounded if they are trying to copy text using Drag and Drop. This is because copying requires the CTRL key to be held while dragging the text. With the Right-Drag method, the right mouse button is used when dragging. When the right mouse button is released at the destination, a pop-up menu appears. The pop-up menu lets you choose Move, Copy, or Cancel. This provides more control because there is no need to use the CTRL key when copying, and you have the option of canceling the move or copy. The Right-Drag pop-up menu is shown in the illustration to the right.

Hands-On 2.10 Use Drag and Drop and Right Drag

In this exercise, you will use Drag and Drop and the Right-Drag method to rearrange paragraphs.

Use Drag and Drop

1. If necessary, scroll down until the paragraphs with the headings About Flexico, FlexMax Styles, and Delivery and Availability are all visible on the screen.
   Drag and Drop is most effective for moving or copying a short distance on the screen.
2. Follow these steps to move the Delivery and Availability paragraph and heading.

   A Select from the empty paragraph above the Delivery and Availability heading to the end of the paragraph as shown in the illustration.

   B Release the mouse button.

   C Position the mouse pointer on the selected text, and drag the text up until the move pointer is just above the About Flexico heading, as shown here.

   D Release the mouse button to drop the text above the About Flexico heading.

Announcement
San Francisco, Ca—Today's Date—Flexico, Inc. today announced the FlexMax fabric for active wear. FlexMax fabric is ideally suited for active wear such as biking, hiking, and aerobics attire. This revolutionary fabric is designed by Flexico and allows for maximum range of motion while providing support, comfort, and moisture protection.

About Flexico
Founded in 1988, Flexico is a leading manufacturer of fabrics for active wear and outdoor activities. Flexico fabrics are used in fine active wear products worldwide.

FlexMax Styles
Initially, FlexMax fabric will be available in two weights and a variety of colors. Contact Flexico or your distributor for information and samples.

Delivery and Availability
FlexMax products are expected to reach retailers shelves by the third quarter of this year. Look for the distinctive Flexico logo and the FlexMax trademark. FlexMax products will be available at most quality sporting goods stores.

If you selected the empty paragraph above the text as shown and dropped the text in the empty space above the About Flexico heading, then your paragraphs should be properly spaced.

Use Right Drag

3. Follow these steps to move the FlexMax Styles paragraph and heading.

Ⓐ Select from the empty paragraph above the FlexMax Styles heading to the end of the paragraph as shown here; then release the mouse button.

Ⓑ Position the mouse pointer on the selected text, and press and hold the right mouse button.

Ⓒ Drag the mouse up while holding the right button until the move pointer is positioned just above the About Flexico heading, as shown here.

Delivery and Availability
FlexMax products are expected to reach retailers shelves by the third
Look for the distinctive Flexico logo and the FlexMax trademark. Fle
be available at most quality sporting goods stores.

About Flexico
Founded in 1988, Flexico is a leading manufacturer of fabrics for acti
outdoor activities. Flexico fabrics are used in fine active wear produc

FlexMax Styles
Initially, FlexMax fabric will be available in two weights and a variet
Flexico or your distributor for information and samples.

Ⓓ Release the mouse button, and choose Move Here from the pop-up menu that appears. Notice that the pop-up menu would have allowed you to cancel the move if desired.

Move a Sentence

4. Use any of the move techniques you have learned thus far to move the last sentence in the Announcement paragraph as shown in the following illustration. You can use Cut and Paste, Drag and Drop, or Right Drag.

Move the selected sentence to this location in front of the previous sentence. When the move is complete, you will need to insert a space after the moved sentence.

Announcement
San Francisco, Ca.—Today's Date—Flexico, Inc. today announced the FlexMax fabric for active wear. FlexMax fabric is ideally suited for active wear such as biking, hiking, and aerobics attire. This revolutionary fabric is designed by Flexico and allows for maximum range of motion while providing support, comfort, and moisture protection.

The Format Painter

The Format Painter lets you copy text formats from one location to another. This is convenient if you want the same format(s) applied to text in different locations. The Format Painter copies all text formats, including the font, font size, color, and character effects. The Format Painter saves time and helps create consistent formatting throughout a document. The Format Painter can also be used to copy paragraph formats, such as alignment settings.

QUICK REFERENCE: COPYING TEXT FORMATS WITH THE FORMAT PAINTER

- Click on the text with the format(s) you wish to copy.
- Click the Format Painter once if you want to copy formats to one other location, or double-click if you want to copy to multiple locations.
- Select the text at the new location(s) that you want to format. If you double-clicked in the previous step, the Format Painter will remain active, allowing you to select text at multiple locations. You can even scroll through the document to reach the desired location(s).
- If you double-clicked in the first step, then click the Format Painter button when you have finished. This will turn off the Format Painter.

Hands-On 2.11 Use the Format Painter

Format Text

1. Click on the Announcement heading (just above the first large paragraph of text).
2. Choose Format→Font to display the Font dialog box.

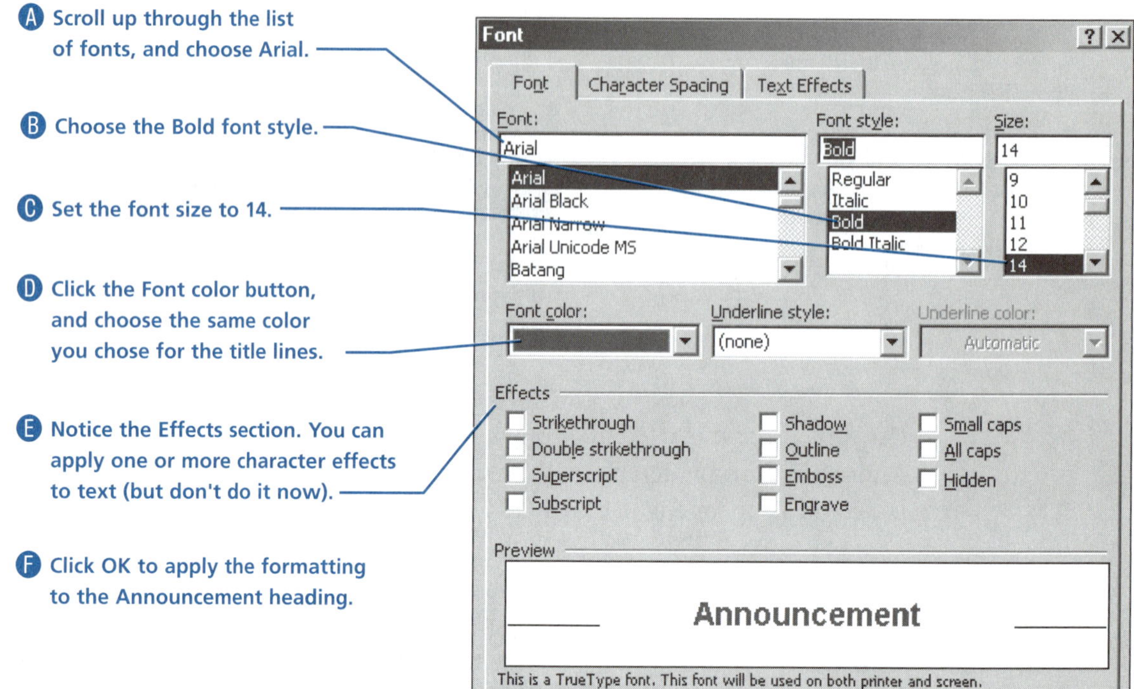

Notice that you were able to format the word Announcement without actually selecting it. You can format a single word by clicking on the word and applying the desired formats.

Copy Formats to One Location

3. Make sure the insertion point is on the Announcement heading.
4. Click the Format Painter button on the Standard toolbar.
   An animated paintbrush icon will be added to the I-beam pointer once it is positioned over the document.
5. Drag the mouse pointer across the Delivery and Availability heading and release the mouse button.
   The Arial, 14pt, bold, colored formats should be copied to the heading. The animated paintbrush icon also vanished because you clicked the Format Painter button just once in the previous step. If you want to copy formats to multiple locations, you must double-click the Format Painter. Actually, the 14pt heading is too large for these paragraphs. In the next few steps, you will change the size to 12pt for the Announcement heading and then copy the formats to the other headings in the press release.

Copy Formats to Several Locations

6. Click anywhere on the Announcement heading.
7. Click the Font Size 14 drop-down button on the Formatting toolbar, and choose 12.
   Once again, you can format an individual word by just clicking on the word and applying the desired formats.
8. Double-click the Format Painter.
9. Select the Delivery and Availability heading by either dragging the mouse over it or by clicking in front of it in the margin.
10. Select the FlexMax Styles heading to copy the formats to that heading.
11. If necessary, scroll down, and then select the About Flexico heading.
12. Click the Format Painter to turn it off.
13. Scroll through your document, and take a moment to appreciate your work.
14. Feel free to experiment with any of the techniques you have learned in this lesson.
15. When you have finished, save the changes to your document; then close the document.
    Continue with the end-of-lesson questions and exercises.

Concepts Review

True/False Questions

1.	The zoom control changes the size of printed text.	TRUE	FALSE
2.	The Formatting toolbar can be used to set all text formats and character effects.	TRUE	FALSE
3.	Normal view is the default view in Word 2002.	TRUE	FALSE
4.	The Format Painter is used to copy and paste text.	TRUE	FALSE
5.	Manual page breaks remain in place until the user removes them.	TRUE	FALSE
6.	The Right-Drag method displays a pop-up menu when the mouse button is released.	TRUE	FALSE
7.	The Office Clipboard can hold up to 12 cut or copied items.	TRUE	FALSE
8.	Items must be pasted from the Office Clipboard in the same order that they were placed on the Clipboard.	TRUE	FALSE

Multiple-Choice Questions

1. In order to copy text formats to several locations in a document, you must
   a. click the Format Painter button and then select the desired text.
   b. double-click the Format Painter button and then select the desired text.
   c. use the Copy button.
   d. This cannot be done in Word.

2. Which of the following statements can be used to describe manual page breaks?
   a. Manual page breaks remain in place until they are deleted.
   b. Manual page breaks are inserted by the user.
   c. Manual page breaks can be inserted by pressing CTRL+ENTER.
   d. All of the above

3. What is the percentage range of the zoom control?
   a. 25%–200%
   b. 10%–500%
   c. 25%–500%
   d. None of the above

4. Which key should you press if you want to copy while using drag-and-drop?
   a. SHIFT
   b. CTRL
   c. ALT
   d. HOME

Skill Builders

Skill Builder 2.1 Alignment and Formatting Practice

1. Click New to start a new document.
2. Click the Center button.
3. Tap ENTER several times to space down to 2″.
4. Set the font to Arial, the point size to 18, and turn on bold.
5. Click the drop-down button on the Font Color button (on the right end of the Formatting toolbar), and choose your favorite color.
6. Type **The Wilson Family**, and tap ENTER *twice.*
   Notice you can apply text formats prior to typing text. The formats remain in effect until you change them or move the insertion point to a location with different formats.
7. Set the font size to 14.
8. Type **Is Having a**, and tap ENTER twice.
9. Set the font size to 18.
10. Type **Big Yard Sale**, tap ENTER twice, and set the alignment to Left.
11. Set the font to Times New Roman, the size to 14, turn off bold, and set the color to black.
12. Complete the document as shown below. You will need to apply bold formatting to the date and time as shown.
13. Save the document as **Skill Builder 2.1**, then close the document.

The Wilson Family

Is Having a

Big Yard Sale

Stop by our home at 22 Maple Street in Walnut Grove on July 21 for the yard sale of the summer! We'll have furniture, toys, electronics, antiques, and much more. We start at 8:00, so arrive early and be prepared to find bargains, one-of-a-kind items, and rare antiques!

Skill Builder 2.2 The Office Clipboard, Format Painter, and Drag and Drop

In this exercise, you will open a document on your exercise diskette. You will use the Office Clipboard to rearrange paragraphs, the Format Painter to paint formats, and Drag and Drop to move blocks of paragraphs.

Use the Office Clipboard

1. Open the document named Skill Builder 2.2 on your exercise diskette.
   Notice that the document contains a list of professional contacts. In the next few steps, you will use the Office Clipboard to reorganize the contacts by contact type. In other words, all of the attorneys will be grouped together, followed by the designers, then the bookkeepers.
2. Choose Edit→Office Clipboard from the menu bar.
   The Clipboard task pane appears, displaying the Office Clipboard. You must have the Office Clipboard displayed if you want to cut or copy multiple items to it.
3. If necessary, click the Clear All button to clear the clipboard.
4. Select the first attorney contact—David Roberts, Attorney—by clicking in front of the contact in the left margin.
   This will select the entire paragraph, including the paragraph mark.
5. Click the Cut button and the item will appear on the clipboard.
6. Select the next attorney—Lisa Wilson, Attorney—and Cut it to the clipboard.
7. Cut the remaining attorney contacts to the clipboard. Use Undo if you make a mistake. However, be careful because even if you use Undo, the item you cut will remain on the clipboard.
8. Now Cut the designer contacts to the clipboard.
   The bookkeeper contacts should now be grouped together in the document.
9. Tap ENTER to position the insertion point on a new line below the bookkeeper contacts.
10. Click the Paste All button on the Office Clipboard to paste the attorney and designer contacts.
    Notice that the contacts are pasted in the order they were cut, thus grouping the attorneys together and the designers together.

Create Headings

11. Click in front of the first bookkeeper contact, and tap ENTER to create a blank line.
12. Click on the blank line, and type **Bookkeepers**.
13. Use this technique to create an **Attorneys** heading above the first attorney contact, and a **Designers** heading above the first designer contact.

Use the Format Painter

14. Click on the Professional Contacts heading at the top of the document.
15. Double-click the Format Painter .
16. Click the Bookkeepers heading to copy the formats to that heading.
17. Click the Attorneys and Designers headings.
18. Turn off the Format Painter .
19. Select the Professional Contacts heading, and increase the size to 14.

Use Drag and Drop

20. Select the Attorneys heading and the four attorney contacts by dragging in the left margin.
21. Release the mouse button.
22. Position the mouse pointer on the selection, and drag up until the pointer is just in front of the Bookkeepers heading.
23. Release the mouse button to move the Attorneys block above the Bookkeepers.
24. Now move the Designers heading and the designer contacts above the Bookkeepers.

Create Space and Center the Title

25. Position the insertion point just in front of the Attorneys heading, and tap ENTER to create a blank line between the Professional Contacts heading and the Attorneys heading.
26. Insert blank lines above the Designers and Bookkeepers headings.
27. Click on the Professional Contacts heading, and click the Center Align button.
28. Use ENTER to push the entire document down to approximately the 2″ position.
29. Save the changes, and close the document when you have finished.

Skill Builder 2.3 Create a Memorandum

1. Follow these guidelines to create the memorandum shown below.
   - Position the MEMO TO: line approximately 2" down from the top of the page.
   - Double space between all paragraphs, and apply bold to the lead words MEMO TO:, FROM:, DATE:, and SUBJECT:.
   - Apply bold formatting as shown in the body paragraph.
2. Save the memo with the name **Skill Builder 2.3**, and then close the document.

MEMO TO: Jason Alexander

FROM: Tamika Jackson

DATE: Today's Date

SUBJECT: Monthly Sales Meeting

Our monthly sales meeting will be held in the conference room at **10:00 a.m.** on **Thursday, July 24**. Please bring your sales forecast for August and any important accounts that you wish to discuss. I will give you a presentation on our new products that are scheduled for release in September. I look forward to seeing you then.

xx

Skill Builder 2.4 Formatting Skills

1. Follow these guidelines to create the document shown below.
   - Begin the document 2" down and enter all text. Center the titles as shown. Notice the dashes between the locations and days of the week in the Hands-On Workshops list and the other lists. These are em dashes inserted using the Special Characters tab of the Symbols dialog box. An easy way to insert these dashes is to insert the first one, select it, and copy it with the Copy command. Then, paste the dash at every other location where it is needed.
   - Format the first title line with an Arial, bold, 16pt font. Apply a color to the title.
   - Use the Format Painter to copy the formats to the subtitle, then change the font size of the subtitle to 14pt.
   - Format the Hands-On Workshops heading with an Arial, bold, 12pt font, and apply the same color you applied to the titles.
   - Use the Format Painter to copy the formats from the Hands-On Workshops heading to the Seminar Series heading and the Internet Events heading.
2. Save the document with the name **`Skill Builder 2.4`**, and then close the document.

Southern California Computer Training

Summer Training Schedule

The following schedule is for hands-on workshops, seminars, and Internet events for July, August, and September. If you plan on attending an event, make your reservations early as we have limited seating. You should also pick up your training materials at least one week prior to your event.

Hands-On Workshops
Irvine—Tuesday, July 20
Los Angeles—Wednesday, July 21
San Diego—Wednesday, August 18
Riverside—Tuesday, September 21

Seminar Series
Irvine—Wednesday, July 21
Los Angeles—Thursday, August 19
Riverside—Wednesday, September 22

Internet Events
Los Angeles—Friday, August 20
Woodland Hills—Thursday, September 2

Assessments

Assessment 2.1 Create a Memorandum

1. Follow these guidelines to create the memorandum shown below.
   - Begin the document 2″ down from the top of the page.
   - Boldface the lead words MEMO TO, FROM, DATE, and SUBJECT as shown.
   - Use the em dash after the department names.
   - Type your initials at the bottom of the memo.
2. Save the document to your exercise diskette with the name **`Assessment 2.1`**.
3. Print the document, and then close it.

MEMO TO: Mark Paxton

FROM: Tamara Niu

DATE: Today's Date

SUBJECT: Purchase Orders

The following departments have requested that purchase orders be issued for the specified products. Please conduct the necessary research and issue purchase orders as soon as possible.

Marketing—A cordless mouse that can be used at least six feet away from the base unit.

Systems—A flatbed scanner with high resolution. It should have software that allows enhancing of images even as scanning is taking place.

Research—A video camera that is supported by the Universal Serial Bus (USB) standard. The price should be lower than what we paid for the analog camera.

xx

Assessment 2.2

1. Open the document named Assessment 2.2 on your exercise diskette.
2. Follow these guidelines to modify the memorandum.
    - Apply bold formatting as shown below.
    - Insert the Do Not Try to Please Everyone line and the paragraphs following it as shown below, including the initials line and the attachment line.

MEMO TO: Office Staff

FROM: Ariel Ramirez

DATE: Today's Date

SUBJECT: Multiple Supervisors

Most executive assistants at our firm have multiple supervisors. Therefore, we are offering the following suggestions to make your work easier.

Prioritize—What is important may take preference over what is urgent. Which project can be delayed? Overall, which has the greatest importance to our firm? Evaluate and schedule your time accordingly.

Refuse Assignments—If you do not have the time, ask your supervisor if someone else can do the assignment. It's better to say no than to not meet the deadline.

Enjoy Multiple Projects—Learn to enjoy the challenge of switching from one project to another. You may not be able to finish them all, but realize the contribution you have made to each one.

Do Not Try to Please Everyone—There is no way you will please all of your supervisors all of the time. Set your own approval rating and go with it.

Listed on the attached sheet are some related workshops you may want to attend. Contact Human Resources for registration forms.

xx
Attachment

(Continued on the next page)

3. Tap (ENTER) once after the Attachment line; then insert a page break.
4. Follow these guidelines to create the following page.
   - Start the title line 2″ down.
   - Center and bold the title as shown.
   - Apply the color of your choice to the title.
   - Double-space between all paragraphs.

RECOMMENDED WORKSHOPS

How to Mange Your Boss, April 23, Holiday Inn, Fremont, Phoenix Extension

The Perfect Support Person, April 30, Hyatt at the Airport, ProPeople Associates

Prioritizing Made Easy, May 5, Sheraton at the Wharf, CareerTech

Office Procedures for the Executive Assistant, May 7, SF Marriott, Phoenix Extension

5. Save the changes, print the document, and then close it.

Assessment 2.3

1. Open the document named Assessment 2.3.
2. Follow these guidelines to modify the document until it matches the following document.
   - Rearrange the paragraphs into groups as shown, using Cut and Paste, drag-and-drop, or the Office Clipboard. Use whichever method you prefer. The rearranged paragraphs should match the following example.
   - Insert a title, headings, and empty paragraphs as shown in the example.
   - Format the title and headings with an Arial bold font and a sea-green color. The title should have a font size of 16.
   - Use (ENTER) to push the entire completed document down to the 2″ position.
3. Save the document, print the document, and then close it.

Bay Area Environmental Groups

Marin County
Marin Wetlands Conservation Corps, Marin County
Mt. Tamalpais Hiking Club, Marin County
John Muir Society, Marin County
Redwood Preservation Group, Marin County

East Bay
East Bay Conservation Corps, East Bay
El Cerrito Wetlands Restoration, East Bay
San Pablo Reservoir Water Reclamation, East Bay
Citizens for Environmental Restoration, East Bay

South Bay
South Bay Water Restoration, South Bay
San Jose Environmental Corps, South Bay
Gilroy Preservation Society, South Bay
Bay Wildlife Foundation, South Bay

Critical Thinking

Critical Thinking 2.1 On Your Own

Tanisha Johnson is the Director of Human Resources for Big Time Video Distributors. Tanisha works hard to provide Big Time employees with a variety of attractive fringe benefits. She realizes this is necessary in today's competitive job market. Recently, Tanisha set up the Big Time Discounts program with other local businesses. Through this program, Big Time employees are issued a Big Time discount card. The card gives Big Time employees a 10% discount on the products or services they purchase from participating businesses.

Set up a memorandum from Tanisha Johnson to the Big Time employees announcing the program. Let the employees know that the effective date will be the beginning of next month and that all employees are eligible to participate. Let them know that a 10% discount will be given to them on all purchases. Mention that the participating businesses list will be issued within a few days. Save your completed memorandum as **`Critical Thinking 2.1`**, then close it.

Critical Thinking 2.2 On Your Own

Tanisha Johnson has prepared the memorandum that was set up in Critical Thinking 2.1 but she changes her mind and decides not to send the memo until the participating businesses list is completed. Open the Critical Thinking 2.1 memorandum and save it as **`Critical Thinking 2.2`**. Add a second page to the memorandum that includes the following participating businesses list. You can use the TAB key to line up the list entries. Also, bold the headings as shown.

Discount Provider	**Contact**	**Number**
West Side Chiropractic	Dave Smith	223-1345
The Panda Restaurant	Sam Chin	223-0909
Spiffy Cleaners	Carol Caruso	222-9090
Southside Cinemas	Ken Turner	221-2121
Dave's Auto Repair	Dave Adams	221-4545

Include a centered title at the top of the second page. Edit the memorandum text on the first page to indicate that the participating businesses list is attached. Your memorandum should also have an attachment notation. Save the changes to the document, and then close it.

Critical Thinking 2.3 **Web Research**

Veronica Smith was recently promoted to Vice President of Operations for Veritime Systems. Veritime develops transaction processing systems and employs more than 1,500 people. One of Veronica's primary goals is to streamline the procurement process. She realizes that Veritime's procurement processes are outdated and too centralized. Veronica wants to push decision making down to the departmental level and use the Internet to streamline processes and ultimately save money.

The first directive that Veronica issues is to push purchasing decisions for office supplies down to the various department managers. Set up a memorandum from Veronica to all departmental managers. The memo should state that office supply purchases can now be made at the department level. Use Internet Explorer and a search engine of your choice to locate three office supply companies that allow purchases to be made from their Web sites. Add a second page to your memorandum listing the approved Web-based office supply stores. Include the URLs and 800 numbers of the stores. Save your completed memorandum as **`Critical Thinking 2.3`**.

Critical Thinking 2.4 **With a Group**

In this exercise, you will work with the same classmate that you worked with to set up Health-e-Meals.com in Critical Thinking 1.5. Health-e-Meals.com has been in business for over two years, and you have had tremendous success. The credit line that was secured through Citizen's Bank has allowed Health-e-Meals to surpass even your most optimistic projections. During this time, you have hired 16 employees to do everything from delivery to office management. To celebrate your success, you and your classmate have decided to organize a company Christmas party.

Set up a memorandum to all employees announcing the Christmas party. Praise your employees for their hard work and the success of the company. Let them know how optimistic the future looks and how you look forward to the coming year. Have your classmate write an attachment page outlining the details of the Christmas party. The date, time, location, and agenda should be included. Have your classmate save the attachment page in a separate file from your memorandum. Open your classmate's attachment page, and copy and paste the information onto a new page (second page) of your memorandum. Save the completed memorandum as **`Critical Thinking 2.4`**.

LESSON 3

Professional Writing and Editing Tools

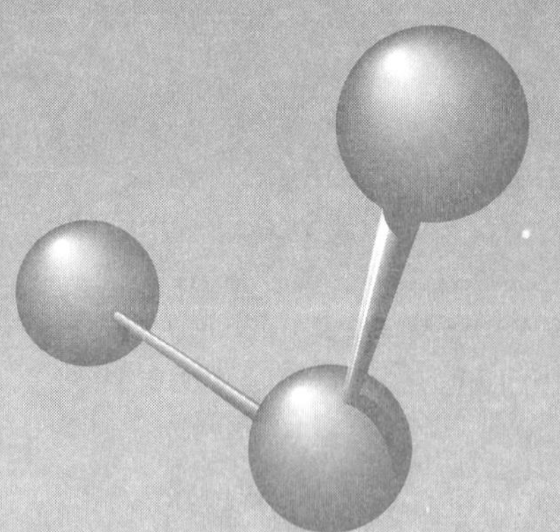

In this lesson, you will use the Office Assistant, online Help, and professional writing and editing tools. The Office Assistant and online Help allow you to get assistance at any time. Word 2002 provides spell checking, grammar checking, and a powerful thesaurus. Word 2002 even has automatic spell checking and grammar checking that check your work as you write. Another powerful tool in Word 2002 is Find and Replace. Find and Replace is especially useful for finding and replacing text in large documents. Once you master the writing tools in Word 2002, you'll be able to write business documents, research papers, and reports with confidence.

IN THIS LESSON

Word 2002 Core MOUS Objectives Covered in this Lesson

MOUS Objective Number	MOUS Objective Description	Concept Page References	Exercise Page References
W2002-1-1	Insert, modify and move text and symbols	85	85–87
W2002-1-3	Correct spelling and grammar usage	80–82, 84	81–83, 84

See the Lesson 3 Web Page at: labpub.com/learn/bc/word1/lesson3

Case Study

Sarah Thomas is a Health Science major at Upper State University. In order to fulfill the requirements of her Nutritional Studies class, Sarah has chosen to write a research paper on diabetes. Sarah is enthusiastic about this topic since one of her family members was recently afflicted with diabetes. Sarah takes full advantage of the powerful writing and editing tools in Word 2002. She uses the spelling and grammar checkers to proof her paper prior to submission. She uses the thesaurus to find the best words to express her ideas. Finally, Sarah uses the find and replace feature to make changes and ensure consistency throughout her paper.

MANAGING DIABETES

Exercise and a healthy diet are important tools in the prevention and management of diabetes. It is estimated that diabetes affects the lives of over 17 million Americans. This potentially life threatening disease can affect people with a variety of problems including heart disease, kidney failure, and blindness.

With Type I diabetes, the pancreas can't manufacture enough insulin. Insulin is a hormone that helps manage blood sugar levels in the body. In people with Type III diabetes, the body's cells cannot use the insulin produced by the pancreas. In both types of diabetes, sugar builds up in the bloodstream. Without proper treatment, high blood

A polished paper, thanks to Word 2002's writing tools.

The Office Assistant

The Office Assistant is an interactive Help tool available in all Office XP applications. The Assistant monitors your activities and provides tips, suggestions, and alert messages whenever it assumes you need assistance. For example, the Assistant recognizes certain phrases such as salutations beginning with the word Dear. The Assistant displays a speech balloon when it recognizes such a phrase. The speech balloon contains the suggestion or alert message. The Assistant can also be configured to display a tip of the day when Word is started.

Assistant offering assistance

Using the Assistant to Get Help

The Assistant's speech balloon contains a search box where you can enter phrases and questions. When you click the Search button, the Assistant interprets the phrase or question in the search box and displays a list of topics relating to the search box text. When you click a topic, Word displays a Help window providing you with detailed help information.

Controlling the Assistant

You can control all aspects of the Assistant. For example, you may not want the Assistant to display a tip of the day, or you may want to turn the Assistant off. You can set options for the Assistant in the Office Assistant dialog box. The following Quick Reference table outlines various methods of controlling the Assistant.

QUICK REFERENCE: CONTROLLING THE OFFICE ASSISTANT

Task	Procedure
Display the Assistant's speech balloon (four different methods).	■ Click anywhere on the Assistant. ■ Press F1. ■ Click the Help button on the Standard toolbar. ■ Choose Microsoft Word Help from the Help menu.
Close the speech balloon.	Click anywhere in the document, or tap ESC.
Display Office Assistant dialog box.	Display the speech balloon, and click the Options button.
Change animated character.	Display the Office Assistant dialog box, click the Gallery tab, use the Next button to browse the available characters, choose a character, and click OK.
Temporarily hide the Assistant.	Choose Help→Hide the Office Assistant, or right-click the Assistant, and choose Hide from the pop-up menu.
Turn Assistant off completely.	Display the Office Assistant dialog box, and uncheck the Use the Office Assistant box.
Unhide the Assistant or turn on the Assistant.	Choose Help→Show the Office Assistant.

Hands-On 3.1 Use the Office Assistant

In this and the following exercise, you will use the Assistant to learn more about inserting dates.

Display the Speech Balloon

1. Start Word, and the Assistant may appear.
2. If the Assistant is not visible on your screen, choose Help→Show the Office Assistant.
   This text shows the default Assistant character known as "Clippit." The Assistant on your machine may be different.
3. Click the Assistant and the speech balloon will pop up.
4. Click anywhere in the document window to close the speech balloon.
5. Position the mouse pointer on the Assistant, and drag the Assistant to a new screen location.
   You can always reposition the Assistant even if the speech balloon is displayed.

Get Help

6. Click the Assistant to display the speech balloon.
7. Follow these steps to get help on inserting the date in documents.

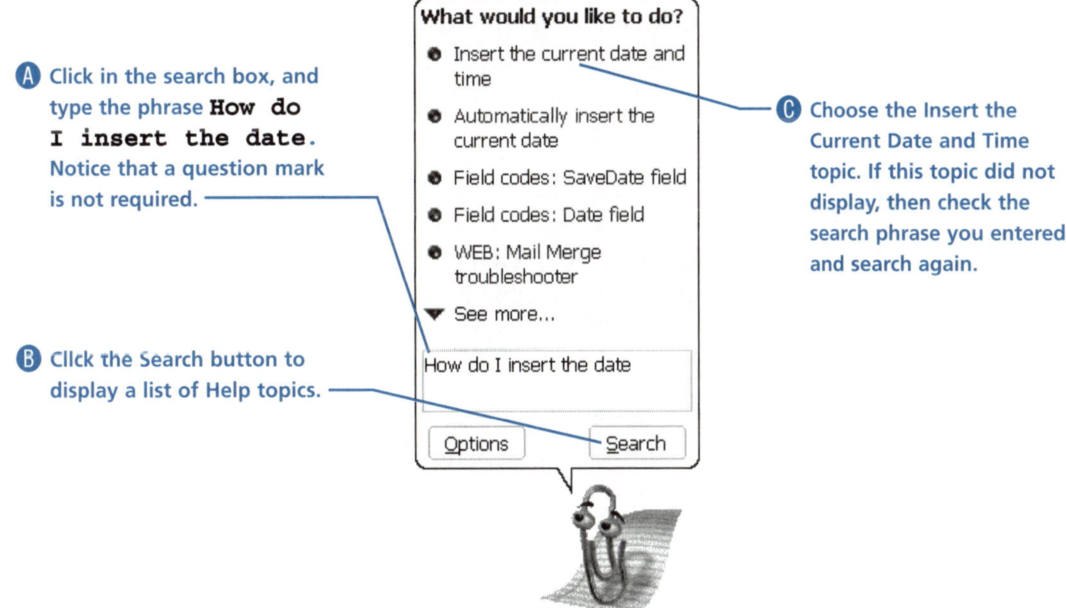

Word will display a Help window relating to inserting the date and time.

(Continued on the next page)

8. For now, click the Close button at the top–right corner of the Help window.
9. Type the word **date** in the Assistant's search box.
10. Click the Search button, and a list of topics will appear.
Notice that Insert the Current Date and Time is one of the topics. This is the same topic you searched for previously when you entered the search phrase "How do I insert the date." This example shows that it isn't always necessary to type long phrases in the search box. Often, a single word is enough to locate a desired topic.

Check Out the Options

11. Click the Options button on the speech balloon.
12. If necessary, click the Options tab in the dialog box that appears.
13. Click the Question Mark button at the top-right corner of the dialog box, and then click on any option check box.
Word will provide a ScreenTip describing the purpose of the option.
14. Tap the ESC key to close the ScreenTip.
15. Feel free to get help on the various Office Assistant options. You may also want to click the Gallery tab in the dialog box to check out the other Assistant characters. If you are studying in a computer lab, it is recommended that you not change any options.
16. Close the Office Assistant dialog box when you have finished.

Online Help

Word's online Help puts a complete reference book at your fingertips. Help is available for just about any topic you can imagine. Online Help is important because Microsoft does not provide reference manuals with Office XP. The reference manuals are now integrated into online Help.

Locating Help Topics

Your goal when using online Help is to locate Help topics. There are several different search methods you can use to locate topics. All Help topics have key words that identify them. For example, a Help topic that discusses printing documents can probably be located by including the key word printing in your search method. Regardless of which search method you use, the goal is to locate a topic. Once you locate the desired topic, you can display it and follow the instructions in the topic.

When Help Is Available

In Word 2002, you can display the Help window directly only when the Office Assistant is turned off. You learned how to turn off the Office Assistant in the previous topic. When the Office Assistant is turned off, the Help window can be displayed using any of the following methods:

- Click the Microsoft Word Help button on the Standard toolbar.
- Press F1.
- Choose Help→Microsoft Word Help from the menu bar.

The following Quick Reference table describes the various methods for locating Help topics.

QUICK REFERENCE: LOCATING HELP TOPICS

Search Method	Procedure
Contents	The Contents method is useful if you are trying to locate a topic but you aren't really sure how to describe it. The Contents method lets you navigate through a series of categories until the desired topic is located.
Answer Wizard	The Answer Wizard lets you find topics the same way that you find them with the Office Assistant. You type a phrase into a search box and execute a search.
Index	The Index method lets you locate a topic by typing key words. An alphabetically indexed list of topics is displayed from which you can choose the desired topic. This method is most useful if you know the name of the topic or feature for which you need assistance.

The Help Window Toolbar

The Help window contains a toolbar to assist you with online Help. The following illustration defines the buttons on the Help toolbar.

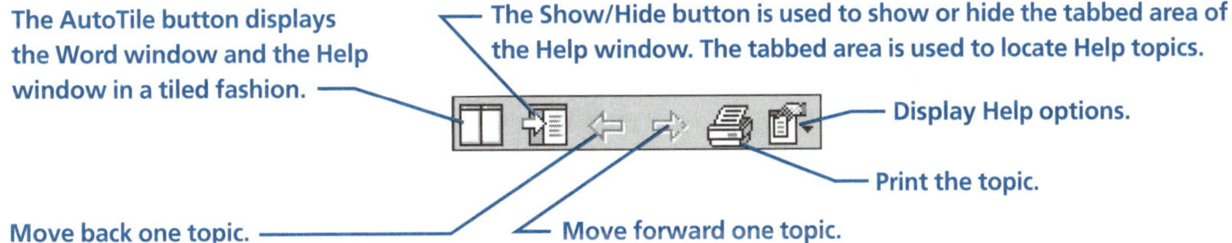

Hands-On 3.2 Use Online Help

Turn Off the Office Assistant

1. Click the Office Assistant, and then click the Options button.
2. Make sure the Options tab is active, and remove the check from the Use the Office Assistant box.
3. Click OK, and the Office Assistant will vanish.
   Once the Office Assistant is turned off, commands that would normally display the Office Assistant display the Help window instead.

Use an Index Search

4. Choose Help→Microsoft Word Help from the menu bar.
   The Help window will be displayed. If the Office Assistant had been active, this command would have popped up the Assistant's speech balloon.
5. If the tabbed area of the Help window is not displayed, then click the Show button on the Help toolbar.

(Continued on the next page)

6. Click the Index tab.
7. Type the word **`date`** in the Type Keywords box, and click the Search button.
   The topic Insert the Current Date and Time should appear in the lower part of the Help window along with other Help topics.
8. If necessary, click the Insert the Current Date and time Topic.
   The Help information for that topic will appear in the right side of the Help window.
9. Take a moment to read the help information; then click the blue Field hyperlink that appears in Step 5.
   A definition of the term Field appears.

Experiment with Help

10. Feel free to experiment with Help. Try using the Contents method to locate Help topics, and try using the Index method to locate additional topics.
11. When you have finished, click the Close ☒ button on the Help window.

Spell Checking

Word checks a document for spelling errors by comparing each word to the contents of a main dictionary. The main dictionary is a standard, college-level dictionary. The spell checker also looks for double words such as *the the*, words with numbers such as *2001budget*, and a variety of capitalization errors.

Custom Dictionaries

Word actually compares your document with two (or more) dictionaries: the main dictionary and one or more custom dictionaries. Custom dictionaries contain words such as last names or company names that may not be in the main dictionary. You can add words to a custom dictionary during a spell check. For example, you may want to add last names or company names you frequently use in your work. The spell checker will ignore those words during future spell checks. Word also lets you use dictionaries for languages other than English. You can even purchase dictionaries with specific terminology, such as medical or legal terminology.

Automatic Spell Checking

Word can automatically check your spelling as you type. Word flags spelling errors by underlining them with wavy red lines. You can correct a flagged error by right-clicking the error and choosing a suggested replacement word or other option from the pop-up menu that appears.

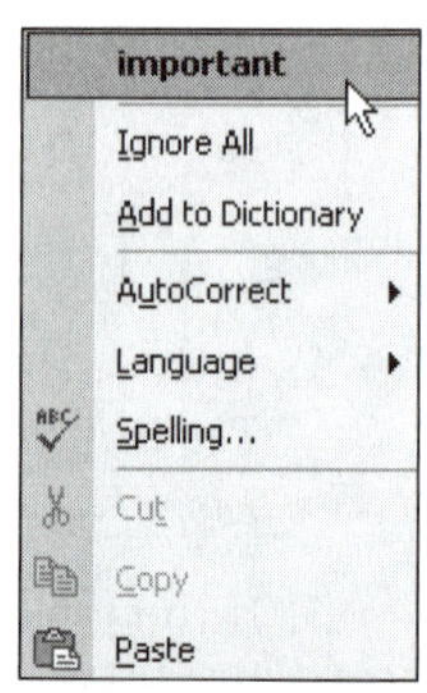

Spell Check Pop-Up Menu

Hands-On 3.3 Use Automatic Spell Checking

Correct Spelling Errors

1. Open the document named Hands-On Lesson 3 on your exercise diskette.
   This document has plenty of spelling errors for you to correct.

2. Notice the word *iportant* in the first sentence has a wavy red underline.
   Misspelled words are identified by wavy red underlines.

3. *Right-click* the word *iportant,* and the following pop-up menu will appear.
   Take a few moments to study the following illustration.

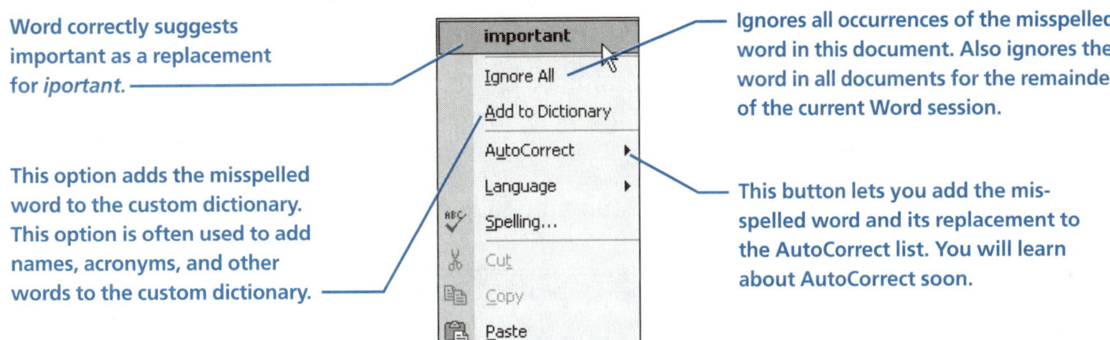

4. Choose important from the top of the list as shown in the preceding illustration.
   Important will replace iportant.

5. *Right-click* the word *millionAmericans* on the second line of the first paragraph, and choose *million Americans* from the pop-up menu.

Double Word and Capitalization Errors

6. Notice the double word *with with* on the third line.
   Word reports these types of errors as well.

7. *Right-click* the second occurrence of *with,* and choose Delete Repeated Word from the pop-up menu.

8. *Right-click* the word WIth at the start of the second paragraph.

9. Choose With from the pop-up menu.
   As you can see, the spell checker looks for spelling, double words, and capitalization errors. You can always correct spelling as you type by right-clicking words with wavy red underlines and choosing an option from the pop-up menu.

Grammar Checking

Word has a sophisticated grammar checker that can help improve your writing skills. Like the spell checker, the grammar checker can check grammar as you type. The grammar checker "flags" grammar errors by underlining them with wavy green lines. You can correct a flagged error by right-clicking the error and choosing a replacement phrase or other option from the pop up menu. Be careful when using the grammar checker, however, because it isn't perfect. There is no substitute for careful proofreading.

The Spelling and Grammar Dialog Box

FROM THE KEYBOARD

Press F7 to start Spelling and Grammar checker

The Spelling and Grammar dialog box is useful when you are spell checking and/or grammar checking a large document. It also provides access to customization options. For example, you use the Spelling and Grammar dialog box to choose a customized dictionary for the spell checker and to choose the writing style for the grammar checker. The Spelling and Grammar dialog box is displayed with the Tools→Spelling and Grammar command or by clicking the Spelling and Grammar button on the Standard toolbar.

Hands-On 3.4 Use the Spelling and Grammar Dialog Box

Use the Spell Checker

1. Click the Spelling and Grammar button on the Standard toolbar.
   The spell check will begin, and the speller should stop on the misspelled word tretment *in the second paragraph.*
2. Take a few moments to study the following illustration.

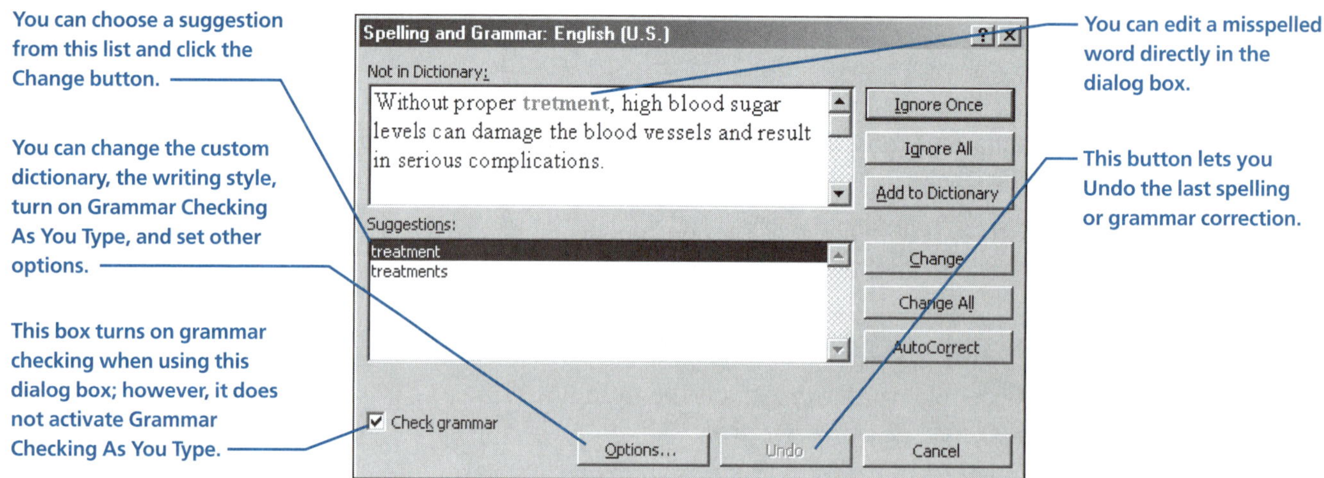

Use the Grammar Checker

3. Make sure that the Check Grammar box is checked.
   This will ensure that the grammar checking portion of this exercise works as it should.
4. Choose treatment from the Suggestions list, and click the Change button.
   Now the grammar checker should detect a grammatical error.

5. Follow these steps to explore the grammar checker options:

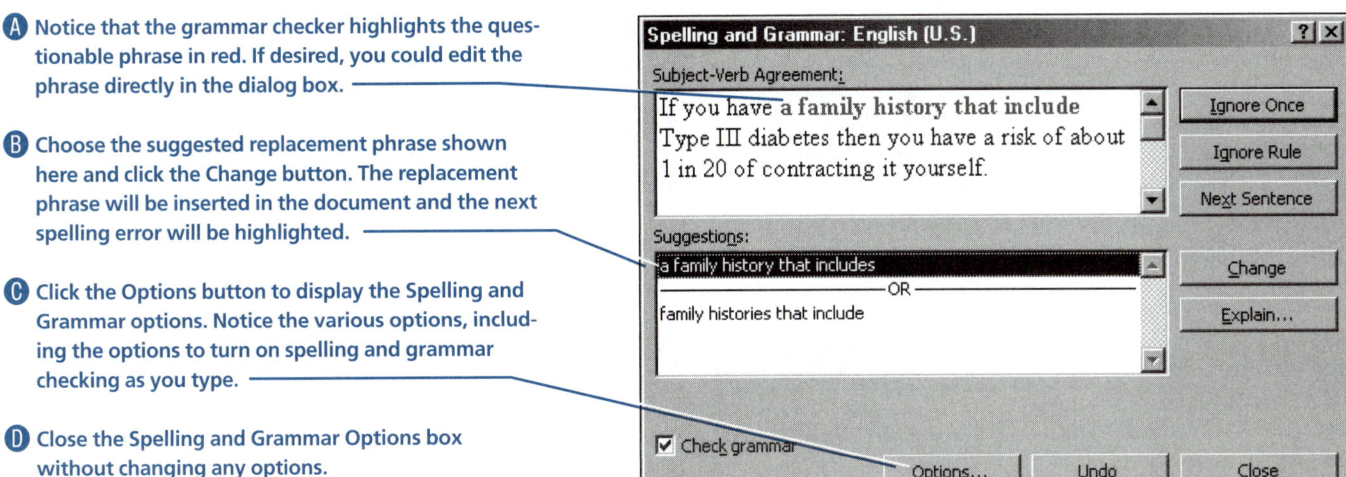

6. Use the following guidelines to spell check and grammar check the remainder of this document.

- Use your best judgment to determine the correct spelling of all misspelled words.
- Use your best judgment to determine the correct grammar if Word reports grammar errors.
- From time-to-time, messages may pop up helping you with reported spelling and grammar errors. The messages will vanish as soon as you take any kind of action.

Thesaurus

The thesaurus can help improve your vocabulary and writing skills by providing synonyms (words with the same meaning) for words or phrases. The thesaurus can help you choose just the right words or phrases to accurately express your ideas. You can easily display of list of synonyms by right-clicking a selected word or phrase and choosing Synonyms from the pop up menu that appears. The thesaurus dialog box can also be used to display antonyms (words or phrases with the opposite meaning). You display the Thesaurus dialog box with the Tools→Language→Thesaurus command.

FROM THE KEYBOARD

SHIFT+F7 to display the Thesaurus dialog box

Hands-On 3.5 Use the Thesaurus

1. Scroll up and right-click the word *manufacture* in the first line of the second paragraph.
2. Choose Synonyms from the pop-up menu.
3. Choose *produce* from the synonym list.
4. Use the preceding steps to replace the word *manage* with *control* on the second line of the second paragraph.
5. Click anywhere on the word *control,* and choose Tools→Language→Thesaurus from the menu bar.
6. Follow these steps to explore the thesaurus dialog box.

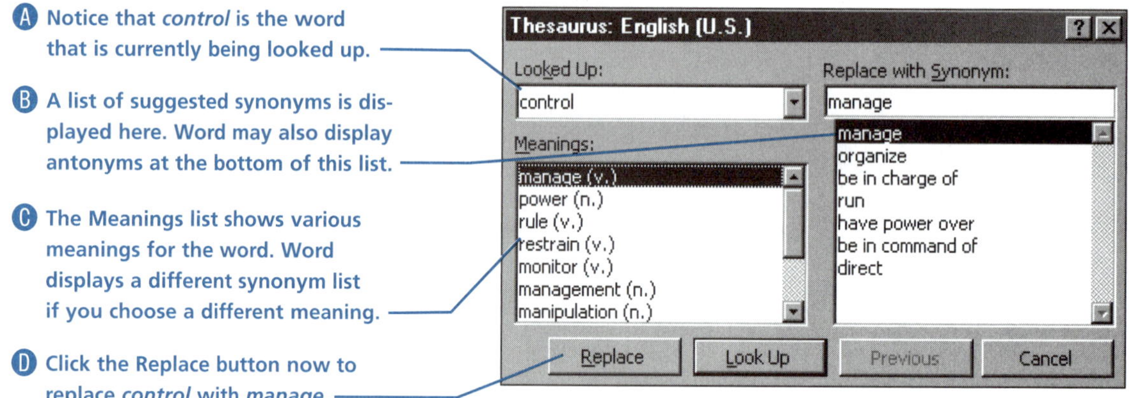

7. Right-click the word *manage,* and choose *control* from the Synonyms list on the pop-up menu.
8. Feel free to experiment with the thesaurus.
9. Save your document when you have finished experimenting.

Find and Replace

FROM THE KEYBOARD

Press CTRL+F for Find
Press CTRL+H for Replace

Word's Find command lets you search a document for a particular word or phrase. You can also search for text formats, page breaks, and a variety of other items. Find is often the quickest way to locate a phrase, format, or item in a document. The Replace option lets you replace the found phrase, format, or item with a replacement phrase, format, or item. The Find and Replace dialog box is displayed with either the Edit→Find command or the Edit→Replace command.

Hands-On 3.6 Use Find

Find a Word

1. Position the insertion point at the top of the document, and make sure that no text is selected.
2. Choose Edit→Find from the menu bar.
3. Follow these steps to search for the word *pancreas*.

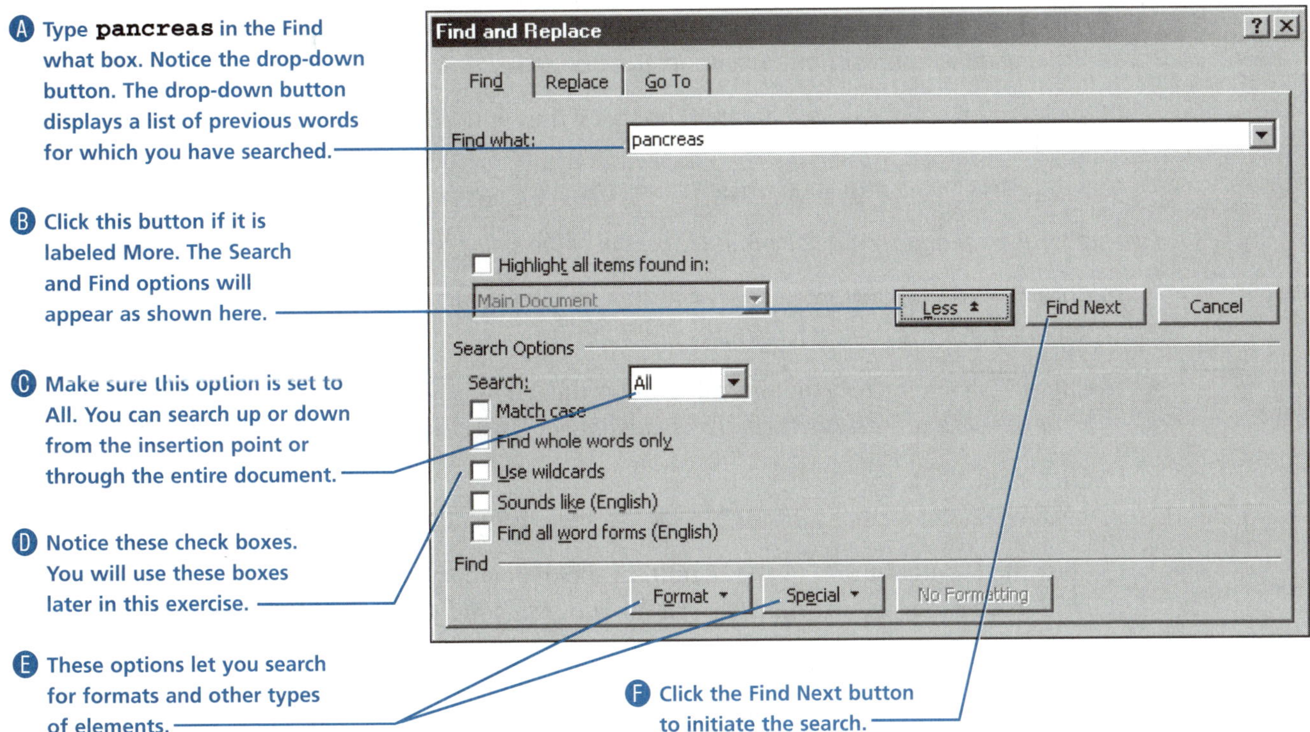

Find Another Word

4. Click in the Find What box, delete *pancreas* and type **With** (with a capital W) in its place.
5. Click the Find Next button, and *with* should be located in the second paragraph.
6. Click Find Next again, and the word *Without* should be located in the second paragraph. *Notice that With was found even though it is part of the word Without. By default, Find is not case-sensitive, and it doesn't recognize the difference between a whole word or part of the word. You will change this, however, in the next few steps.*

(Continued on the next page)

Use Match Case

7. Click the Match Case check box under the search options.
   This box instructs Word to find only occurrences of the search string with the same matching case.

8. Click the Find Next button, and Word will locate the capitalized word *With* further down in the document.

9. Click Find Next again, and Word will indicate the entire document has been searched.
   Word skipped over several occurrences of with *in lowercase.*

10. Click OK on the message box, then uncheck the Match Case check box.

Search for a Whole Word

11. Scroll to the top of the document, and click the insertion point anywhere on the document title. Notice you can scroll while the Find and Replace box is open, although you may need to move the box out of your way.

12. Check the Find Whole Words Only check box.

13. Click Find Next several times until Word indicates that the entire document has been searched.
    Notice that the word without *was not located this time.*

14. Click OK on the message box, then uncheck the Find Whole Words Only check box.

Search for Text Formats and Tab Characters

Notice the Format and Special buttons at the bottom of the dialog box.

15. Click the Special button, and a list of items will appear.
    You can search a document for the presence of any item.

16. Choose Tab Character (the second item on the list).
    Word will place a ^t character in the Find What box. This character tells Word to search for a tab.

17. Click Find Next.
    Word will select the space at the start of the first main paragraph. A tab created this space.

18. Click the Format button at the bottom of the dialog box.
    The Format button lets you search for specific fonts, paragraph formats, and other formats.

19. Choose Font from the list.

20. Choose Bold from the Font Style list, and click OK.
    The words Format: Font: Bold should appear below the Find What box.

21. Remove the ^t character from the Find What box; then click the Find Next button.
    Word should select the title because it is in bold.

22. Click the Cancel button to close the Find and Replace dialog box.

23. Click anywhere on the title to remove the selection.

Use Replace

24. Press CTRL+H to display the Find and Replace dialog box.
Notice that the Replace tab is active in the dialog box. The shortcut keystroke you use determines which tab displays when the dialog box appears. Notice that there are tabs for Find, Replace, and Go To. Go To is covered later in this lesson.

25. Click the No Formatting button at the bottom of the dialog box.
This turns off the bold setting that you searched for earlier in this exercise. In the next step, you will begin replacing the Roman numeral III with II.

26. Type the Roman numeral **III** (3 capital I's) in the Find What box and **II** in the Replace box.

27. Click the Find Next button.
Word will locate and select the first occurrence of III.

28. Click the Replace button.
Word replaces III with II and selects the next occurrence of III in the document.

29. Now click Replace All, and Word will replace all occurrences of III with II.
Word should indicate that three replacements were made.

30. Click OK to dismiss the message box.
Be careful with Replace All because you may make accidental replacements. For example, if you replace cat *with* dog, *then words like* catapult *may become* dogapult. *You should use the Find Whole Words Only option if the word you are replacing might be part of a larger word (like* cat *and* catapult*).*

31. Now use Replace to replace the word *running* with *walking*. Make the replacements one at a time (rather than using Replace All).
Notice that Word maintains the appropriate capitalization for each replacement.

32. Feel free to experiment with Find and Replace.

33. Close the Find and Replace dialog box when you have finished, but leave the document open.

Word Count

The word count feature counts the number of words, sentences, paragraphs, and pages in a document. Word count can be useful if you need to adjust your document to a specific length. For example, students who are creating reports or research papers often have length constraints. Word count is particularly useful to word processing professionals who bill clients by the word or page. You initiate word count with the Tools→Word Count command.

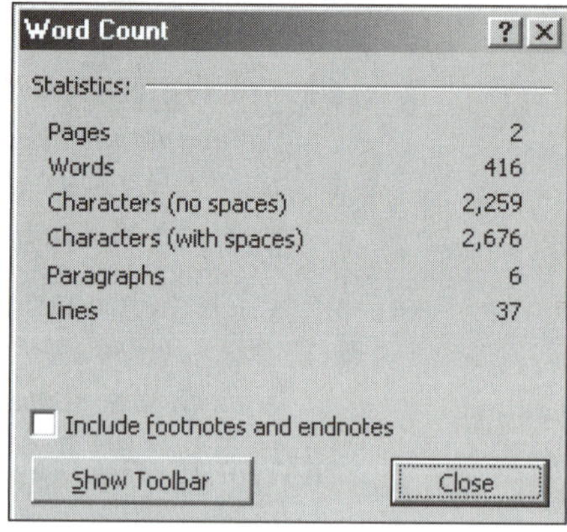

Word Count Statistics

Hands-On 3.7 Use Word Count

1. Click anywhere in the document to make sure no words are selected.
2. Choose Tools→Word Count from the menu bar.
   Word will analyze the document and display the statistics.
3. Take a few moments to study the results; then click the Close button.
4. Save the changes to the document; then close the document.

Recently Used File List

Word and other Office applications list up to nine of the most recently used files at the bottom of the File menu. You can open any of these documents by choosing them from the list. This is often the most efficient way to open a recently used document. The following Quick Reference steps explain how to adjust the number of files displayed on the Recently Used File List.

QUICK REFERENCE: MODIFYING THE RECENTLY USED FILE LIST

- Choose Tools→Options from the menu bar.
- Click the General tab.
- Adjust the number of entries in the Recently Used File List box.

Hands-On 3.8 Use the Recently Used Files List

1. Choose File from the menu bar.
   You will notice up to nine recently used documents are listed at the bottom of the menu. The Hands-On Lesson 3 document should be at the top of the list because you used it in the previous exercise.
2. Choose Hands-On Lesson 3 from the list, and the document will open.
   Leave the document open; you will continue to use it in the next exercise.

The Go To Command

The Go To command lets you rapidly locate a specific page in a document. Go To can also be used to locate objects (which you have not learned about) such as bookmarks, tables, footnotes, and endnotes. You choose the object you wish to go to in the Go To tab of the Find and Replace dialog box. You can display the Go To tab of the Find and Replace dialog box by choosing Edit→Go To from the menu bar. You can also display the Go To tab by double-clicking the page number section of the status bar.

FROM THE KEYBOARD

CTRL+G to display Go To dialog box

Hands-On 3.9 Go To a Page

Use the Keyboard

1. Press CTRL+G, and the Go To tab of the Find and Replace dialog box will appear.
2. Type **2** into the Enter page number box, and click the Go To button.
   The insertion point should move to the top of page 2.
3. Click the Close button on the dialog box.

Use the Status Bar

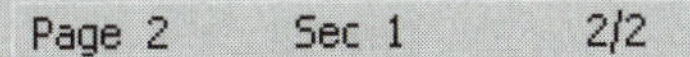

4. Double-click anywhere on the page number section of the status bar to display the Go To tab of the Find and Replace dialog box.
   Notice that you can go to other locations, such as Sections, Lines, etc.
5. Type **1** into the Enter Page Number box, and then click the Go To button.
6. Close the Find and Replace dialog box.

Hyphenation

Word lets you hyphenate text automatically or manually. With automatic hyphenation, Word hyphenates words whenever it determines that hyphenation is necessary. With manual hyphenation, Word searches the document for words to hyphenate. When a word requiring hyphenation is located, Word prompts you to confirm the hyphen location within the word. Hyphenation is most useful in documents with short line lengths, such as documents containing newspaper style columns.

QUICK REFERENCE: HYPHENATING TEXT

To Hyphenate a Document Automatically:

- Choose Tools→Language→Hyphenation from the menu bar.
- Check the Automatically Hyphenate Document box, and click OK.

To Hyphenate a Document Manually:

- Choose Tools→Language→Hyphenation from the menu bar.
- Click the Manual button.
- If Word identifies a word to hyphenate and you want the hyphen positioned at the location Word proposes, click Yes. If you want the hyphen positioned at a different location in the word, then use the arrow keys on the keyboard to adjust the position, and then click Yes.

The Hyphenation Zone

The Hyphenation dialog box contains a Hyphenation Zone setting. The hyphenation zone lets you adjust the sensitivity of the hyphenation. You can widen the hyphenation zone by entering a larger number in the Hyphenation Zone box. This will reduce the number of words that are hyphenated. Likewise, you can increase the number of words that are hyphenated by entering a smaller number for the hyphenation zone.

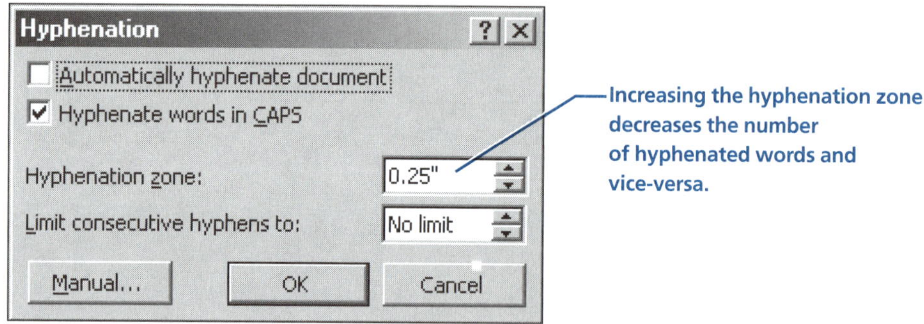

Nonbreaking Hyphens Nonbreaking Spaces

Some phrases (such as easy-to-use) require hyphens between the words in the phrase. You can use nonbreaking hyphens to ensure that all words in the phrase stay together on the same line. If you use nonbreaking hyphens and there is not enough space on a line for the entire phrase, then Word will move the entire phrase to the beginning of the next line. You insert nonbreaking hyphens with the CTRL+SHIFT+- keystroke combination. Likewise, you can insert nonbreaking spaces with the CTRL+SHIFT+SPACE BAR keystroke combination.

Hands-On 3.10 Use Hyphenation

1. Browse through the document and notice that there are no hyphenated words at the ends of the lines.
   This is because automatic hyphenation is turned off.
2. Scroll to the top of the document, and click on the title.
3. Choose Tools→Language→Hyphenation from the menu bar.
4. Make sure the hyphenation zone setting is set to .25", and click the Automatically Hyphenate Document check box.
5. Click OK, and browse through the document counting the number of end-of-line hyphens.
   You will increase the hyphenation zone setting in the next few steps and notice how this affects the number of hyphens.
6. Choose Tools→Language→Hyphenation from the menu bar.
7. Set the hyphenation zone to **.5"** and click OK.
8. Browse through the document, count the number of hyphens.
   The number of hyphens should have been reduced.
9. Choose Tools→Language→Hyphenation from the menu bar.
10. Uncheck the Automatically Hyphenate Document box, and click OK.
11. Browse through the document and notice that all automatic hyphens have been removed.
12. Save the document, close it, and continue with the end-of-lesson questions and exercises.

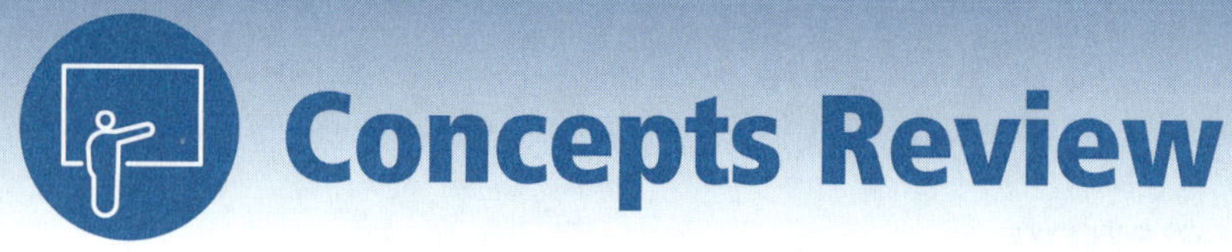

Concepts Review

True/False Questions

1. The Office Assistant cannot be turned off in Word 2002. TRUE FALSE
2. Word marks misspelled words with wavy red underlines. TRUE FALSE
3. You can correct a misspelled word by clicking it with the left mouse button and choosing a suggested replacement from the pop-up menu. TRUE FALSE
4. The Ignore All command on the Spelling and Grammar dialog box ignores a misspelled word for the current spell check only. TRUE FALSE
5. The spell checker can identify certain types of capitalization errors. TRUE FALSE
6. The Go To command can be initiated by pressing ALT+G. TRUE FALSE
7. The thesaurus lets you find and replace misspelled words. TRUE FALSE
8. Increasing the hyphenation zone measurement increases the number of hyphenated words. TRUE FALSE

Multiple-Choice Questions

1. Which of the following statements is true?
   - a. The spell checker uses only a main dictionary.
   - b. The only time a custom dictionary is used is with legal documents.
   - c. The spell checker uses a main and custom dictionary for all spell checks.
   - d. None of the above
2. Which command initiates Word Count?
   - a. Tools→Word Count
   - b. Edit→Word Count
   - c. Format→Word Count
   - d. None of the above
3. What will happen if the Office Assistant is turned off and you click the Help button on the Standard toolbar?
   - a. The Office Assistant will appear.
   - b. You will receive an error message.
   - c. The Help window will appear.
   - d. The Save dialog box will appear.
4. On which menu is a list of the most recently used documents displayed?
   - a. File
   - b. Edit
   - c. Insert
   - d. Format

Skill Builders

Skill Builder 3.1 Use the Office Assistant and Online Help

1. Choose Help→Show the Office Assistant to display the Office Assistant.
2. Click the Assistant to display the speech balloon.
3. Type the phrase **`Office Clipboard`** in the search box, and click the Search button.
4. Click the Display the Contents of the Office Clipboard topic that appears.
5. Take a moment to read the topic.
6. Use the Assistant to locate the Help topic Create and Use Custom Dictionaries.
7. Click the Create and Use Custom Dictionaries topic, then click the Create a New Custom Dictionary hyperlink in the Help window.
8. Take a moment to read the topic, then click the Back button on the Help toolbar to return to the Office Clipboard topic.
   You can always use the Back and Forward buttons to revisit topics.
9. Click the Contents tab.
   The Contents tab contains a series of books that you can expand or collapse to locate a Help topic. This method is most useful if you have a general idea of the topic you are trying to locate but don't know the name of the topic.
10. Feel free to locate various Help topics using the Contents tab.
11. Close the Help window, and hide the Office Assistant with the Help→Hide the Office Assistant command.

Skill Builder 3.2 Spell Checking/Find and Replace

1. Start a new document, and type the business letter shown below. Use Word's automatic spell checking and grammar checking as you type the letter. Format the text with bold and italics as shown.

> Today's date
>
> Mr. Juan Lopez
> Editor-in-Chief
> Western Wildlife Publications
> 1450 Parker Lane
> Ventura, CA 93003
>
> Dear Mr. Lopez:
>
> A short time ago, I subscribed to *Birds of Prey* magazine and I am enjoying it immensely. Your monthly tips have been especially useful. I have spotted more than twenty new species in my local area since I first subscribed to *Birds of Prey*. **Keep up the good work!**
>
> One thing that I would like to see more of in *Birds of Prey* is recommendations on bird watching sites in the Western United States. I am especially interested in bald eagles and golden eagles. I would appreciate any suggestions you may have.
>
> Sincerely,
>
> Jason Torval
> 450 Lighthouse Lane
> Manhattan Beach, CA 90266

2. Press CTRL+H to open the Find and Replace dialog box.
3. Replace all occurrences of Birds of Prey with Bird Watcher.
   Word should automatically italicize the phrase Bird Watcher because Birds of Prey was italicized.
4. Make sure there are no spelling errors in the document.
5. Save the document with the name **`Skill Builder 3.2`**, then close the document.

Skill Builder 3.3 Using the Thesaurus

In this exercise, you will modify the letter you created in the previous exercise.

1. Choose File from the menu bar, and then choose Skill Builder 3.2 from the list of recently used files.
   Suppose you want to use a word other than especially *in the second paragraph.*
2. Right-click anywhere on the word *especially* in the second paragraph.
3. Choose Synonyms from the pop-up menu, and then choose *particularly.*
4. Use the thesaurus to find replacements for the word *useful* in the first paragraph and *appreciate* in the second paragraph.
5. Select the phrase *A short time ago* at the beginning of the first paragraph.
6. Right-click the selected phrase.
7. Choose the replacement phrase *not long ago,* from the Synonym list.
   Notice that Word replaces the phrase but does not capitalize the first word of the sentence.
8. Click Undo to restore the original phrase.
9. Choose Tools→Language→Thesaurus from the menu bar.
10. Choose the replacement phrase *not long ago,* and click Replace.
    In this case, Word should have replaced the phrase and capitalized the first word of the sentence. This is one minor advantage to using the dialog box over the right-click method.
11. Choose File→Save As from the menu bar.
    This command can be used to save a document under a new name.
12. Change the name Skill Builder 3.2 in the filename box to **Skill Builder 3.3**, and click the Save button.
    The Skill Builder 3.2 file remains unchanged, and Skill Builder 3.3 now also resides on your diskette.
13. Close the document, and continue with the next exercise.

Skill Builder 3.4 Editing a Business Letter

1. Open the document on your exercise diskette named Skill Builder 3.4.
2. Use Find and Replace to replace all occurrences of the word *bill* with *account*.
3. Use Find and Replace to replace all occurrences of the word *payment* with *check*.
4. Spell check the entire document.
5. Select the entire document, and change the font size to 12.
6. Use (ENTER) to start the date line at approximately the 2" position.
7. Replace the phrase Today's Date with the current date.
8. Move the address block from the bottom of the letter to the space between the last body paragraph and the complimentary close (Sincerely). If necessary, insert or remove hard returns until there is a double space between the address block and the last body paragraph, and between the address block and the complimentary close (sincerely).
9. Center the three address block lines horizontally on the page.
10. Insert your typist's initials and the document name below the signature block.
11. Save the changes; then close the document.

Assessments

Assessment 3.1

1. Open the document on your exercise diskette named Assessment 3.1.
2. Spell check the document. Use your best judgment to determine which replacement words to use for incorrectly spelled words.
3. Use Find and Replace to make the following replacements. Also, write the number of replacements in the third column of the table.

Word	Replace With	Number of Replacements
breaks	fractures	__________
collarbone	clavicle	__________
movement	range-of-motion	__________

4. Print the document when you have finished.
5. Save the changes; then close the document.

Assessment 3.2

1. Open the document on your exercise diskette named Assessment 3.2.
2. Replace the phrase Today's Date with the current date, using the Date and Time feature. Insert the date as a field so that it updates automatically.
3. Spell check the document. Use your best judgment to determine which replacement words to use for incorrectly spelled words. Assume all proper names are spelled correctly.
4. Use Find and Replace to make the following replacements. Make sure the case (lowercase or uppercase) remains the same for all replacements. Also, write the number of replacements in the third column of the table.

Word or phrase	Replace With	Number of Replacements
Dan	Mr. Heywood	__________
Do not replace Dan in the inside address		
families	people	__________
special consideration	something special	__________

5. Print the document when you have finished.
6. Save the changes; then close the document.

Critical Thinking

Critical Thinking 3.1 On Your Own

Amanda Jackson is the owner of Amanda's Bookstore. Amanda's Bookstore is located in a small community and specializes in fiction and poetry books. For the past 15 years, Amanda has held weekly poetry readings by local and nationally recognized poets. Write a personal business letter to Amanda thanking her for the poetry readings. Let Amanda know that you enjoy the readings very much and that you would like her to hold monthly book signings. Try to sell her on the idea of holding book signings by convincing her that the events will complement the poetry readings by encouraging fiction enthusiasts to visit the store. The address of Amanda's Bookstore is:

Amanda Jackson
Amanda's Bookstore
3420 Colonial Lane
Atlanta, GA 30308

Use Word's spell checker and grammar checker to spell check and grammar check the letter. Use the thesaurus to find replacement words for at least five words in the letter. Save the completed letter as **`Critical Thinking 3.1`**.

Critical Thinking 3.2 On Your Own

Open the letter that you created in Critical Thinking 1.1. Use Word's spell checker and grammar checker to spell check and grammar check the letter. Use the thesaurus where necessary to replace words in the letter. Save the changes to the completed letter, and close it.

Spell check, grammar check, and use the thesaurus on Critical Thinking exercises 1.3, 1.4, 2.1, 2.2, and 2.3. Save the changes to each document, and then close it.

Critical Thinking 3.3 On Your Own

Bill Patterson is the Executive Director of the Southside Coalition for the Homeless. Bill wants to open a new housing center that will provide shelter, meals, counseling, and job training for needy single mothers and their children. Bill has found the perfect building for the new shelter, but he needs to raise $250,000 to renovate and furnish the building. In addition, he needs $185,000 per year for food, medical supplies, staff salaries, and other expenses. Bill has decided to solicit large corporations in the area for donations. He believes this could be a profitable venture for the corporations because they will receive the following benefits:

Tax deductions
Positive publicity in the community
A pool of trained job candidates

Write a letter for Bill requesting donations from the corporations. The letter should specify the total amount of money needed, how it will be spent, and the benefits realized by the corporations. In addition, ask for specific donation amounts. The recommended donation amounts for the building renovation are $10,000, $15,000, and $25,000. The recommended donation amounts for the annual expenditures are $2,500, $5,000, and $10,000.

Spell check and grammar check your letter, and use the thesaurus to choose the right words. In an important letter such as this, choosing the right words can be essential. Save your completed letter as **Critical Thinking 3.3**.

Critical Thinking 3.4 Web Research

Use Internet Explorer and a search engine of your choice to find information on dictionaries that can be used with Word 2002. There are many third-party dictionaries available with legal, medical, and scientific terminology. Try to locate Web sites of companies that offer such products. Create a Word document that documents your findings. Include the company names, Web site URLs, and any other relevant information that you find. Save your document as **Critical Thinking 3.4**.

Critical Thinking 3.5 With a Group

Open the document you created in Critical Thinking 1.5. Work with your classmate to spell check and grammar check the document. Together, use the thesaurus to choose replacement words for several words in the letter. Choose words that enhance the letter and make your sentences stronger. Discuss the various choices with your partner, and try to choose the right word for each occasion. Save the changes to the letter when you have finished.

Open the memorandum you created in Critical Thinking 2.4. Work with your partner to spell check and grammar check the letter. Together, use the thesaurus to choose replacement words for several words. Save the changes to the memorandum when you have finished.

LESSON 4

Creating a Simple Report

In this lesson, you will create a simple report. Reports are important documents often used in business and education. You will format your report using various paragraph formatting techniques. Paragraphs are a fundamental part of any Word document. You will learn how to use Word 2002's Click and Type feature and change line spacing. In addition, you will master indenting techniques using the ruler and the indent buttons on the Formatting toolbar.

IN THIS LESSON

Word 2002 Core MOUS Objectives Covered in this Lesson

MOUS Objective Number	MOUS Objective Description	Concept Page References	Exercise Page References
W2002-2-1	Modify paragraph formats	107–108	107–109

See the Lesson 4 Web Page at: labpub.com/learn/bc/word1/lesson4

Case Study

Bill Nelson is a freshman at West Side Junior College. Bill has enrolled in an information systems course in which Office XP is an important component. Bill has been assigned the task of preparing a report on the importance of computer technology in the twenty-first century. Professor Williams has instructed Bill to use Word 2002. After conducting the necessary research, Bill uses the paragraph formatting techniques in Word 2002 to prepare a report that is easy to read, properly formatted, and has a professional appearance.

COMPUTER TECHNOLOGY IN THE TWENTY-FIRST CENTURY

Our society has changed from a manufacturing-oriented society to an information society. Those with access to capital had power in the early 1900s. In the twenty-first century, however, power will come from access to information. The amount of worldwide information is growing at a rapid pace. Computer technology is responsible for much of this growth, but it can also help us manage the information.

Information management is an important use of computer technology. Daryl Richardson of Harmond Technology describes four other reasons why the average person may want to acquire thorough knowledge of computers.

> Computer skills are becoming more important in the business world. Many companies need employees with excellent computer skills.
>
> The Internet and other information resources provide access to a global database of information.
>
> Computer skills can often simplify ones personal life. Computers can be used to entertain, to manage finances, and to provide stimulating learning exercises for children.
>
> Using computers can provide a sense of accomplishment. Many people suffer from "computerphobia." Learning to use computers often creates a feeling of connection with the information age.

Report Formats

Overview

There are a variety of acceptable report formats. The example below shows a traditional business report in unbound format. Other report formats can be used for research papers and other types of documents.

Traditional Unbound Business Report Format

Double-spacing is typically set before beginning the report. Three double-spaced returns are used to space the title down to approximately the 2" position.

The title is typed in uppercase, centered, and bold face. You can also apply a distinctive font to the title.

The body of the report is double-spaced. The first line of each body paragraph is indented to 0.5".

Quotations and other text you wish to emphasize are single-spaced and indented 0.5" to 1" on the left and right. You should double-space (by tapping ENTER twice) between quotes.

COMPUTER TECHNOLOGY IN THE TWENTY-FIRST CENTURY

Our society has changed from a manufacturing-oriented society to an information society. Those with access to capital had power in the early 1900s. In the twenty-first century, however, power will come from access to information. The amount of worldwide information is growing at a rapid pace. Computer technology is responsible for much of this growth, but it can also help us manage the information.

Information management is an important use of computer technology. Daryl Richardson of Harmond Technology describes four other reasons why the average person may want to acquire thorough knowledge of computers.

> Computer skills are becoming more important in the business world. Many companies need employees with excellent computer skills.
>
> The Internet and other information resources provide access to a global database of information.
>
> Computer skills can often simplify ones personal life. Computers can be used to entertain, to manage finances, and to provide stimulating learning exercises for children.
>
> Using computers can provide a sense of accomplishment. Many people suffer from "computerphobia." Learning to use computers often creates a feeling of connection with the information age.

Click and Type

Click and Type lets you automatically apply formatting in blank areas of a document. Click and Type lets you set paragraph alignments (Align Left, Center, and Align Right), customize tab stops, insert tables, and apply other formats. To use Click and Type, position the mouse pointer in a blank area of a document and double-click. Click and Type inserts hard returns and adjusts the paragraph alignment as necessary to achieve the formatting you desire. Click and Type is only available in Print Layout and Web Layout views. The following illustrations demonstrate the use of Click and Type.

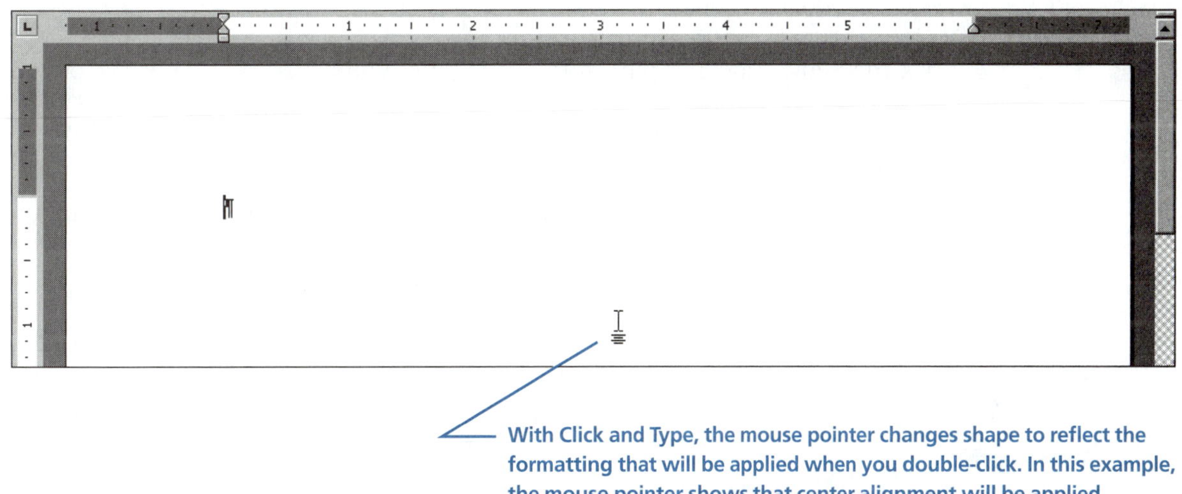

With Click and Type, the mouse pointer changes shape to reflect the formatting that will be applied when you double-click. In this example, the mouse pointer shows that center alignment will be applied.

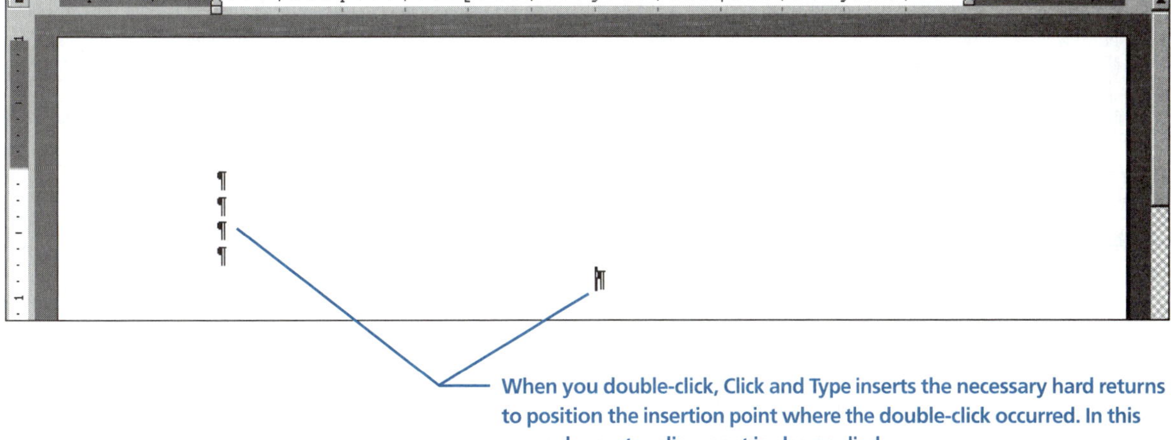

When you double-click, Click and Type inserts the necessary hard returns to position the insertion point where the double-click occurred. In this example, center alignment is also applied.

Hands-On 4.1 Use Click and Type

1. Start Word, and a blank document window will appear.
2. Make sure you are in Print Layout view. If necessary, use the View→Print Layout command to switch to Print Layout view.
3. Slide the mouse pointer to various locations in the blank document, and notice how the mouse pointer changes shape.
   The align left or align right shapes reflect the formatting that would be applied if you were to double-click.
4. Click the Show/Hide ¶ button to display the symbols.
5. Make sure the ruler is displayed at the top of the document window. If necessary, use the View→Ruler command to display the ruler.
6. Follow these steps to use Click and Type to format the title line of the report.

Ⓐ Position the mouse pointer approximately 2" down and centered on the line. You can tell you are two inches down by looking at the vertical ruler. The 1" position on the white section of the vertical ruler means you are 2" down on the page. This is because the ruler's white section begins at the top margin, which is already 1" down from the top of the page.

Ⓑ Double-click when the mouse pointer has the center alignment shape, as shown here.

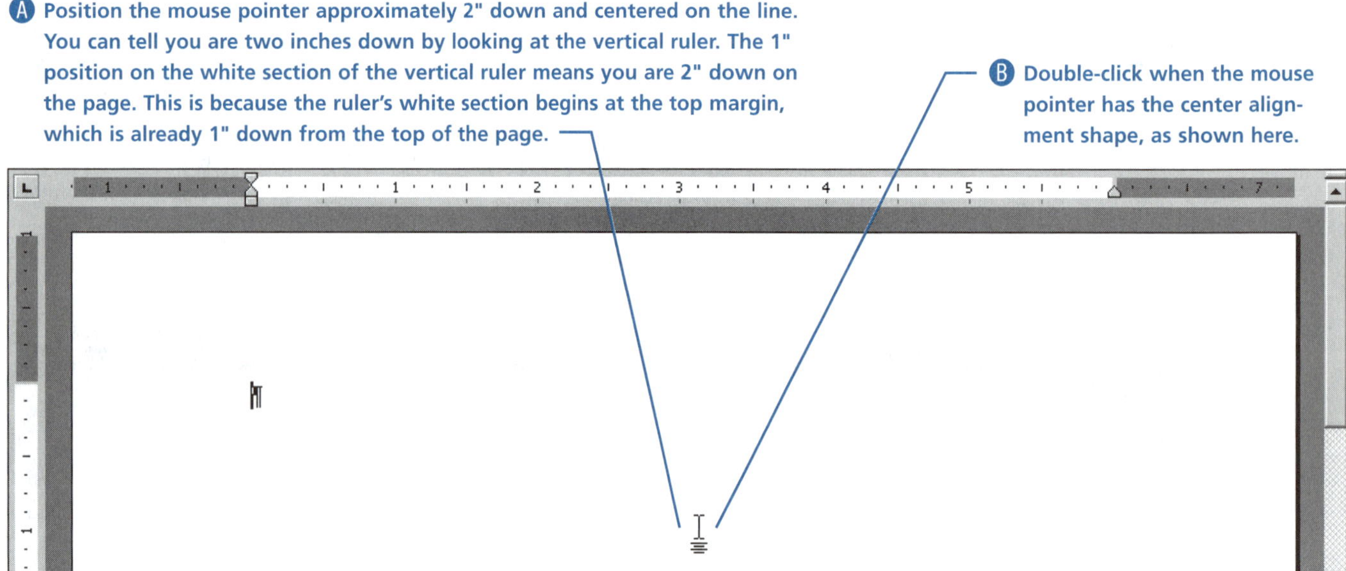

Word inserts paragraph marks as necessary and applies center alignment. Check the Status bar at the bottom of the window to ensure the insertion point is at approximately the 2″ position. As you can see, Click and Type can be useful for rapidly applying formats. However, it does lack the precision that may be required for formatting some types of documents.

7. If the insertion point is not at the 2″ position, use ENTER to insert hard returns as necessary to force it to the 2″ position.
8. Turn on CAPS LOCK, and click the Bold **B** button.
9. Type the report title **`COMPUTER TECHNOLOGY IN THE TWENTY-FIRST CENTURY`**.
10. Turn off Bold, and tap ENTER twice.

11. Slide the mouse pointer to the left end of the current line.

12. Double-click when the mouse pointer has this shape I≡ .
The alignment should change to left, and the insertion point should be positioned two lines below the title. Use Undo and try again if the alignment is not set to left.

13. Save the document to your exercise diskette with the name **`Hands-On Lesson 4`**.

Line Spacing

The Line Spacing button on the Formatting toolbar lets you set the line spacing for one or more paragraphs. Line spacing determines the amount of vertical space between lines in a paragraph. The default line spacing is single. Word makes a single-spaced line slightly higher than the largest character in the line. For example, if you are using a 12-point font, then single line spacing is slightly larger than 12 points. You apply line spacing by selecting the desired paragraph(s) and choosing the desired line spacing from the Line Spacing drop-down list. Line spacing can also be set using the Paragraph box. The following table describes line spacing options available through the Paragraph box.

FROM THE KEYBOARD

CTRL+1 for single spacing
CTRL+5 for 1.5 spacing
CTRL+2 for double spacing

Line Spacing	Description
Single	Default spacing in Word
1.5 Lines	1.5 times single-spacing
Double	Twice single-spacing
At Least	Specifies the minimum line spacing. The spacing may increase if the font size increases. However, the line spacing will never be smaller than the number of points specified in the At Least setting.
Exactly	Fixes the line spacing at the number of points specified. The line spacing remains fixed even if the font size of characters within the line changes.
Multiple	Lets you precisely control the line spacing by setting multiples such as 1.3 or 2.4.

Hands-On 4.2 Set Line Spacing

1. Make sure the insertion point is on the second blank line below the title.

2. Click the Line Spacing drop-down button, and choose 2.0.

3. Tap the TAB key once to create a 0.5″ indent at the start of the paragraph.

(Continued on the next page)

4. Now type the following paragraph, but only tap ENTER after the last line in the paragraph. *The lines will be double-spaced as you type them.*

> Our society has changed from a manufacturing-oriented society to an information society. Those with access to capital had power in the early 1900s. In the twenty-first century, however, power will come from access to information. The amount of worldwide information is growing at a rapid pace. Computer technology is responsible for much of this growth, but it can also help us manage the information.

5. Make sure you tap ENTER after the last line. Then TAB once, and type the following paragraph. *Notice the double-spacing has been carried to the new paragraph.*

> Information management is an important use of computer technology. Daryl Richardson of Harmond Technology describes four other reasons why the average person may want to acquire thorough knowledge of computers.

6. Tap ENTER to complete the paragraph, then press CTRL+1 to set single-spacing. *The shortcut keystrokes can be quite useful for setting line spacing.*
7. Now type the following paragraphs, tapping ENTER twice between paragraphs. There is no need to tab at the beginning of these paragraphs.

> Computer skills are becoming more important in the business world. Many companies need employees with excellent computer skills.
>
> The Internet and other information resources provide access to a global database of information.
>
> Computer skills can often simplify one's personal life. Computers can be used to entertain, to manage finances, and to provide stimulating learning exercises for children.
>
> Using computers can provide a sense of accomplishment. Many people suffer from "computerphobia." Learning to use computers often creates a feeling of connection with the information age.

8. Save the changes, and continue with the next topic.

Indenting Text

FROM THE KEYBOARD

CTRL+M for left indent
CTRL+SHIFT+M to remove left indent
CTRL+T for hanging indent
CTRL+SHIFT+T to remove hanging indent

Indenting offsets text from the margins. The left indent is the most widely used indent. The left indent sets off all lines in a paragraph from the left margin. Likewise, the right indent sets off all lines from the right margin. The first line indent sets off just the first line of paragraphs. This is similar to using TAB at the start of a paragraph. The hanging indent sets off all lines except for the first line.

The Increase Indent button and Decrease Indent button on the Formatting toolbar let you adjust the left indent. These buttons increase or decrease the left indent to the nearest tab stop. The default tab stops are set every 0.5″, so the left indent changes 0.5″ each time you click the buttons. You can also set indents using keystrokes, the Paragraph dialog box, and by dragging indent markers on the horizontal ruler.

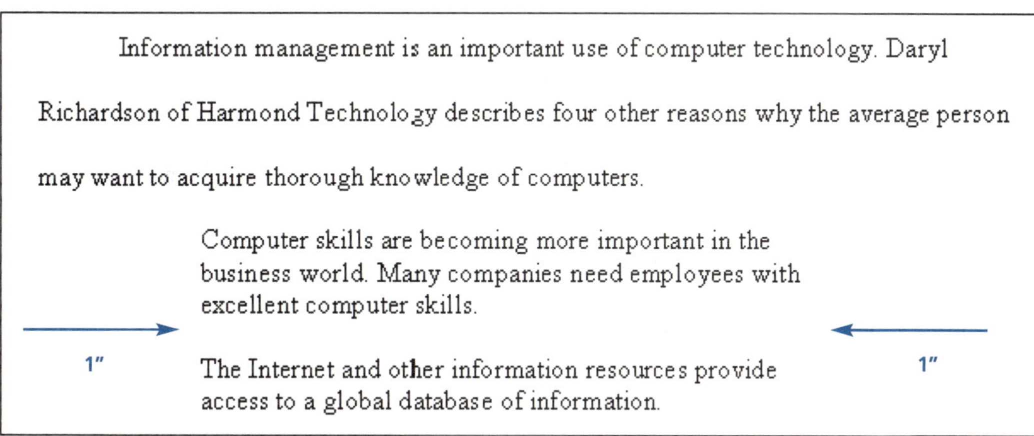

Information management is an important use of computer technology. Daryl Richardson of Harmond Technology describes four other reasons why the average person may want to acquire thorough knowledge of computers.

Computer skills are becoming more important in the business world. Many companies need employees with excellent computer skills.

The Internet and other information resources provide access to a global database of information.

These paragraphs are indented 1″ from the left and right margins.

Hands-On 4.3 Experiment with Left Indents

Indent One Paragraph

1. Click on one of the single-spaced paragraphs you just typed.
2. Click the Increase Indent button near the right end of the Formatting toolbar.
   The paragraph should be indented 0.5″ on the left.
3. Click the Decrease Indent button to remove the indent.

Indent Several Paragraphs

4. Use the mouse to select any part of two or more paragraphs.
   You only need to select part of a paragraph when indenting or applying other paragraph formats.
5. Click Increase Indent twice to create a 1″ left indent on each of the selected paragraphs.
6. Now click Decrease Indent twice to remove the indents.
   You will continue to work with indents in the next Hands-On exercise.

The Horizontal Ruler

You can set indents, margins, and tab stops by dragging markers on the horizontal ruler. When you use the ruler, you can see formatting changes as they are applied. The horizontal ruler is positioned just above the document in the document window. You can display or hide the ruler with the View→Ruler command. The following illustration shows the ruler, the margin boundaries, and the various indent markers.

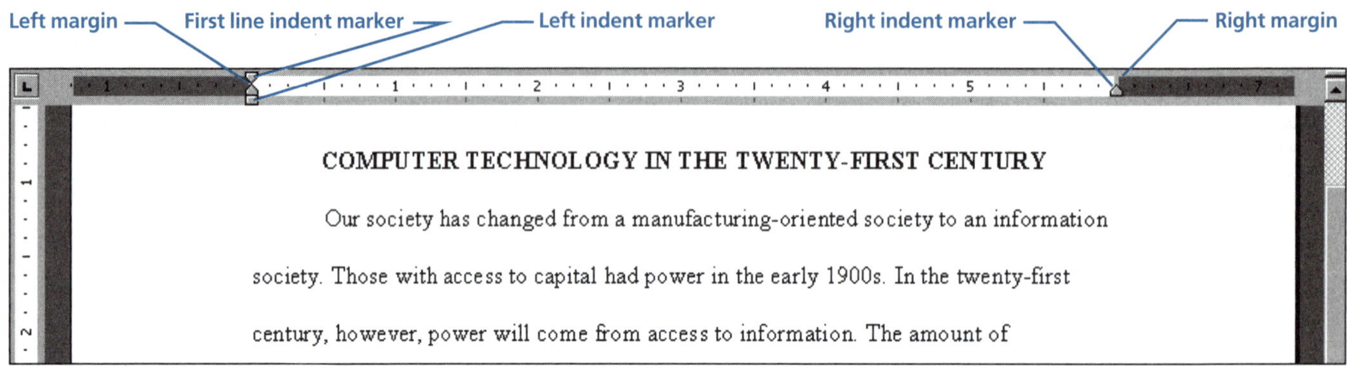

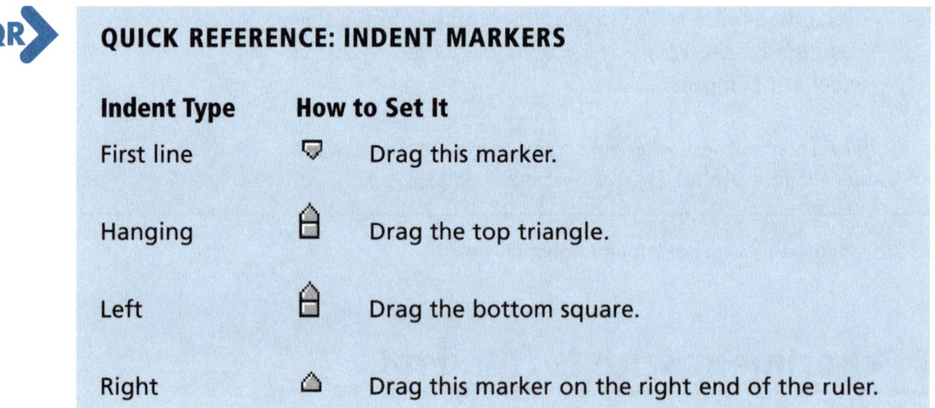

QUICK REFERENCE: INDENT MARKERS

Indent Type	How to Set It
First line	Drag this marker.
Hanging	Drag the top triangle.
Left	Drag the bottom square.
Right	Drag this marker on the right end of the ruler.

Hands-On 4.4 Use the Ruler to Indent Paragraphs

Set Left and Right Indents

1. If necessary, scroll down until the four single-spaced paragraphs at the bottom of your document are visible.
2. Select all four paragraphs by dragging the mouse pointer in the left margin.

3. Follow these steps to adjust the left and right indents.

Ⓐ Position the pointer on the Left Indent marker (the bottom box). A yellow Left Indent ScreenTip will appear, as shown here.

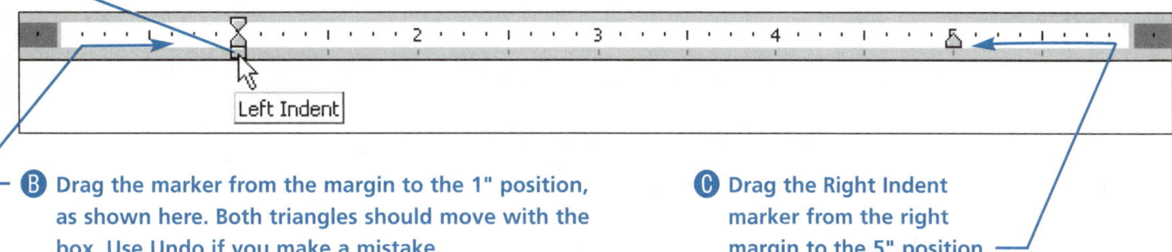

Ⓑ Drag the marker from the margin to the 1" position, as shown here. Both triangles should move with the box. Use Undo if you make a mistake.

Ⓒ Drag the Right Indent marker from the right margin to the 5" position.

Experiment with the Indent Markers

4. Scroll to the top of the document and select both of the large, double-spaced paragraphs. *The easiest way to do this is to drag in the left margin.*

5. Follow these steps to adjust the indent markers.

Ⓐ Notice that the First Line Indent marker is at the 0.5" position. This indent was set when you tapped the TAB key while creating the paragraphs earlier in this lesson. Word automatically converts tabs to first line indents in this manner.

Ⓑ Drag the First Line Indent marker to the right or left, and release the mouse button. Notice that the first line indent only changes in the selected paragraphs.

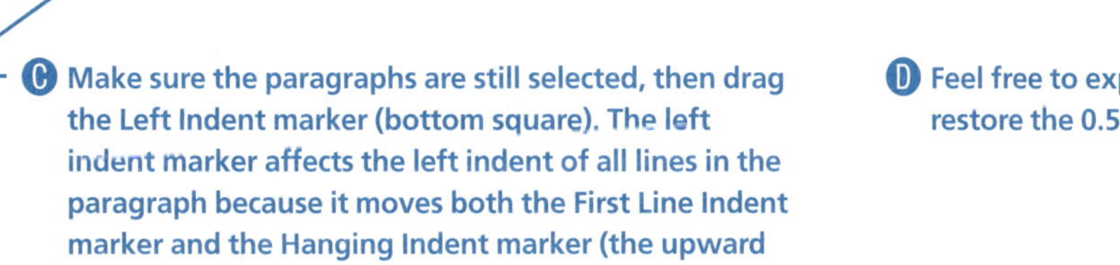

Ⓒ Make sure the paragraphs are still selected, then drag the Left Indent marker (bottom square). The left indent marker affects the left indent of all lines in the paragraph because it moves both the First Line Indent marker and the Hanging Indent marker (the upward pointing triangle).

Ⓓ Feel free to experiment with the indents, but restore the 0.5" first line indents when you finish.

6. Save the changes to your document, and then close the document.

Concepts Review

True/False Questions

1. The Increase Indent button changes the right indent. TRUE FALSE
2. The Decrease Indent button changes the right indent. TRUE FALSE
3. The ruler can be used to indent paragraphs. TRUE FALSE
4. The CTRL+D keystroke combination is used to set double-spacing. TRUE FALSE
5. The CTRL+I keystroke combination is used to set single-spacing. TRUE FALSE
6. The Ruler is displayed with the Edit→Ruler command. TRUE FALSE
7. First Line indents only affect the first line of each selected paragraph. TRUE FALSE
8. The title begins 2″ from the top of the page in a traditional business report. TRUE FALSE

Multiple-Choice Questions

1. In which of the following view modes is Click and Type available?
   a. Print Layout
   b. Web Layout
   c. Outline
   d. Both a and b
2. If the font size of a paragraph is 12 point and the line spacing is set to single, then which of the following is true?
   a. The line spacing is slightly larger than 12 point.
   b. The line spacing is slightly smaller than 12 point.
   c. The line spacing is exactly 12 point.
   d. None of these
3. Which of the following actions should you take to adjust the right indent of three paragraphs?
   a. Drag the Right Indent marker.
   b. Select the paragraphs, and then drag the Right Indent marker.
   c. Select the paragraphs, and tap the Tab key.
   d. All of the above
4. Which command is used to display the horizontal ruler?
   a. View→Ruler
   b. Edit→Display Ruler
   c. Insert→Ruler
   d. File→Ruler

Skill Builders

Skill Builder 4.1 Indents and Line Spacing

1. Start a new document, and use the Line Spacing button to set the line spacing to 2.0.
2. Click the Center button, and tap (ENTER) three times to space down to the 2″ position.
3. Set the font to Arial, bold, 12pt, and type the title shown below.
4. Tap (ENTER), and set the alignment to left.
5. Turn off bold and set the font size to 11.
6. Type the first paragraph shown below, tapping (ENTER) once at the end of the paragraph.
7. Choose Format→Paragraph from the menu bar, and set the line spacing to single and the left and right indents to 1″.
   The Paragraph dialog box is useful when setting several options, or when you want to precisely set line spacing, indents, or other options.
8. Click Italics and type the quotations shown below. Use the Em Dash symbol from the Symbols dialog box between the end of paragraph periods and the author's names. Do not use italics on the author's names.

FAMOUS AMERICAN QUOTATIONS

Quotations have the power to inspire and define moments in our history. They are windows into the minds and lives of great people. Famous Americans certainly have contributed their share of famous quotations.

> *There was never yet an uninteresting life. Such a thing is an impossibility. Inside of the dullest exterior, there is a drama, a comedy, and a tragedy.*—Mark Twain
>
> *We hold these truths to be sacred and undeniable; that all men are created equal and independent, that from that equal creation they derive rights inherent and inalienable, among which are the preservation of life, and liberty, and the pursuit of happiness.*—Thomas Jefferson
>
> *I think, at a child's birth, if a mother could ask a fairy godmother to endow it with the most useful gift, that gift would be curiosity.*—Eleanor Roosevelt

9. Save the document with the name **`Skill Builder 4.1`**.
   You will continue to use the document in the next exercise.

Skill Builder 4.2 Add Another Quotation

In this exercise, you will add a new quotation, and a paragraph to the Skill Builder 4.1 document. The document should be open from the previous exercise.

1. Position the insertion point in front of the word *We* at the beginning of the second quote.
2. Tap (ENTER) twice to push the last two quotations down.
3. Tap (↑) twice to move the insertion point into the blank space between the paragraphs.
4. Now type the following quotation.

> *No one has been barred on account of his race from fighting or dying for America—There are no "white" or "colored" signs on the foxholes or graveyards of battle.—John F. Kennedy*

5. Now add the paragraph shown below to the bottom of the document. Make sure you double-space with (ENTER) between the last quote and the new paragraph. For the new paragraph, set the left and right indents to zero, the first line indent to 0.5″, and the line spacing to 2.0. You will also need to turn off italics.

> Famous quotations help us express those hard-to-find words and feelings that are in all of our hearts. They become a part of our national conscience and memory.

6. Choose File→Save As from the menu bar.
7. Change the name of the document to **`Skill Builder 4.2`**, save it, and close it.

Skill Builder 4.3 Format an Existing Document

In this exercise, you will open a report on your exercise diskette. You will adjust the line spacing and indents and spell check the document.

Adjust the First Line Indent and Line Spacing

1. Open the document named Skill Builder 4.3.
2. Select the entire document by triple-clicking in the left margin, or choose Edit→Select All from the menu bar.
3. Drag the First Line Indent marker to the 0.5″ position on the ruler.
   This will indent the first line of all paragraphs by 0.5″ (including the title).
4. Set the line spacing to double.

Format the Title and Credit Line

5. Use ENTER to push the title down to approximately the 2″ position.
6. Center the title.
   Look at the ruler, and notice that the First Line Indent marker is at the 0.5″ position. This will cause the title to be slightly off center.
7. Set the First Line Indent for the title paragraph to zero.
8. Format the title as Arial Bold, 14pt.
9. Click on the credit line at the bottom of the report.
10. Set the First Line Indent to zero, and right-align the paragraph.
    The paragraph should be flush with the right margin.
11. Format the title "Moss-Gathering" in the credit line with italics.
12. Spell check the entire document. Assume that the names of all people are correct.
13. Save the changes, and close the document.

Skill Builder 4.4 Create an Announcement

1. Follow these guidelines to create the announcement shown below.
   - Begin the announcement 2″ down. Use 2.0 line spacing between all title lines and for the first body paragraph. Use (ENTER) to double-space between the cast member paragraphs. Use 1.0 line spacing within the cast member paragraphs.
   - Use an Arial font for the entire document. Use a font size of 12 for the body paragraphs. All title lines are centered, 14pt, and bold.
   - Use Em Dash symbols after the names of the cast members. Indent the cast member paragraphs 0.5″ on both the left and right.
2. Save the announcement with the name **`Skill Builder 4.4`**, and close the document.

The West Coast Playhouse

Presents

An Evening with Mabel

This fabulous play has been entertaining audiences since its opening night on March 1, 1998. The cast is first-class, and the ambience is magical. You will find this play delightfully humorous and deeply moving.

The Cast

> **Rebecca Thomas**—Rebecca is a graduate of the Smithton School of Dramatic Arts. Rebecca has played lead roles in 17 theatrical productions. She has also appeared on *Saturday Night Live* and other television productions.
>
> **Jim Oliver**—Jim is a recent graduate with a major in drama. Jim was voted the best overall actor in his graduating class, and he has won numerous other awards. We are confident that you will find Jim's performance truly memorable.
>
> **Clara Boyd**—Clara recently moved here from London, England, where she specialized in Shakespearean theatrical performances. Clara is also a world-class pianist.

Assessments

Assessment 4.1 Format an Existing Document

1. Open the document named Assessment 4.1 on your exercise diskette.
2. Apply 2.0 line spacing to the entire document.
3. Center the title, and apply bold formatting to the title.
4. Apply bold formatting to the two capitalized headings.
5. Apply a 0.5″ First Line indent to all body paragraphs except for the headings.
6. Print the document, save the changes, and close the document.

Assessment 4.2 Create a Report Using Indents

1. Use the skills and report formatting knowledge you have acquired to create the report shown below. The single-spaced paragraphs are indented 1″ on both the left and right.
2. Print the report, save it as **`Assessment 4.2`**, but leave it open, as you will continue to use it.

CLASSIFICATIONS OF EMPLOYMENT

CFEB Associates—Company Handbook

It is important that you understand how CFEB Associates classifies its employees. We have established the following classifications for purposes of salary administration and eligibility for overtime payment and benefits.

Full-Time Regular Employees. These are staff members hired to work CFEB's normal, full-time workweek on a regular basis.

Part-Time Regular Employees. These are staff members hired to work at CFEB fewer than thirty-five hours per week on a regular basis.

Exempt Employees. These are staff members of CFEB Associates who are not required to be paid overtime, in accordance with applicable federal wage and hour laws, for work performed beyond forty hours in a workweek.

Nonexempt Employees. These are staff members of CFEB Associates who are required to be paid overtime at the rate of time and one-half their regular rate of pay for all hours worked beyond forty hours in a workweek.

Assessment 4.3 Add Paragraphs to a Document

1. Use the File→Save As command to save Assessment 4.2 with the name **Assessment 4.3**.
2. Add the following two paragraphs to the end of the Assessment 4.3 document. Notice that the first paragraph is indented and single-spaced, and the second paragraph is not indented and double-spaced.
3. If your report wraps to a second page after inserting the text, then remove hard returns from the top of the document until it fits on one page. If necessary, use a Whole Page zoom setting so that you can see the entire document. You should remove enough hard returns to center the document vertically on the page.
4. Print the report, save the changes, and close the document.

> **Temporary Employees**. These are staff members of CFEB Associates who are engaged to work full-time or part-time on the firm's payroll with the understanding that their employment will be terminated no later than upon completion of a specific assignment.

You will be informed of your initial employment classification and of your exempt or nonexempt status during your orientation session. Please direct any questions regarding your employment classification or exemption status to the Director of Human Resources.

Critical Thinking

Critical Thinking 4.1 On Your Own

Alexis Winston is a sophomore at Big State University majoring in computer science. Alexis has completed her freshman courses and is finally taking her first computer science courses. Computer Science 101 provides an introduction to computing theory and requires each student to submit several reports. The topic of the first report assigned by Professor Carpenter is to research trends in computer science and technology. Each student must write a one-page report on the four most relevant computing trends of the twenty-first century. Alexis conducts the necessary research and decides upon the four trends that she considers to be the most relevant. She writes the following report text describing these trends.

The Internet—Use of the Internet has grown exponentially since 1995. The Internet has affected nearly every aspect of the computer world. Use of the Internet for business, education, communication, and other functions will continue to expand exponentially in the near future.

Open source—The move towards open source software (particularly operating systems) appears to be gathering momentum. The driving force behind the open source movement is the emergence of the Linux operating system. Linux has become the operating system of choice for many server systems and applications. Linux is also gaining recognition as a potential operating system for personal computers.

Internet appliances—Computing in the twenty-first century will no longer be restricted to personal computers and larger servers. The emergence of smart appliances and Internet-enabled consumer devices is a major trend. It is estimated that sales of Internet appliances in the United States will reach $15.3 billion by 2004.

Computers on a chip—The semiconductor industry has made remarkable advances in miniaturization and specialization. Soon, the functions of a motherboard will be condensed into a single chip. Single-chip computers will play a major role in a variety of devices from personal computers to cell phones, Internet appliances, and consumer electronics.

Write a one-page report on computing trends of the twenty-first century. Include a title, at least one main body paragraph, and the four trends discussed above. You can retype the trends exactly as they appear above. Format the report using the traditional unbound business report format. Indent the four trends 0.5" on both the left and right.

Spell check and grammar check your report. Use the thesaurus to find replacement words words in the trends shown above. Save your completed report as **`Critical Thinking 4.1`**.

Critical Thinking 4.2 Web Research With a Group

Alexis Winston's CS 101 class incorporates a business component that addresses the impact of computing trends on business. Professor Carpenter has assigned a second report that requires each student to discuss the business implications of one of the trends mentioned in the previous report (the report written in Critical Thinking 4.1). Alexis decides to write her report on companies that will benefit from the emergence of Internet appliances.

Work with your classmate to write a brief, one-page report on four companies that will benefit from the use of Internet appliances. Together, use Internet Explorer and a search engine of your choice to get information about the companies. You can choose any four companies. Some examples of companies that may benefit from this trend include Wind River Systems, Network Appliance, Cisco Systems, and Intel. Write a brief description of how each company may benefit from the use of Internet appliances. You can visit the Web sites of the companies or search for relevant articles on the Web. Position the information on the four companies below the main body paragraph, and indent them 1" on both the left and right. Use the unbound business report format with a title, at least one body paragraph, and the four indented paragraphs on the companies. Save your completed report as **Critical Thinking 4.2**.

LESSON 5

Margins and Lists

In this lesson, you will expand upon the formatting techniques you learned in the previous lesson and you will use margins, bulleted lists, and hanging indents to create a more sophisticated document. You will also learn how to customize bulleted and numbered lists, and you will work with outline-style numbered lists.

IN THIS LESSON

Word 2002 Core MOUS Objectives Covered in this Lesson

MOUS Objective Number	MOUS Objective Description	Concept Page References	Exercise Page References
W2002-2-1	Modify paragraph formats	129	129–130
W2002-2-3	Apply bullet, outline, and numbering format to paragraphs	123–126	124–128
W2002-3-3	Modify document layout and Page Setup options	122	122

See the Lesson 5 Web Page at: labpub.com/learn/bc/word1/lesson5

Case Study

Lisa Madison has found the summer job that most students dream about: she is a whitewater-rafting guide for Outdoor Adventures. Outdoor Adventures has been wooing thrill seekers for 25 years with rafting trips, helicopter skiing, wilderness trekking, and other high-octane adventures. Recently, Lisa realized that many guests have been forgetting to bring items, while others have been getting lost on the way to the starting points. Lisa decides to take charge of this situation using the power of Word 2002. She designs a pre-trip checklist that includes a list of recommendations, a bulleted list of items to bring, and directions to the starting points. With her take-charge attitude and her Office XP skills, Lisa should have no problem navigating the turbulent waters awaiting her in today's rough-and-tumble business world.

OUTDOOR ADVENTURES

Pre-Trip Checklist

The following checklist and directions will help you prepare for your trip. Also, remember to keep three important things in mind:

1. Pack light—We have limited space on our rafts, and you must carry all of your belongings with you. You will make more friends if you pack light.

2. Bring waterproof bags—One thing you can count on is that you bag(s) will get wet. Make sure they are waterproof and they float.

3. No valuables please—Leave valuables such as camcorders and cameras at home. Inexpensive 35mm cameras are the safest bet.

Checklist:

- o Sunglasses
- o Sunscreen
- o Insect repellant
- o Three sets of dry clothing
- o Tennis shoes
- o A warm, waterproof jacket

Directions:

Upper Granite Canyon—Take Highway 240 to the Forest Lake exit. Take Forest Lake Drive to Creekside Lane, and look for the starting point.

Middle Granite Canyon—Take Highway 240 to the Pine Meadows turnoff. Go right for two miles until you see a fork in the road. Go right for one mile to the starting point.

Margins

Margins determine the overall size of the text area on a page. In Word, the default top and bottom margins are 1″, and the left and right margins are 1.25″. You can set margins by dragging the margin boundaries on the rulers. You can also use the File→Page Setup command and set the margins in the Margins tab of the Page Setup dialog box. Margin settings are applied to the entire document or to an entire section (if the document has multiple sections). Sections are not discussed in this lesson.

Differences Between Margins and Indents

The margins determine the space between the text and the edge of the page. Indents are used to offset text from the margins. For example, imagine a document has a 1″ left margin, and one of the paragraphs in that document has a 0.5″ indent. The margin plus the indent will position the paragraph 1.5″ from the edge of the page. If the margin were changed to 2″, then the indented paragraph would be positioned 2.5 ″ from the edge of the page (the 2″ margin plus the 0.5″ indent).

Hands-On 5.1 Set Margins

1. Start Word, and choose File→Page Setup from the menu bar.
   The Page Setup dialog box lets you adjust a number of important settings that affect pages; for example, margins, paper size, page orientation, and headers and footers.
2. Make sure the Margins tab is selected, and notice the default settings for the margins.
3. Change the top margin to 1.5″ and the left and right margins to 1″.
4. Click OK to apply the changes.
   The top of the vertical ruler will have a 1.5″ dark gray area representing the top margin. Also, the Status bar will indicate that the insertion point is at the 1.5″ position.
5. Set the font size to 14, and type the following text. Use (ENTER) to double-space between the title and subtitle and to triple-space between the subtitle and body paragraph. Also, use (ENTER) to double-space after the body paragraph.

> OUTDOORS ADVENTURES
>
> Pre-Trip Checklist
>
> The following checklist and directions will help you prepare for your trip. Also, remember to keep three important things in mind:

6. Format the title with an Arial 18 pt bold font, and the subtitle with an Arial 16 pt bold font.
7. Save the document with the name **`Hands-On Lesson 5`**.
   You will continue to enhance this document throughout the lesson.

Setting Margins with the Rulers

You can set all four margins by dragging the margin boundaries on the rulers. The benefit of this technique is that you can see the effect immediately in the document. If you press the ALT key when dragging a margin boundary, Word displays the precise margin measurements on the rulers. However, you must press ALT after you have begun dragging the margin boundary.

Hands-On 5.2 Change Margins with the Ruler

1. Follow these steps to adjust the margins.

A Position the mouse pointer here on the top margin boundary so that a double-headed arrow will appear.

B Drag the margin boundary down until the numeral 2 appears at the top of the ruler. This indicates that the margin is set to 2".

C Try adjusting the top margin again but press and hold the ALT key after you begin dragging. Word will display the margin measurements on the ruler.

D Set the top margin to 2".

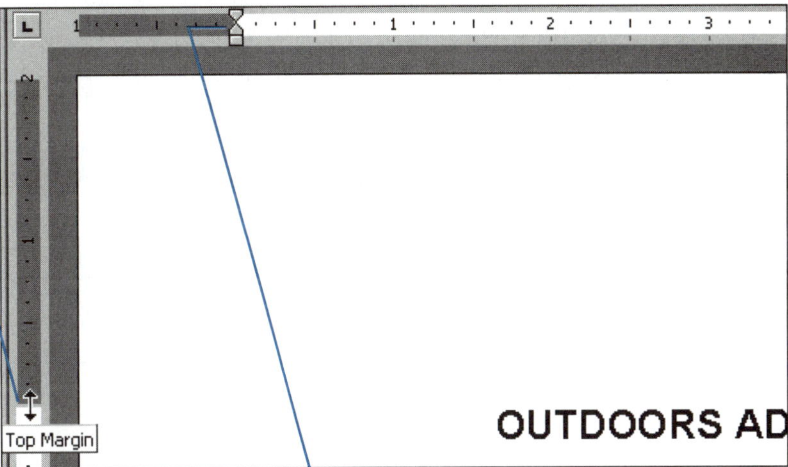

E Try changing the left margin by dragging this margin boundary. However, be patient because the indent markers may prevent the double-headed arrow from appearing. When you have finished, make sure the left margin is set to 1".

Bulleted and Numbered Lists

You can create bulleted and numbered lists with the Bullets and Numbering buttons on the Formatting toolbar. In Word, a list is a series of two or more paragraphs. You can apply bullets and numbers to paragraphs by selecting the paragraphs and clicking the desired button. For a new list, you can turn on bullets or numbers when you begin typing the list. Word will format the first paragraph with a bullet or number. When you complete the paragraph and tap ENTER, Word formats the next paragraph with a bullet or number. In a numbered list, Word numbers the paragraphs sequentially. Paragraphs in a numbered list are automatically renumbered if paragraphs are inserted or deleted.

AutoFormat as You Type

You can also start a bulleted list by typing an asterisk * followed by a space or a tab at the beginning of a new paragraph. When you complete the paragraph and tap ENTER, Word converts the asterisk to a bullet character. Likewise, you can begin a numbered list by typing 1 followed by a space or tab and tapping ENTER. This feature is known as AutoFormat as You Type.

Turning Bullets and Numbering Off

You can remove bullets or numbers from paragraphs by selecting the paragraphs(s) and clicking the Bullets button or the Numbering button. If you are typing a list, you should complete the list by tapping ENTER after the last paragraph in the list. You can then turn off bullets or numbering for the first paragraph following the list by clicking the Bullets button or the Numbering button.

Hands-On 5.3 Bullets and Numbers

Create a Numbered List

1. Position the insertion point at the bottom of the document.
   The insertion point should be on the second blank line below the body paragraph.
2. Click the Numbering button on the Formatting toolbar.
   The indented numeral 1 appears followed by a period.
3. Type the following text, inserting the Em Dash symbol as shown.

> 1. Pack light—We have limited space on our rafts, and you must carry all of your belongings with you. You will make more friends if you pack light.

4. Tap ENTER once after typing the text.
   Notice that Word begins the next paragraph with the numeral 2. Paragraphs are numbered sequentially unless you tell Word otherwise. You will learn how to change the starting number later in this lesson.
5. Tap ENTER again, and numbering will be turned off for the new paragraph.
   Word assumes you want to turn off numbering when you tap ENTER without typing any text.
6. Click the Numbering button again.
   Word will number the new blank paragraph with the numeral 2. Word continues the numbering from the previous list.
7. Type the following text.

> 2. Bring waterproof bags—One thing you can count on is that your bag(s) will get wet. Make sure they are waterproof and they float.

8. Tap ENTER and notice that Word creates a double-space and starts the numbering at 3.
   Word now understands that you want a double-space between each paragraph in the list.
9. Type the following text.

> 3. No valuables please—Leave valuables such as camcorders and cameras at home. Inexpensive 35mm cameras are the safest bet.

10. Tap ENTER and another double-space will be inserted.
11. Click the Numbering button to turn off numbering for the new paragraph.

Create a Bulleted List

12. Type **`Checklist:`** and tap (ENTER) once.
13. Click the Bullets button on the Formatting toolbar.
    Word will most likely insert a round • bullet (although another bullet style may appear). Also, the bullet may be indented further than the numbers in the numbered list.
14. Type **`Sunglasses`**, and tap (ENTER).
    Word formats the new paragraph with the bullet style.
15. Complete the following checklist.

> Checklist:
> - Sunglasses
> - Sunscreen
> - Insect repellant
> - Three sets of dry clothing
> - Tennis shoes
> - A warm, waterproof jacket

16. Tap (ENTER) twice after the last list item to turn off bullets.

The Bullets and Numbering Dialog Box

The Format→Bullets and Numbering command displays the Bullets and Numbering dialog box. The Bullets and Numbering dialog box lets you choose a style for your bulleted or numbered list, customize lists, and create outline numbered lists.

Built-in Bullet and Numbering Styles

Word provides seven built-in styles for bulleted and numbered lists. The styles are displayed in style galleries in the Bullets and Numbering dialog box. You can easily change the appearance of a bulleted or numbered list by choosing a style from the style galleries. The following illustration shows the built-in bullet and number styles available.

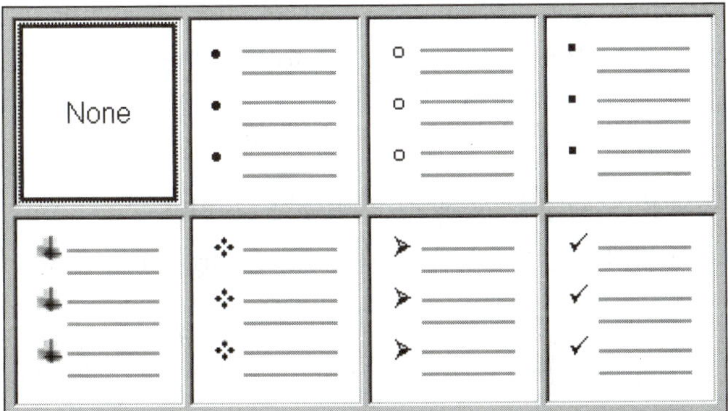

Bullet style gallery

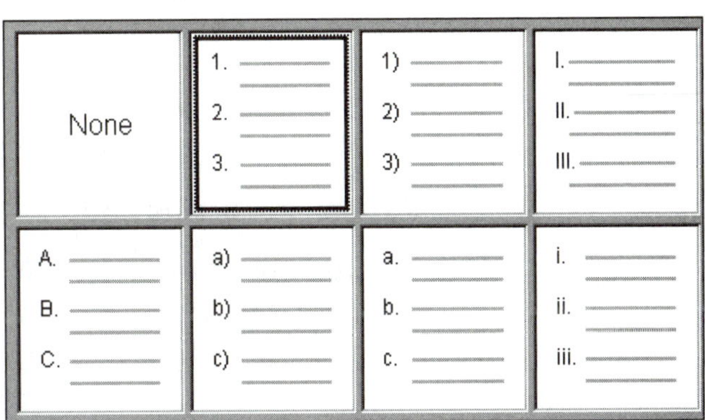

Number style gallery

Hands-On 5.4 Change the Bullet Style

1. Select the bulleted list as shown below.

Checklist:
- Sunglasses
- Sunscreen
- Insect repellant
- Three sets of dry clothing
- Tennis shoes
- A warm, waterproof jacket

2. Choose Format→Bullets and Numbering from the menu bar.
3. Choose the Circle bullet style from the bullets gallery, and click OK.

Customizing Bullet and Number Styles

You can customize the built-in bullet and number styles in several ways. For example, you may want to use a bullet character other than the built-in bullet characters, or you may want to change the default indentation of a particular built-in bullet or number style. These and other customization options are available in the Customization dialog box. To display the Customization dialog box first display the Bullets and Numbering dialog box, and then choose a bullet or number style from the style galleries, and click the Customize button.

Resetting Customized Bullet and Number Styles

Once you customize a built-in bullet or number style, the new customized style replaces the built-in style in the style gallery from that point onward. Fortunately, the Bullets and Numbering dialog box contains a Reset button that restores a style in the gallery to its original built-in format. To reset a style, you choose the style from the style galleries and click the Reset button.

Modifying List Numbering

Many documents have more than one numbered list. In some documents, you may want the numbering to continue sequentially from one list to the next. For example, if one list ends with the numeral 4 you may want the next list to begin with the numeral 5. Then again, you may want the numbering in each new list to begin with 1. Fortunately, Word has two options on the Numbered tab of the Bullets and Numbering dialog box that let you control the list numbering:

- **Restart numbering option—**This option forces a list to begin with the number 1.
- **Continue previous list option—**This option forces the numbering to continue from the previous list.

Hands-On 5.5 Experiment with Customization

1. Scroll up, and click anywhere on the first numbered paragraph.
2. Choose Format→Bullets and Numbering from the menu bar.
   Notice the seven different number styles in the gallery. As with bullets, you can apply a style by choosing it from the gallery and clicking OK. When you use the Numbering button on the Formatting toolbar, it always applies the most recently used number style.
3. Notice the Restart Numbering and Continue Previous List options below the number styles.
   These options are used to adjust the starting number of a numbered list. These options will not be available for the paragraph numbered 1 because it is the first numbered paragraph in the document.
4. Click the Customize button.
5. Follow these steps to explore the Custom Numbered List dialog box.

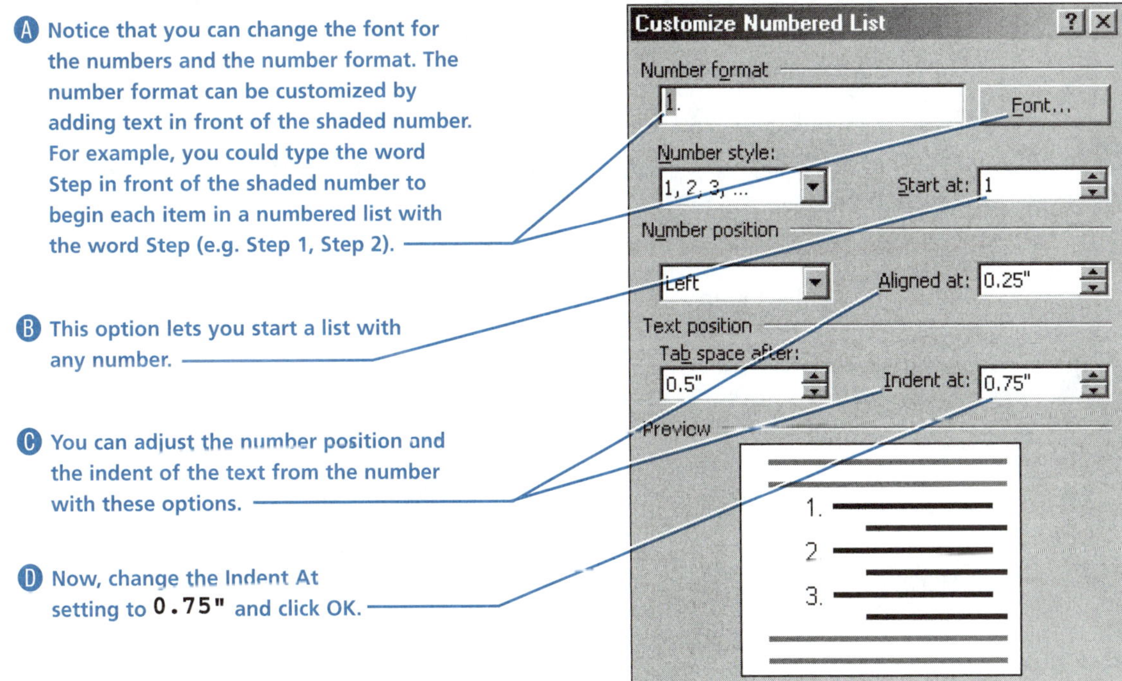

The new number style should be applied to all numbered paragraphs. This will move the text following the number to the 0.75" position.

6. Make sure the insertion point is somewhere on the first paragraph in the numbered list.
7. Choose Format→Bullets and Numbering from the menu bar.
   The current number style should be highlighted in the gallery.
8. Locate the Reset button at the bottom of the dialog box.
   The Reset button will be available because the current number style has been customized.
9. Click the Reset button.

(Continued on the next page)

10. Click Yes on the message box that appears.
    Word asks if you want to restore the gallery position to the default style. Each style has a position in the gallery. When you reset a style, you are resetting a particular gallery position to the default formats for that position. Notice that the Reset button is no longer available. The Reset button is only available if the highlighted gallery style has been customized.

11. Click OK, and the numbered paragraphs will be restored to their original format.
    Keep in mind that you can customize bullet styles in a similar manner to number styles.

Adjusting Bullet and Number Alignment with the Ruler

You can easily adjust the indents of bulleted and numbered lists and the text following the bullets and numbers by dragging markers on the ruler. This technique is useful because it can be applied to specific paragraphs without changing the built-in styles in the style galleries. Drag the First Line Indent marker to adjust the bullet position and a Left Tab marker to adjust the text position.

Hands-On 5.6 Adjust Bullet Position and the Text Indent

1. Scroll to the bottom of the document, and select all of the bulleted paragraphs.
2. Follow this step to adjust the First Line Indent marker.

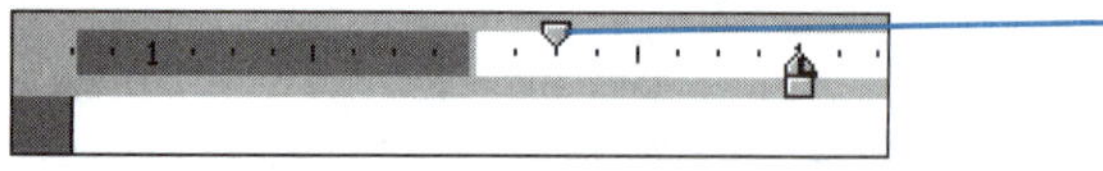

A Drag the First Line Indent marker to the 0.25" position on the ruler as shown here. The bullets will move over to the 0.25" position. As you can see, the First Line Indent marker determines the bullet position.

3. Follow these steps to adjust the Left Tab marker.

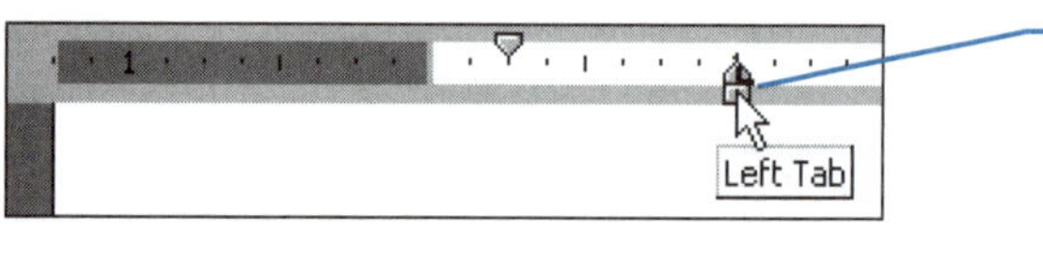

A Position the mouse pointer on the Left Indent marker (the bottom square) and a Left Tab ScreenTip will appear. Notice a Left Tab marker is superimposed on the indent marker. The Left Tab marker appears whenever a paragraph has bullets or numbers.

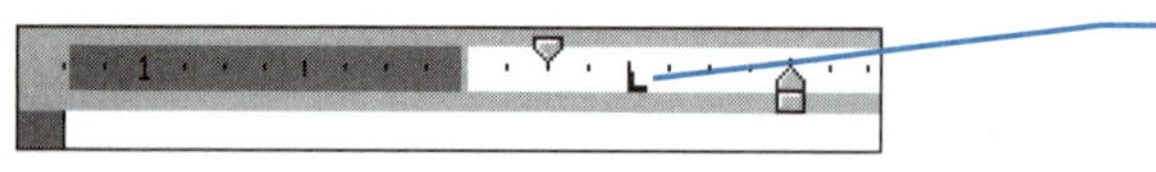

B Drag the Left Tab marker until it is positioned at the 0.5" position as shown here. The bullet text should now be aligned at the 0.5" position.

4. Follow these steps to adjust the Hanging Indent marker.

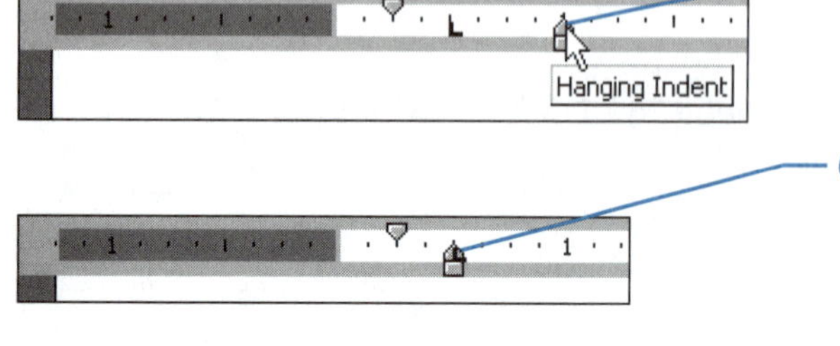

A Position the mouse pointer on the Hanging Indent marker (the upward pointing triangle) and a Hanging Indent ScreenTip will appear.

B Drag the Hanging Indent marker until it is positioned at the 0.5" position as shown here. You won't notice any change in the alignment at this point. You will learn about hanging indents in the next topic.

The bulleted checklist should have the appearance and alignment shown below.

> 3. No valuables please—Leave valuables such as camcorders and cameras at home. Inexpensive 35mm cameras are the safest bet.
>
> Checklist:
> - o Sunglasses
> - o Sunscreen
> - o Insect repellant
> - o Three sets of dry clothing
> - o Tennis shoes
> - o A warm, waterproof jacket

5. Save the changes, and continue with the next topic.

Hanging Indents

The Hanging Indent marker (upward-pointing triangle) offsets all lines of a paragraph except for the first line. Hanging indents are often used in bibliographic entries, glossary terms, and bulleted and numbered lists. You create hanging indents by dragging the Hanging Indent marker on the ruler or with the Paragraph dialog box.

> Middle Granite Canyon—Take Highway 240 to the Pine Meadows turnoff. Go right for two miles until you see a fork in the road. Go right for one mile to the starting point.

A paragraph with a hanging indent

Hands-On 5.7 Create Hanging Indents

1. Position the insertion point on the second blank line below the checklist.
2. Type **`Directions:`** and tap ENTER.
3. Type the following text. As you type, Word may underline various words or phrases with wavy green (grammar suggestion) or red (spelling suggestion) lines. You can remove the red or green underlines by right clicking them and choosing Ignore Once from the pop-up menu. In addition, the street names (Forest Lake Drive and Creekside Lane) may be underlined with purple dotted lines. These Smart Tag indicators give you various options. You can remove a smart tag by pointing to the underlined street name, clicking the Smart Tag Options button that appears, and choosing Remove This Smart Tag.

> Upper Granite Canyon—Take Highway 240 to the Forest Lake exit. Take Forest Lake Drive to Creekside Lane and look for the starting point.

(Continued on the next page)

4. Click anywhere on the paragraph you just typed.
5. Follow these steps to create a hanging indent.

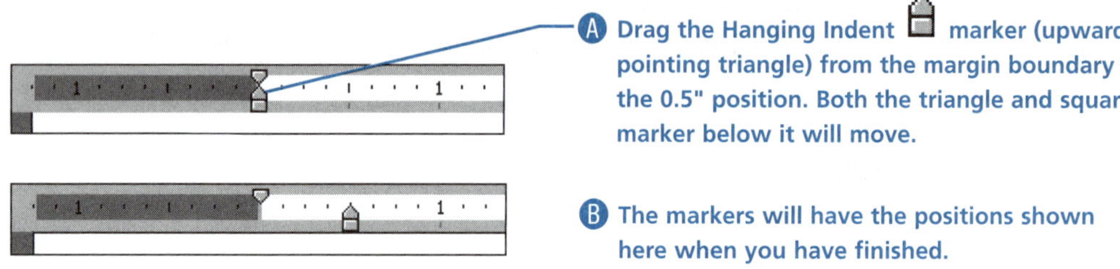

The formatted paragraph should match the following example. Notice how the second line is indented, but the first line remains at the margin.

> Upper Granite Canyon—Take Highway 240 to the Forest Lake exit. Take Forest Lake Drive to Creekside Lane and look for the starting point.

6. Now click the Increase Indent button to increase both the First Line indent and the Hanging indent.
7. Position the insertion point at the end of the paragraph (to the right of the period).
8. Tap ENTER twice, then type the following text.

> Middle Granite Canyon—Take Highway 240 to the Pine Meadows turnoff. Go right for two miles until you see a fork in the road. Go right for one mile to the starting point.

9. Tap ENTER twice, and drag the First Line Indent marker and the Hanging Indent marker to the 0″ position on the ruler.
10. Save the changes, and continue with the next topic.

Outline-Style Numbered Lists

An outline-style numbered list can have up to nine levels of numbers or bullet characters. Outline-style lists are often used in the legal profession where multiple numbering levels are required. You format paragraphs as an outline-style numbered list by displaying the Bullets and Numbering dialog box and choosing the desired style from the style gallery on the Outline Numbered tab.

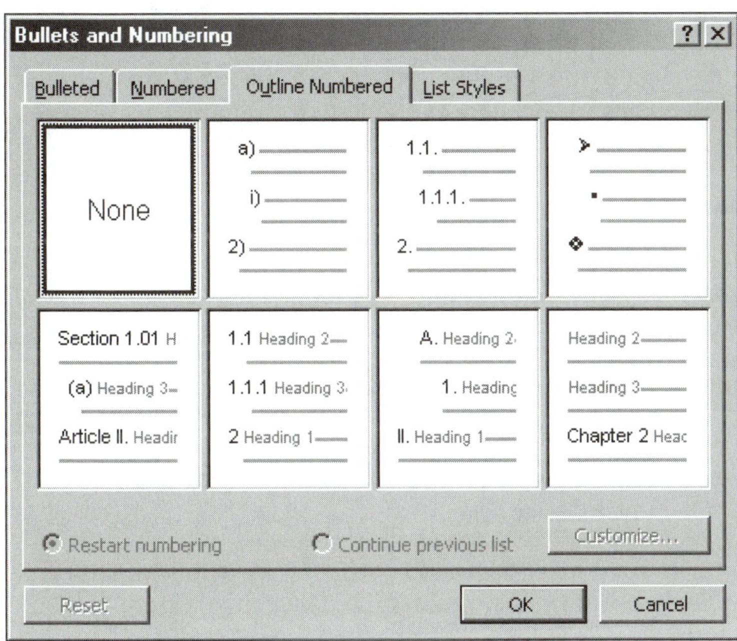

Outline numbered list styles

Promoting and Demoting List Items

FROM THE KEYBOARD

TAB to demote
SHIFT+TAB to promote

The Increase Indent button and the Decrease Indent button are used to promote or demote paragraphs in an outline-style numbered list. The Increase Indent button indents selected paragraphs one level, thus demoting them one level. The Decrease Indent button reduces the indentation level and thus promotes the paragraph one level.

Hands-On 5.8 Create a Policies and Procedures Page

In this exercise, you will use outline-style numbered lists to create a policies and procedures page at the end of the document.

Set Up the New Page

1. Make sure the insertion point is at the end of the document and that the paragraph has no indents set.
2. Press CTRL+ENTER to insert a page break.
   Notice that the top margin is still set to 2".
3. Click the Center button.

(Continued on the next page)

4. Type **OUTDOOR ADVENTURES**, and tap ENTER twice.
5. Type **Policies and Procedures**, and tap ENTER three times.
6. Click the Align Left button.

Create an Outline-Style Numbered List

7. Choose Format→Bullets and Numbering from the menu.
8. Click the Outline Numbered tab.
9. Click the first style in the gallery. If the Reset button is available at the bottom of the dialog box, click it to restore the style to the default setting. The style should match the example shown to the right.

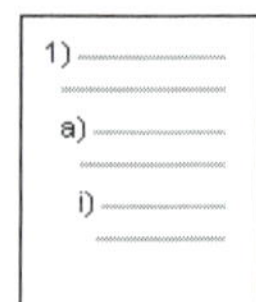

10. Click OK to apply the style.
11. Type **Medical and Injury**, and tap ENTER.
    The heading Medical and Injury should be preceded by the number 1 followed by a closing parenthesis, and the number 2) should be applied to the new paragraph.
12. Click the Increase Indent button to demote the new paragraph.
    The number 2) should now become the letter a).
13. Type **All guests must have medical insurance**, and tap ENTER.
    The new paragraph will be preceded by the letter b).
14. Complete items b) and c) as shown below, tapping ENTER once after each paragraph. The insertion point should be on the new paragraph d) when you have finished.

```
1) Medical and Injury
   a) All guests must have medical insurance
   b) All guests must sign an injury waiver
   c) All guests agree to pay out-of-pocket medical expenses including:
   d)
```

15. Click the Increase Indent indent to demote the new paragraph.
    The new paragraph will be preceded by the letter i).
16. Type **Injuries resulting from on-trip accidents**, and tap ENTER.
17. Complete the document as shown on the following page. You should double-space between the three list headings as shown. When you do this, the outline numbering will be turned off for the new heading paragraph. Turn the numbering on again using the Numbering button on the Formatting toolbar. Finally, format the title with an Arial 18 pt bold font and the subtitle with an Arial 16 pt bold font.
18. Save the changes, and close the document.

OUTDOOR ADVENTURES

Policies and Procedures

1) Medical and Injury
   a) All guests must have medical insurance
   b) All guests must sign an injury waiver
   c) All guests agree to pay out-of-pocket medical expenses including:
      i) Injuries resulting from on-trip accidents
      ii) Aero medical evacuation
      iii) Rehabilitation costs

2) Cancellations and Refunds
   a) A full refund will be given for cancellations with 60 days notice
   b) A 50% refund will be given for cancellations with 30 days notice
   c) No refund for cancellations with less than 30 days notice

3) Alternate Trip Destinations and Cancellations
   a) Your trip may be cancelled for any of the following reasons:
      i) Inclement weather
      ii) Poor water flow
      iii) Insufficient number of guests
      iv) Unavailability of a guide
   b) Your trip destination may be changed for any of the following reasons:
      i) Inclement weather
      ii) Poor water flow
      iii) Insufficient guest turnout requiring reorganization of trips

Concepts Review

True/False Questions

1.	Margins can be set with the ruler.	TRUE	FALSE
2.	The File→Page Setup command displays a dialog box that can be used to adjust margins.	TRUE	FALSE
3.	Bullets can be offset from the margins.	TRUE	FALSE
4.	Numbering always continues sequentially from one list to the next in documents with multiple lists.	TRUE	FALSE
5.	Bullet formats are carried to the next paragraph when ENTER is tapped.	TRUE	FALSE
6.	Bullet formats cannot be changed once ENTER is tapped.	TRUE	FALSE
7.	Only the first line of a paragraph is indented when a hanging indent is applied.	TRUE	FALSE
8.	Outline-style numbered lists can have up to seven numbering levels.	TRUE	FALSE

Multiple-Choice Questions

1. Which of the following keys is used to display measurements on the ruler while the margin boundary is dragged?
   a. ALT
   b. SHIFT
   c. CTRL
   d. None of the above

2. Which command displays the Bullets and Numbering dialog box?
   a. Format→Bullets and Numbering
   b. Edit→Bullets and Numbering
   c. Format→Paragraph
   d. None of the above

3. Which technique indents the bullets in a bulleted list?
   a. Select the desired paragraphs, and drag the First Line Indent marker.
   b. Select the desired paragraphs, and drag the Left Tab symbol on the indent marker.
   c. Use the TAB key.
   d. None of the above

4. Which technique should you use to indent the text in a bulleted list?
   a. Select the desired paragraphs, and drag the First Line Indent marker.
   b. Select the desired paragraphs, and drag the Left Tab symbol on the indent marker.
   c. Use the TAB key.
   d. None of the above

Skill Builders

Skill Builder 5.1 Create a Personal Business Letter

In this exercise, you will create the document shown on the following page.

Set-Up the Letter

1. Start a new document, and Choose File→Page Setup from the menu bar.
2. Set the left and right margins to 1″ and click OK.
3. Type the date, address, salutation, and first paragraph as shown on the following page.

Create the Numbered List

4. Tap (ENTER) twice after the first main paragraph, and then click the Numbering button. *It's OK if the number style and indentation are different than shown on the following page. You will adjust the style and indentation soon.*
5. Type the three numbered paragraphs, tapping (ENTER) once after each paragraph.
6. Tap (ENTER) twice after the third numbered paragraph. *This will turn off numbering.*
7. Now complete the document as shown on the following page. Turn bullets on and off as necessary, and tap (ENTER) either once or twice between paragraphs as shown. Don't be concerned with text formats or bullet alignments at this point. You will be instructed to make those changes in the following steps.

Format the Lists and Headings

8. Select the three paragraphs in the numbered list.
9. Drag the First Line Indent marker to the 0″ position on the ruler to align the numbers with the left margin.
10. Drag the Left Tab marker and the Hanging Indent marker to the 0.5″ position on the ruler. This will indent the text 0.5″ from the numbers.
11. Now align the bulleted paragraphs the same way.
12. Format the headings with bold as shown on the following page.
13. If necessary, use the Format→Bullets and Numbering command to choose the numbering style and bullet style shown on the following page.
14. Save the document with the name **`Skill Builder 5.1`**, then close the document.

(Continued on the next page)

Today's Date

Mr. Dave Olson, President
Financial Freedom Network
300 South Meyers Fork Road
San Jose, CA 95136

Dear Mr. Olson:

I recently attended your quick start seminar on tax planning for retirement, and I was impressed with both the speaker and content of the presentation. I spoke with Mr. Barry after the presentation, and he asked me to provide you with three types of feedback:

1. Topics that I feel should be included in next year's presentation
2. Ways to improve the presentation
3. Comments on the facilities

I have organized my comments into the three lists that follow.

Topics to Include Next Year
- ✓ Information on 401K plans
- ✓ Method for calculating projected net worth
- ✓ Planning for children's college expenses

How to Improve the Presentation
- ✓ Make it longer (8 hours).
- ✓ Include more visuals.
- ✓ Have multiple speakers.

About the Facilities
- ✓ The food was excellent.
- ✓ The chairs were a little uncomfortable.
- ✓ The employees were very friendly and helpful.

Mr. Olson, I hope my feedback helps you plan for and improve next year's presentation. Please feel free to contact me if you need additional information.

Sincerely,

Richard Ellison, Seminar Participant
2400 Fairview Lane
Richmond, CA 94803

Skill Builder 5.2

1. Start a new document.
2. Set the top margin to 2″ and the left and right margins to 1.5″.
3. Follow these guidelines to create the document shown below.
   - Use a Times New Roman 16 pt font for all text except for the title and subtitle. Use an Arial Bold 18 pt font for the title and an Arial Bold 16 pt font for the subtitle.
   - Use ENTER to create the single-, double-, and triple-spacing shown below.
   - Use the bullet style shown below.
4. Save the document as **`Skill Builder 5.2`**, and close the document.

Baron's Model Train Supply

Going Out of Business Sale

Baron's Model Train Supply has provided the widest selection of model train accessories for over 43 years, but our lease has run out. We have decided to close up shop and liquidate our inventory. Please stop by before the end of June to take advantage of rock-bottom prices and a wide selection of accessories and collectibles. Here is just a sample of what you will find.

Accessories

- ❖ Scenery
- ❖ Tracks and switches
- ❖ Buildings

Collectibles

- ❖ Antique locomotives
- ❖ Antique cabooses
- ❖ Figures: Switchmen, engineers, animals, and more

Skill Builder 5.3

In this exercise, you will open a document on your exercise diskette. You will format the document until it matches the document on the following page.

1. Open the document named Skill Builder 5.3.
2. Set the left and right margins to 1″.
3. Look at the document on the following page, and notice the title shown at the top of the document. Insert the title, separating it from the first body paragraph with three hard returns. Format the title with an Arial 14 pt bold font and Center align the title.
4. Select the first three body paragraphs, and apply double-spacing to them. Adjust the first line indent of the first three body paragraphs to 0.5″.
5. Apply the bullet style shown on the following page to the next three paragraphs. Use ENTER to double-space between the paragraphs.
6. Indent the last paragraph 1″ on both the left and right as shown. You will also need to insert hard returns above and below the paragraph with the phrase "Lough adds a powerful statement".
7. Your completed document should match the document on the following page.
8. Save the changes to the document, and close it.

ELECTRIC CARS

Many people are not aware that electric cars have been used in the United States for nearly ninety years. In fact, before the introduction of the gasoline automobile, approximately 50,000 electric cars soared down American streets. Presently, electric cars are gaining attention as an effective means of improving our air quality, reducing pollution, and reducing the need to import oil into the United States.

Often referred to as "zero-emission vehicles," electric cars have the distinct advantage of releasing little or no pollution, reducing the amount of carbon monoxide in our air. Electric cars are also quieter than gasoline-fueled cars, and the batteries that power these cars have the potential to be recharged through renewable sources such as wind and solar power.

Steven Lough of Eco-Motion Electric Cars in Seattle, WA highlights a few of the many benefits of electric cars. A summary of his points follows:

- Electric cars are affordable. A used car in good condition sells for about $2,900 and new models start at $8,900.
- Electric cars are three times more efficient per dollar than gasoline-fueled cars. They improve air quality, limit pollution, and lessen U.S. dependence on imported coal and oil.
- Electric cars will improve over time. Already new batteries—including metal-nickel-hydride batteries and lithium batteries—are being researched. In the coming years these batteries will be available, doubling and tripling the per charge rate of these automobiles.

Lough adds a powerful statement, that:

> There are alternatives [to gasoline automobiles and the pollution and expense associated with them]...There is carpooling, public transportation, bicycles, telecommunications, and yes, electric cars.

Assessments

Assessment 5.1

1. Follow these guidelines to create the document shown below.
   - Set the top margin to 2″.
   - Insert the date as a field using the Insert→Date and Time command.
   - Use the bullet style shown for the bulleted list.
2. Print the document, save it with the name **`Assessment 5.1`**, and close the document.

Current Date

Mr. John Upshaw
1204 Wilkins Drive
Sacramento, CA 90518

Dear Mr. Upshaw:

I am pleased to inform you that you have won the grand prize in our sweepstakes contest. Please contact me as soon as possible to verify receipt of this letter. You may contact me in any of the following ways.

- ➢ Stop by our office at 2400 Gerber Road.
- ➢ Call 1-916-682-9090 between the hours of 9:00 a.m. and 5:00 p.m.
- ➢ Write to me at the address listed on this letterhead.

I look forward to hearing from you soon. Please be prepared to present us with your verification number. Your verification number is JB101.

Sincerely,

Jerry Williams
Prize Notification Manager

Assessment 5.2

1. Follow these guidelines to create the document shown below.
   - Set the top margin to 2″ and the left and right margins to 1″.
   - Use an Arial Bold 16 pt font for the title and a Times New Roman 14 pt font for all other text.
   - Center the title, and use three hard returns after the title.
   - Use single-spacing and double-spacing as necessary to format the document as shown.
   - Set the First Line indent of the two body paragraphs to 0.5″ as shown. Adjust the indents of the numbered paragraphs and the quotation as shown.
2. Print the document, save it with the name **`Assessment 5.2`**, and close the document.

SUCCESS

The quest for success is a driving force in the lives of many Americans.

This force drives the business world and often results in huge personal fortunes.

However, success can come in many forms, some of which are listed below.

1. Many people in America view success monetarily.
2. Our society also views public figures such as movie stars, athletes, and other celebrities as being successful.
3. Educational achievement such as earning an advanced degree is often perceived as successful.

It is easy to see that success means many things to many people. The poet

Ralph Waldo Emerson provides this elegant definition of success:

> To laugh often and much; to win the respect of intelligent people and the affection of children; to earn the appreciation of honest critics and endure the betrayal of false friends; to appreciate beauty, to find the best in others; to leave the world a bit better, whether by a healthy child, a garden patch or a redeemed social condition; to know even one life has breathed easier because you have lived. This is to have succeeded.

Assessment 5.3

1. Follow these guidelines to create the document shown below.
   - Set the top margin to 2″.
   - Center the title, and use three hard returns after the title.
   - Use an Arial Bold 16 pt font for the title and a Times New Roman 14 pt font for all other text. Apply bold to the list headings as shown.
   - Apply line spacing, indents, and bullets as shown.
2. Print the document, save it with the name **`Assessment 5.3`**, and close the document.

THE GOLDEN STATE

With more than thirty million people, California has become the most populous state in America. From the beaches of Southern California to the great redwood forests of Northern California, the Golden State is home to a diverse population and a vibrant economy.

A recent poll asked Californians to list the five things they liked best about life in California. The same poll also asked them to list the five biggest drawbacks to life in the Golden State. The poll results appear below.

Five Best Things
- Climate
- Cultural attractions
- Economic opportunities
- Educational opportunities
- Recreational activities

Five Biggest Drawbacks
- Air pollution
- Cost of living
- Crime
- Taxes
- Traffic and congestion

Critical Thinking

Critical Thinking 5.1 On Your Own

Jessica Owens is a student at Mid Town High School. Jessica has always dreamed of working in the film industry. Jessica chose to attend Mid Town High primarily because they offer college prep classes for film majors. Jessica just started her first film class, Film 101. Her instructor, Ms. Watkins, has asked students to prepare brief reports on their favorite films. Each report must include a report title and a brief paragraph describing the purpose of the report. In addition, Jessica must include brief paragraphs on her favorite comedy, drama, action, and love story films. The paragraphs should describe why she likes each film and why she believes the film is the best of its category.

Prepare a report using the criteria described above. Include a paragraph describing your favorite film in each category. Use a bulleted list for the category paragraphs. Save the completed report as **`Critical Thinking 5.1`**.

Critical Thinking 5.2 On Your Own

Jack Dennings loves to cook! He finds that the best way to relieve a little tension is to cook up a storm for friends and family. Recently, Jack started a monthly gourmet meal event at his home. Each month, he invites a group of friends and/or family to enjoy his feast. While preparing this month's menu, Jack was perusing his grandmother's recipes when he came across his childhood favorite—Glazed Garlic Prawns.

One of Jack's pet peeves is organization. He has computerized all of his menus by scanning or retyping them into Word documents. His grandmother's Glazed Garlic Prawns recipe was scribbled on a piece of paper as shown below:

Ingredients
1 pound of peeled prawns
1 tablespoon olive oil
1/4 cup coarse sea salt
3/4 cup chicken broth
2 tablespoons finely minced garlic
3 tablespoons fresh lemon juice
1/4 cup finely chopped parsley

Directions: 1. Rinse the prawns, pat dry, and brush with olive oil. 2. Spread the salt on a large plate and roll the prawns in the salt. Preheat the broiler. 3. Place the prawns directly on a rack and broil 4 inches from the heat 2 minutes per side. 4. Meanwhile, heat the chicken broth in a small saucepan over medium heat. Add the garlic, and cook for 2 minutes, stirring constantly. Add the lemon juice and parsley, and cook for 1 minute. Transfer the sauce to a serving bowl. Serve the prawns and dipping sauce immediately.

Enter the recipe above into a Word document. Use a descriptive title, put the ingredients in a bulleted list with the heading "Ingredients," and put the directions in a numbered list with the heading "Directions." If necessary, adjust the indents of the numbered list to allow the numbers to align with the bullets and the bullet text to align with the numbered text. Also, make sure you give Grandma credit for the recipe. Save the completed document as **`Critical Thinking 5.2`**.

Critical Thinking 5.3 Web Research

Bud Richardson works as an Administrative Assistant for Fremont Investment Group. Each month, Jerry Wilkins, Fremont's Chief Investment Advisor, sends a letter to his clients with his top stock picks of the month. Bud has been asked to prepare this month's letter and an attached stock pick page. Jerry's top technology recommendations for this month are 1. Oracle (ORCL), 2. Sun Microsystems (SUNW), 3. Cisco Systems (CSCO), 4. BMC Software (BMCS), and 5. Microsoft (MSFT). His top Dow Jones Industrial Average picks are 1. Citigroup (C), 2. Boeing Aircraft (BA), 3. Microsoft (MSFT), 4. Gillette (G), and 5. IBM (IBM).

Prepare a business letter to Fremont's clients from Jerry informing them that Jerry's top technology and Dow picks are attached. Use Internet Explorer to navigate to the Web site of a company that offers free stock quotations. Get the current stock price for each of the stocks listed above. Include an attachment page with a heading for each group of stocks, a brief paragraph describing some rationale for choosing the stocks, and a numbered list. The numbered lists should be numbered from 1 to 5 with each numbered item including the company name, stock symbol, and current price. Make sure the numbering starts over at 1 for the second list. Thus, each list will be numbered from 1 to 5. Save the completed document as **Critical Thinking 5.3**.

Critical Thinking 5.4 With a Group

Health-e-Meals.com has been in business for over three years now and employees 42 people. Your classmate and you have done a remarkable job building the business. However, you realize that you cannot continue to grow at this rate without having a formal business plan and goals in place. You and your classmate have decided to develop a business plan to help you with strategic planning and to help secure additional credit lines and financing. Part of the business plan is a list of the top five financial goals and the top five customer service goals for the next year.

Create a Word document that lists the top five financial goals and the top five customer service goals of Health-e-Meals.com in the current fiscal year. Have your classmate determine the top five financial goals, and you determine the top five customer service goals. Use numbered lists to format the goals. Include a title and headings in the document. Save the completed document as **Critical Thinking 5.4**.

LESSON 6

Creating a Flyer

Word is a versatile program that gives you many options for designing documents. When you need to create a flyer, Word allows you to change the page orientation from tall (portrait) to wide (landscape). You can also add a border to a page. Like all of the Office XP programs, Word features an extensive library of clip art you can use to add visual interest to images. Much of this clip art is available online and does not take up space on your hard drive. The Insert Clip Art task pane and the Clip Organizer make accessing the clip art collection easy. By the end of this lesson, you will be able to design custom flyers with Word that are visually attractive and effective.

IN THIS LESSON

Word 2002 Core MOUS Objectives Covered in this Lesson

MOUS Objective Number	MOUS Objective Description	Concept Page References	Exercise Page References
W2002-1-4	Apply font and text effects	167–168	168–169
W2002-3-3	Modify document layout and Page Setup options	148–149, 151–152, 164–165	149–150, 153–154, 165–167
W2002-5-1	Insert images and graphics	154–157, 160	157–159, 160–163

See the Lesson 6 Web Page at: labpub.com/learn/bc/word1/lesson6

Case Study

Nick manages an office equipment outlet in a medium-sized town. There's quite a bit of small business activity in the town. Most of these businesses depend on several computers. But when he visits offices, Nick notices that these computers are often set up very inefficiently. For example, he sees keyboards that are set too high for good typing posture and the mouse positioned so that the user must reach awkwardly to maneuver it. Ergonomics is the science of designing and setting up equipment and furniture in ways that workers find comfortable and efficient. One of Nick's sales associates has developed an hour-long presentation covering how to set up an ergonomically sound office space. He decides to mail a flyer to businesses in his area to promote this presentation, which will help generate interest in office furniture among new and established businesses. Nick designs a flyer like the one below for distribution to businesses in their area.

Brown bag discussion

The Ergonomically Challenged Office

- How the setup of your office equipment can affect your productivity and health.
- Questions and answers about your computer workstation.

Where: THE BAKERY CAFÉ

When: Tuesday, September 26th at 12 Noon

A catered lunch will be provided.

Nick's flyer features clip art and a shadowed page border.

Page Orientation and Size

Setting the Page Orientation

When designing a specialized document such as a flyer, you may wish to make changes to the default page orientation and size. There are two types of page orientation:

- **Portrait (tall)**—This is the default page orientation. Most documents use this orientation.
- **Landscape (wide)**—This orientation sets the page horizontally. It is especially useful for the display of long lines of information.

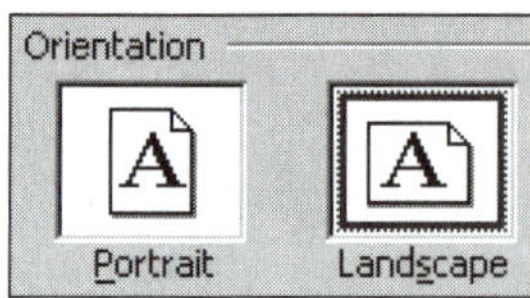

The Orientation setting in the Page Setup dialog box.

Setting the Paper Size

Most documents use the standard letter-size page. However, Word supports the use of many other standard paper sizes, and allows you to set a custom page size when necessary.

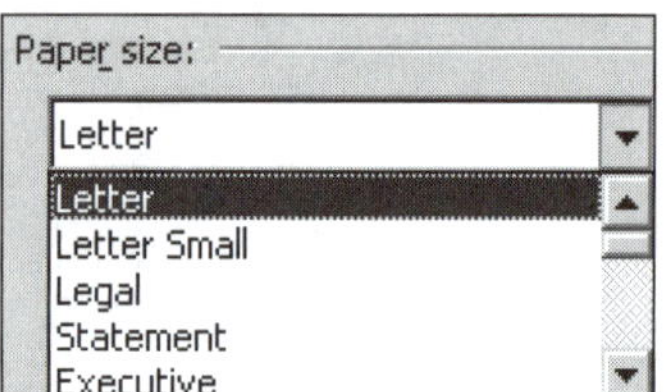

Word allows you to choose from a wide variety of paper sizes, and also supports setting a custom paper size.

Setting the Page Alignment

You can also tell Word how to vertically align the contents of an entire page. For example, a formal letter will usually be centered on the page. Although you could use extra paragraphs at the top to manually align a page, it is much easier to let Word make the alignment adjustment for you. The table below illustrates the effect of each page alignment setting.

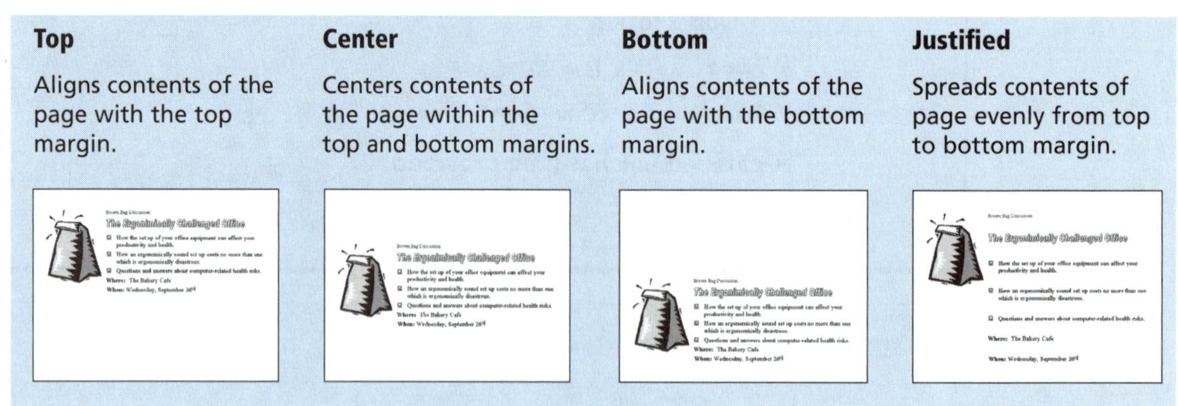

Top	Center	Bottom	Justified
Aligns contents of the page with the top margin.	Centers contents of the page within the top and bottom margins.	Aligns contents of the page with the bottom margin.	Spreads contents of page evenly from top to bottom margin.

QUICK REFERENCE: SETTING PAGE ORIENTATION AND LAYOUT AND ALIGNMENT

Task	Procedure
Change the page orientation	■ Choose File→Page Setup from the menu bar. ■ Choose the Margins tab. ■ Select the desired page orientation.
Change the paper size	■ Choose File→Page Setup from the menu bar. ■ Choose the Paper tab. ■ Select the desired page size from the Paper drop-down list. ■ If the necessary page size is not listed, scroll to the bottom of the list, choose Custom, and manually enter the custom page size.
Change the page alignment	■ Choose File→Page Setup from the menu bar. ■ Choose the Layout tab. ■ Select the desired vertical alignment in the Page section of the dialog box.

Hands-On 6.1 Adjust the Page Setup Settings

In this exercise, you will change the page orientation and alignment.

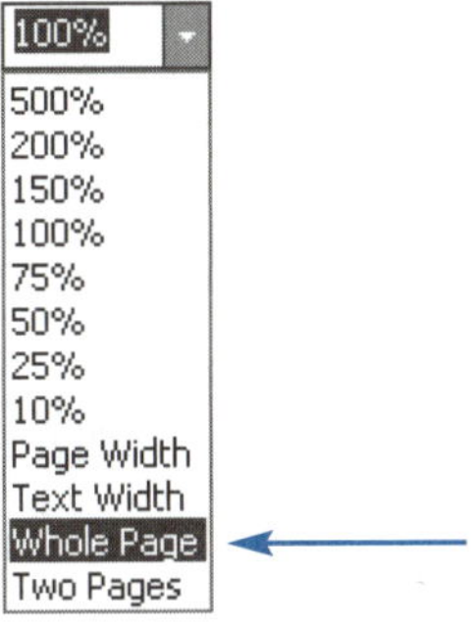

1. Start Word, then choose View→Print Layout from the menu bar.
2. Choose Whole Page from the zoom box on the Word toolbar.
   The page is currently in the default portrait (tall) orientation. Viewing the whole page allows you to see this clearly.

Adjust the Page Orientation and Margins

3. Choose File→Page Setup from the menu bar.
4. Choose the Margins tab, then set the page orientation to Landscape.

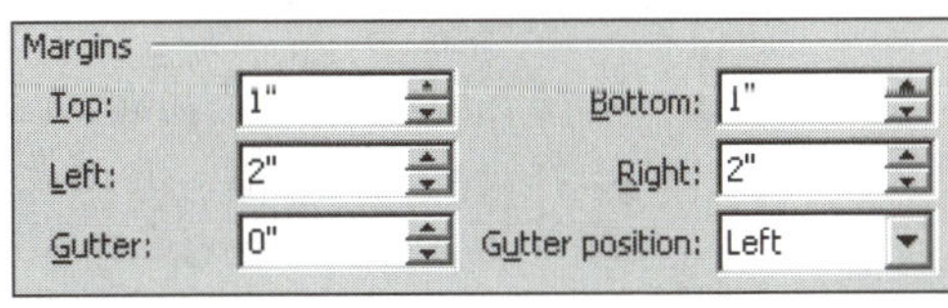

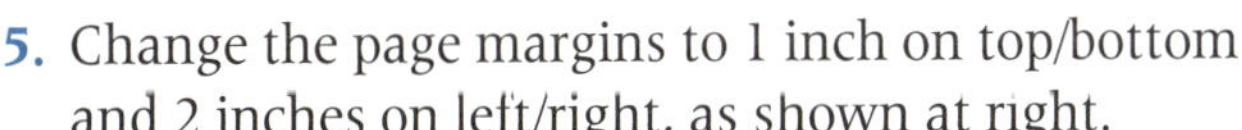

5. Change the page margins to 1 inch on top/bottom and 2 inches on left/right, as shown at right.

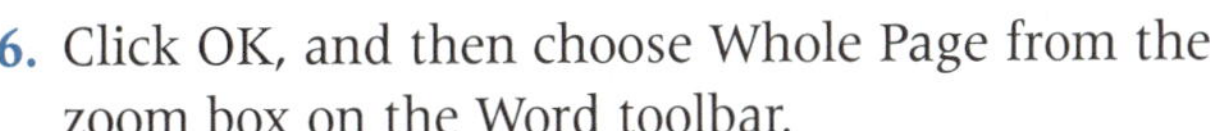

6. Click OK, and then choose Whole Page from the zoom box on the Word toolbar.
   Now the page is oriented in landscape (wide) configuration. By zooming the page again, you obtained a closer view. This is because the monitor is wider than it is tall, and thus fits the portrait page orientation better.

(Continued on the next page)

View the Paper Size Options

7. Choose File→Page Setup from the menu bar.
8. Choose the Paper tab, then click the Paper Size drop-down list near the top of the dialog box.
   This list contains all of the paper sizes pre-programmed for use with Word.
9. Tap the L key on the keyboard.
   The first page size matching the letter L appears.
10. Tap the L key several more times to display other paper sizes that begin with this letter.
    When you view a drop-down list, this keyboard shortcut scrolls to the first item that begins with the letter you tapped.
11. Tap the C key on the keyboard until the Custom Size setting appears.
    This is a quick shortcut to get to the Custom paper size setting. If the paper size you need is unavailable, you can always create a custom setting.
12. Tap the HOME key to jump up to the Letter size setting at the top of the list.

Adjust the Page Vertical Alignment

13. Choose the Layout tab, then choose Center as the Vertical Alignment setting.

14. Click OK.
    The insertion point now blinks at the center of the page to reflect the centered vertical alignment setting.

Creating a Page Border

Word allows you to place a border around any page. You can adjust the color, line thickness, and other features of the border. You can even select various images to display around the border of a page. Word allows you to adjust the distance from the page margin that any border appears.

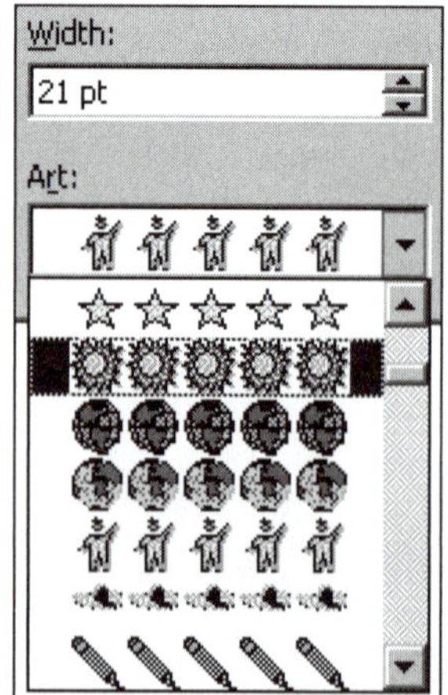

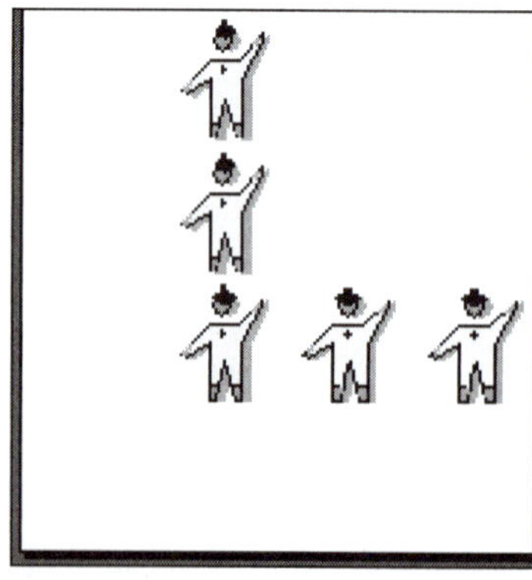

You can choose images to appear around the border of a page.

The Borders and Shading Dialog Box

The Borders and Shading dialog box allows you to select and adjust any page border. You use the same dialog box to edit the borders of other objects such as images, tables, and around paragraphs. This dialog box displays a preview of how your page border will appear after you apply the command.

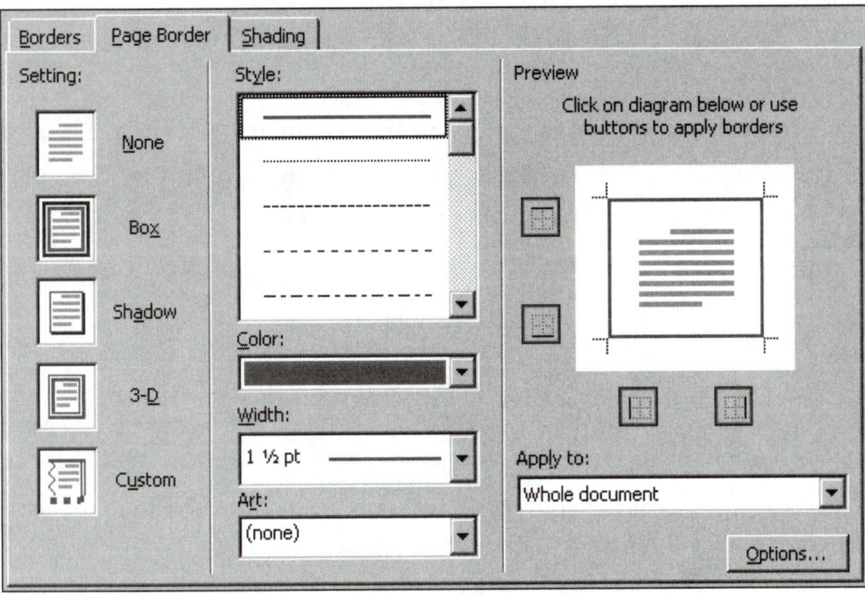

The Borders and Shading dialog box includes a tab for setting page borders.

A New Unit of Measure: The Point

A point (pt) is 1/72 of an inch. This is a common unit of measure in printing and is used by Word for many settings, such as page border margins, paragraph spacing, and other adjustments that benefit from this fine unit of measure.

TIP!

72 points = 1 inch. 36 points = ½ inch. 24 points = ⅓ inch.

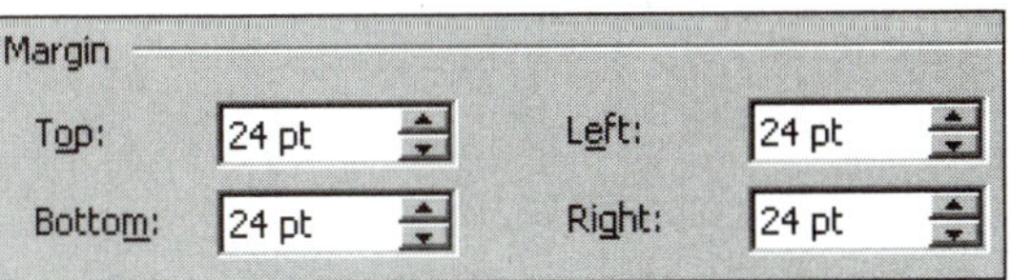

The page border option box is an example of a Word setting that uses points. In this case, each margin is set to 24 points (⅓ of an inch).

Adjusting the Page Border Margins

You can adjust the default margin settings for any page border. Normally, page border margins are set to one-third of an inch (24 points). Since most printers cannot print on the first quarter to-half-inch of the page, this setting works well with most printers. You adjust the page border margins from the options dialog box.

QUICK REFERENCE: APPLYING PAGE BORDERS

Task	Procedure
Apply a preset border to a page	■ Place the insertion point on the page to receive a border. ■ Choose Format→Borders and Shading from the menu bar. ■ Choose the Page Border tab. ■ Select the desired preset border from the items on the left side of the dialog box.
Apply a custom border to a page	■ Place the insertion point on the page to receive a border. ■ Choose Format→Borders and Shading from the menu bar. ■ Choose the Page Border tab. ■ Select the desired line style, color, and thickness from the drop-down lists in the center of the dialog box. ■ Click the desired borders to receive the line style or click a preset style icon on the left side of the dialog box to apply the custom line settings to all borders.
Apply artwork as the page border	■ Place the insertion point on the page to receive a border. ■ Choose Format→Borders and Shading from the menu bar. ■ Choose the Page Border tab. ■ Choose the desired artwork from the Art box and click OK.
Adjust the margins for a page border	■ Place the insertion point on the page on which you wish to adjust the page border margins. ■ Choose Format→Borders and Shading from the menu bar. ■ Choose the Page Border tab. ■ Click the Options button, make the desired margin adjustments, and click OK.

Hands-On 6.2 Apply a Page Border

In this exercise, you will apply a page border and change the margin from 24 points to 36 points (½ inch).

Add a Page Border

1. Choose Format→Borders and Shading from the menu bar.
2. Choose the Page Border tab.
3. Follow these steps to create a page border:

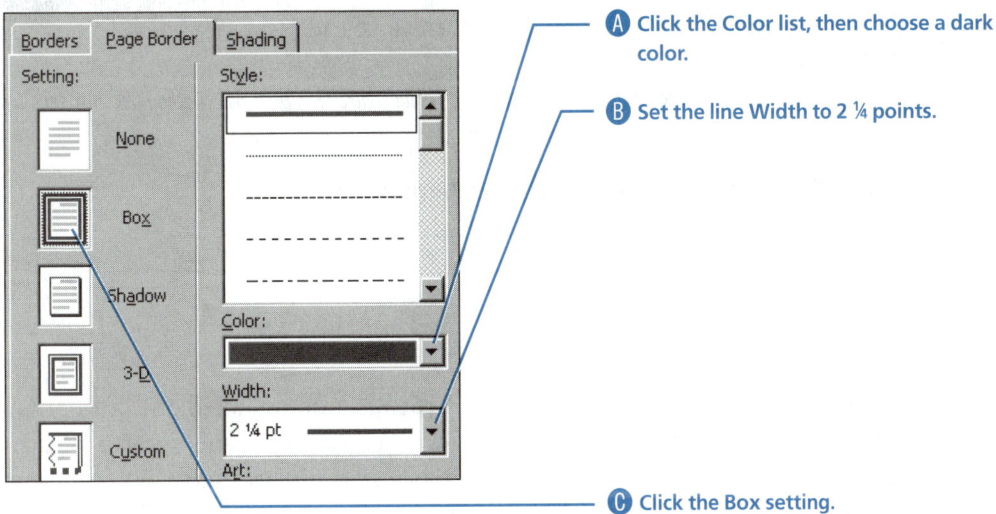

A border appears around the preview item according to your settings.

4. Click the None setting on the left side of the dialog box.
   The border disappears.
5. Follow these steps to place a border at the top and bottom of the page:

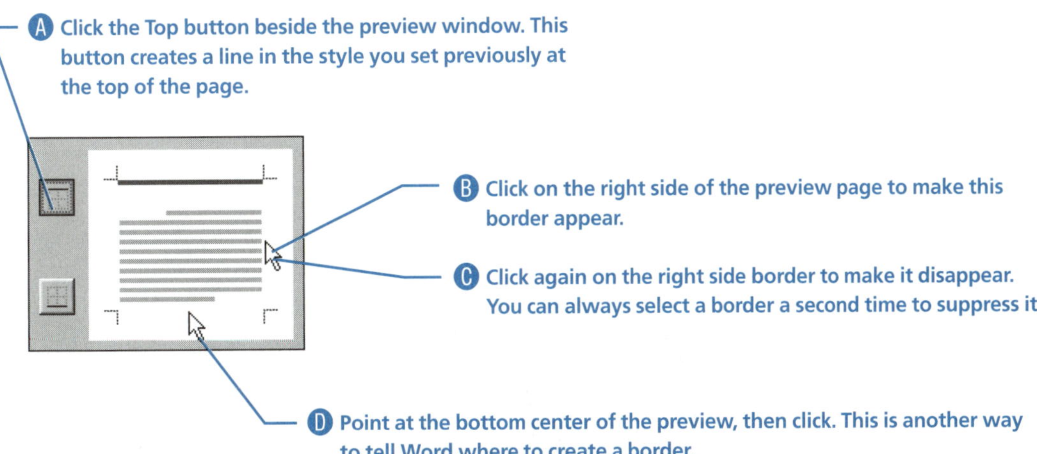

It's easy to set or customize the border settings with the preview box.

(Continued on the next page)

6. Click the Shadow setting box to create a shadowed border.
   This gives you a border around all four edges, with a shadow on the bottom and right sides of the border.

View the Border Margins

Now you will check the margins used for your page borders.

7. Click the Options button near the lower-right corner of the dialog box.
8. Click the Measure From drop-down list.
   Notice that you can measure the page border margin from either the edge of the paper or the edge of the text margin.

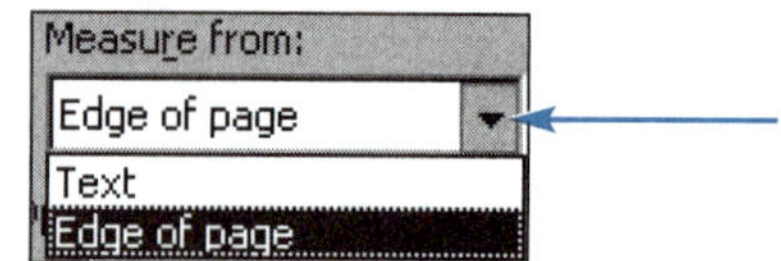

9. Click the Cancel button, then click OK to close the dialog box.
   Your page border settings should be visible. Notice that the bottom and right borders appear thicker than the others. This reflects the shadow setting.
10. Save the document as **`Hands-On Lesson 6`**.

Using Clip Art

Office XP and Word 2002 include a clip art collection installed on your hard drive, even more clip art items are available online. Word gives you a variety of methods to locate and insert clip art images into your documents. Once you have placed a clip art image, you can also change its size and location on the page. Some clip art images are animated, and will display dynamically when viewed in a Web browser.

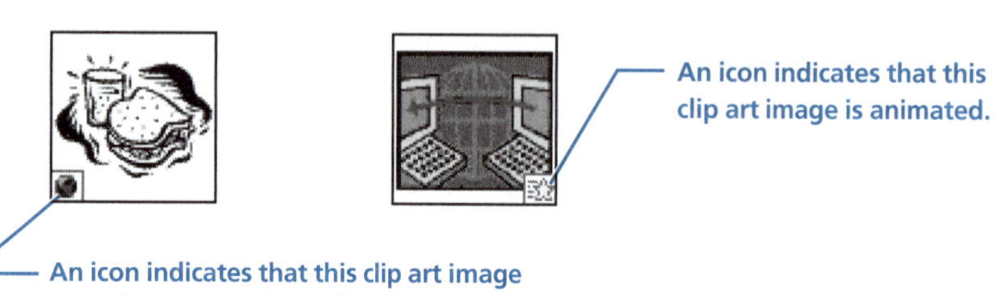

An icon indicates that this clip art image is animated.

An icon indicates that this clip art image came from the online collection.

Inserting Clip Art

Word offers two primary methods to locate and place clip art images into your documents.

- **The Insert Clip Art Task Pane**—This method allows you to search for images by entering key words. When you search on a key word, the Task pane displays thumbnails of all images located by your search.

The Insert Clip Art task pane makes searching for and reviewing clip art found with search keywords easy.

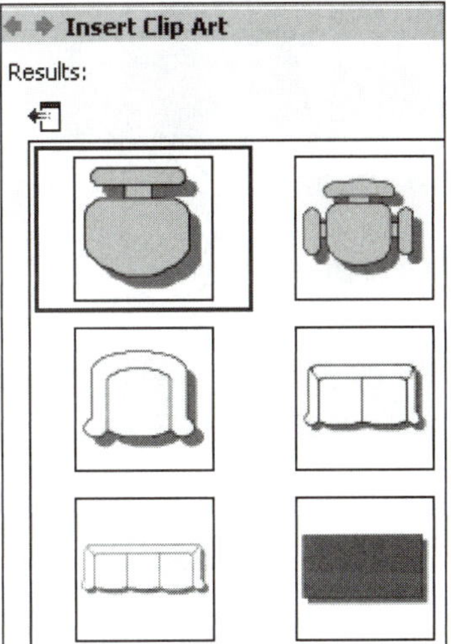

- **The Clip Organizer**—This method allows you to navigate among the major categories of clip art, viewing thumbnail images of the entire collection.

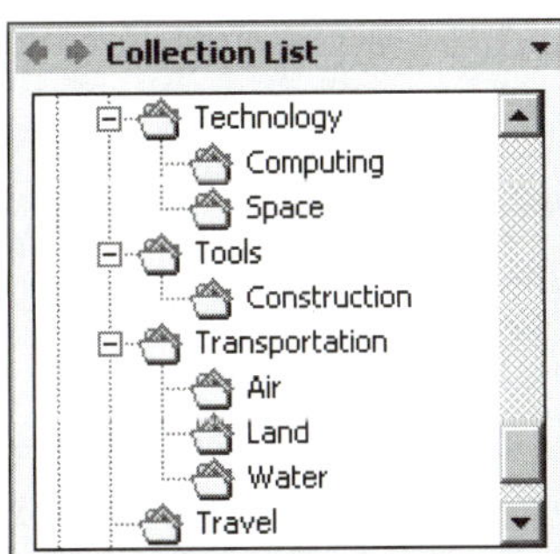

The Clip Organizer arranges clip art into folders.

Searching for Clip Art with Key Words

Each clip art image is associated with one or more key words to help you locate the images you need. Clip art images accessed from the Web may change from time-to-time.

This clip art image has several key words associated with it.

Media Types

The clip art collections feature four primary media types. Each media type has specific characteristics that may suit it for a particular project. For example, a printed flyer will not benefit from a movie file. A document to be saved as a Web page, however, might benefit from the use of an animated (movie-type) image. The four media types are described below.

- **Clip Art**—These are images drawn by graphic artists.
- **Photographs**—These are photographs.
- **Movies**—These may be simple animated pictures or brief video clips.
- **Sounds**—These are sound effects, such as the noise made by a car horn or a modem establishing an online connection.

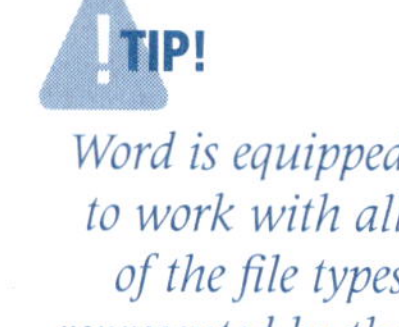

Word is equipped to work with all of the file types represented by the clip art collections.

Items from each media type may reside in one of several file types. A file type is a specific method for saving computer data. Word files use the Word document file type. Picture files come in a variety of files types. For example, a photograph might be in a format optimized for print, such as tag image format file (TIFF), or in a format optimized for the Web, such as the JPEG file interchange format.

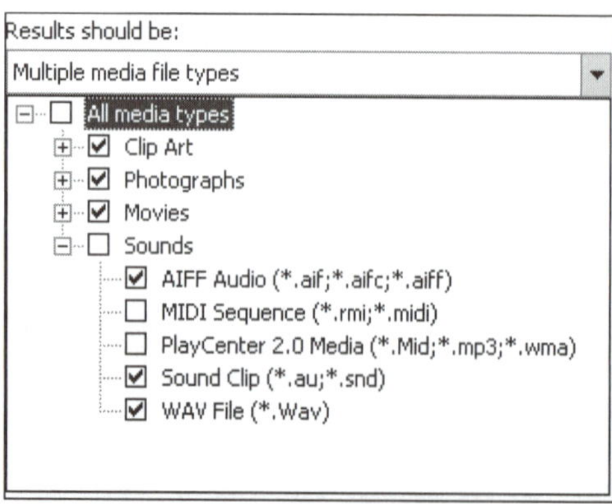

The Results Should Be box allows you to include or exclude specific media types and file types from your searches.

QUICK REFERENCE: INSERTING CLIP ART

Task	Procedure
Insert clip art with the task pane	■ Choose Insert→Picture→Clip Art from the menu bar. ■ Enter one or more key words to search for images, then click Search. ■ Click the thumbnail of the image to be inserted. ■ To perform a new search, click the Modify button at the bottom of the task pane.
Insert clip art with the Clip Organizer	■ Choose Insert→Picture→Clip Art from the menu bar. ■ Click the Clip Organizer link near the bottom of the task pane. ■ Navigate to locate the image you need among the folders in the Collections List, or use the Search button to perform a keyword search. ■ Choose Insert→Picture→Clip Art from the menu bar. After you find the picture, click on the drop-down list button on the picture and choose copy from the pop-up menu. ■ Click where you wish the picture to be placed in your document, then click the Paste button on the Word toolbar.

TIP!

You can also drag-and-drop the image from the Clip Organizer window onto your document.

Hands-On 6.3 Find and Insert Clip Art

In this exercise, you will search for a piece of clip art and place it on your document. Initially, you will just search clip art on the hard drive. Later, you will extend the search to include online images.

Insert Clip Art from the Task Pane

1. Choose Insert→Picture→Clip Art from the menu bar.
   The Insert Clip Art task pane will appear. Depending on how your system is configured, you may also see an invitation to add clips from your hard drive to the Clip Art Organizer. Since this could take several minutes or more to accomplish, you should skip adding clips.
2. Click Later if an Add Clips To Organizer dialog box appears. Otherwise, continue with the next step.
3. Follow these steps to limit your search to clip art on the hard drive:

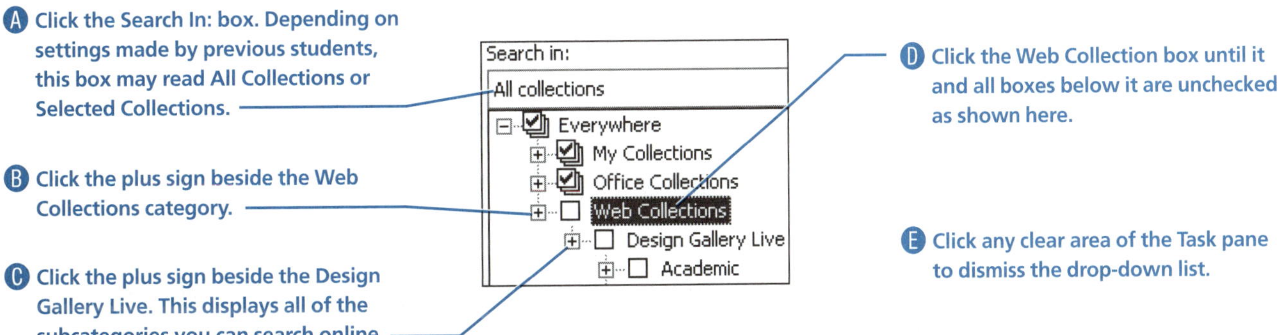

Now that you have deactivated searching the Web collection, let's search for clip art stored on your computer.

(Continued on the next page)

4. Follow these steps to search for clip art:

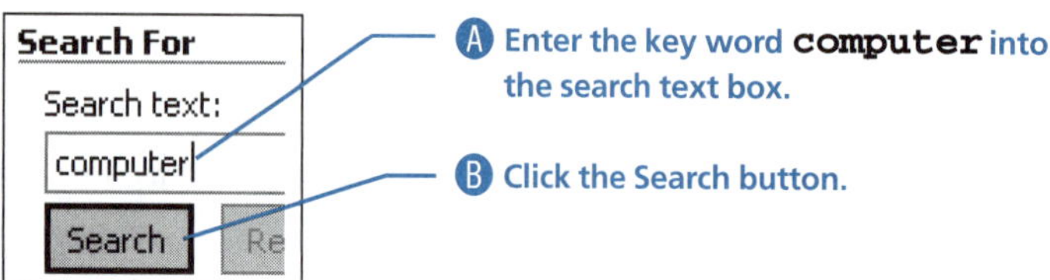

The task pane displays all of the clip art files found by your search. This search is fast because it is searching only your hard drive.

5. Point (don't click) on any clip art picture in the task pane.
   A note pops up, describing details about the picture.

6. Click on any clip art picture in the task pane.
   After a brief pause, the picture is placed in your document at the insertion point. It's very easy to review clip art and insert selected items into your documents.
7. Click on the newly inserted clip art picture.
   Notice that the picture now has a set of small squares around its edges. These are called handles. Later in this lesson you will learn how to manipulate handles to scale an item.
8. Tap the DELETE key to delete the clip art picture.

Limit the Media Types in a Search

In addition to controlling the collection you search, you can limit your search to specific media.

9. Click the Modify button near the bottom of the task pane.
   The Search text box is restored, ready for you to modify your search.
10. Replace *computer* with the word **people** in the Search text box, and tap ENTER.
    Several pictures will appear. As before, this search is limited to items stored on your hard drive, so the selection is relatively small. Now you will make it even smaller by limiting your search to photographs.
11. Click the Modify button, then follow these steps to limit the media types:

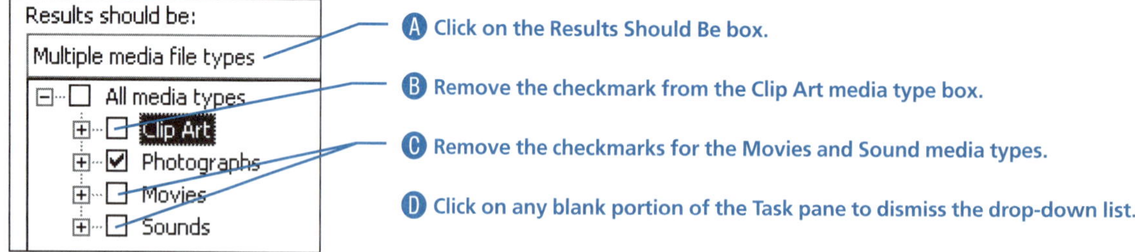

12. Click the Search button.
    Notice that only two items appear—the two photographs. Limiting the media file types on a search can be useful if you only want to consider specific types of images.

13. Click the Modify button, then follow these steps to resume searching all media types.

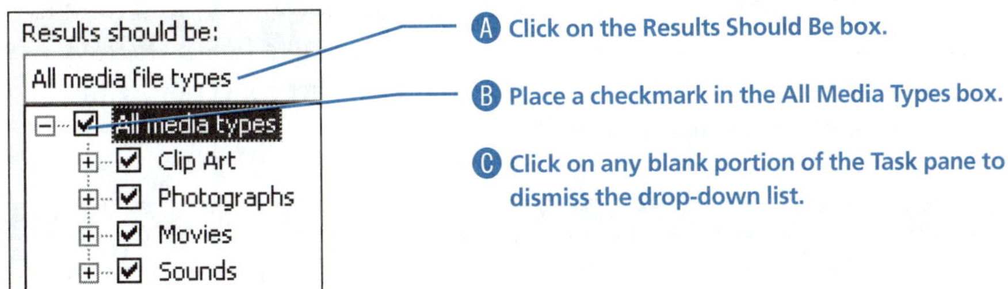

Search the Web Collection

Now that you have searched the hard drive clip art, let's see the additional items you can locate online.

14. Replace *people* with the word **lunch** in the Search text box, then tap ENTER.
    No search results are displayed, since none of the clip art on your hard drive matches the search key word.
15. Click the Modify button near the bottom of the task pane.
16. Click Selected Collections in the Search in box, then double click the checkbox for the Web Collections item to place a checkmark. Make sure that the checkbox has multiple squares below it as shown at right, not just one.

17. Click the Search button to repeat your search on the keyword *lunch*.
    There will be a pause as the Web Collection is added to your search. When the results appear, notice that many items are displayed. The Web Collection of clip art is much more extensive than that on your hard drive. Notice the small globe icon at the lower-left corner of each image from the Web Collection.
18. Click the Expand Task Pane button near the top of the task pane, as shown at right.
    The task pane doubles in size to show a larger selection of clip art. There may be a pause as clip art thumbnail images download to the task pane display.

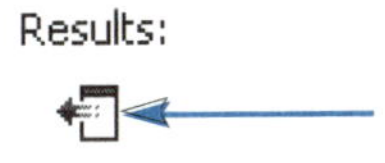

19. Click the Narrow Task Pane button.

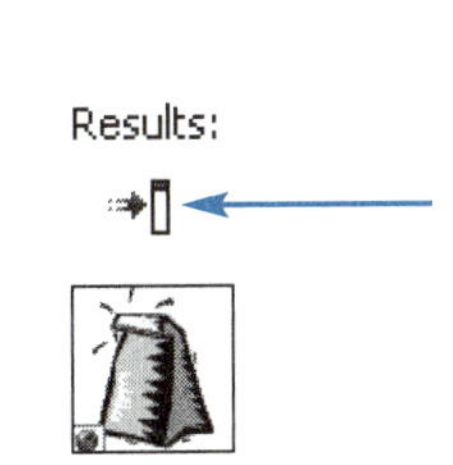

20. Click the lunch bag image near the top of the display.
    The image is placed in your document.
21. Close ☒ the task pane.

Using the Clip Organizer

The Clip Organizer featured on Office XP programs allows you to search for clip art in a Collection List view and to perform searches like those you just conducted with the task pane. The Clip Organizer also allows you to add your own pictures to the clip art collection. Thus, the Clip Organizer is a more versatile view for finding and selecting clip art.

The Clip Organizer allows you to search the collection by category in the Collection List view. You can also add your own images to the collection.

The My Collections Folder

The Clip Organizer also allows you to save pictures to one or more folders within a My Collections folder. You can even save a picture found in the online Web Collections and place it on your hard drive for use when you are offline.

Hands-On 6.4 Work with the Clip Organizer

Start the Clip Organizer

1. Choose Insert→Picture→Clip Art from the menu bar. Click Later if an Add Clips To Organizer dialog box appears.

TIP!

If the Clip Organizer window appears small, you can resize or maximize the window as necessary.

2. Click the Clip Organizer link near the bottom of the task pane. Click Later if an Add Clips To Organizer dialog box appears.
After a pause, the Clip Organizer window appears.

Search for Clip Art in the Collection List View

3. Follow these steps to navigate in the Collection List view:

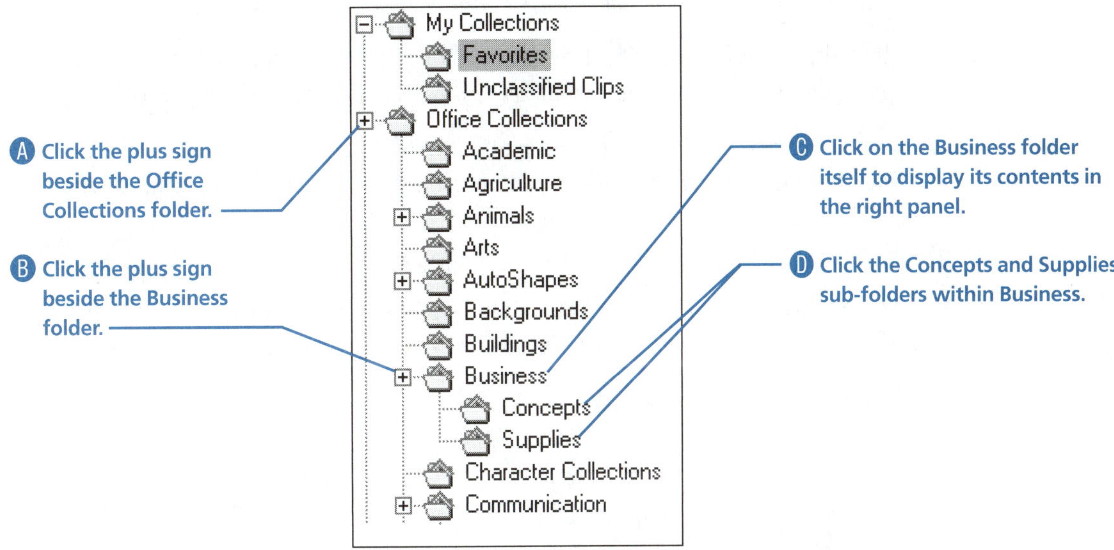

The Clip Organizer stores images in a folder structure.

4. Follow these steps to continue to search the online Collection List:

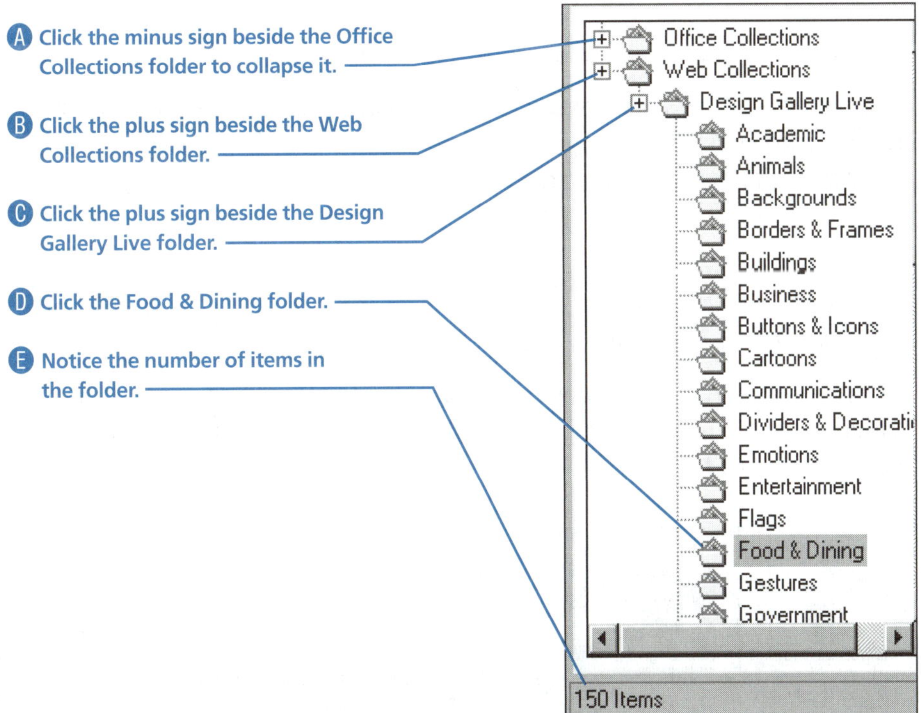

There will be a pause as thumbnail images for the online clip art downloads to the Clip Organizer. Depending on the speed of your Internet connection, several seconds or more may pass before all of the thumbnail images appear.

(Continued on the next page)

5. Scroll twice down the list of Food & Dining thumbnail images. Each time you scroll there will be a pause as the Clip Organizer loads fresh thumbnails.
With about 150 clips to view, this could be a tedious way to search online clip art. Fortunately, the clip organizer gives you a method to search similar to the task pane.

6. Click the Search [Search...] button on the Clip Organizer toolbar.
Notice that your most recent search key word(s) appears in the Search text box.

7. Replace the word *lunch* with **bag** and tap (ENTER).
After a pause, the search results appear, much as they did in the task pane in the previous exercise.

Place Clip Art from the Clip Organizer

Now you will place an image into your document. However, you must copy and paste from the Clip Organizer; you cannot simply click to insert the image as you were able to do from the task pane.

8. Follow these steps to select and copy the clip art image:

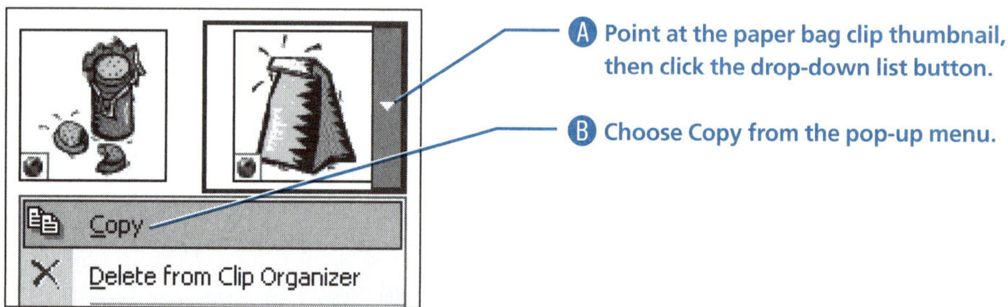

The clip art image is now copied to the Windows clipboard.

9. Click anywhere on the Word document to make it the active window, then click Paste on the Word toolbar.
The clip art image is pasted at the insertion point.

Copy an Online Clip Art Picture to Your Collection

Once you find a useful online picture, you can copy it to your personal clip art collection. Then it will be available even when you are not online.

10. Click its button on the Windows Taskbar to make the Clip Organizer the active window again. Choose any picture displayed in the Clip Organizer, then follow these steps to add it to your personal clip art folder:

There will be a brief pause as the online clip art picture is copied to your hard drive.

11. Click the Collection List [Collection List...] button on the Clip Organizer toolbar. Scroll to the top of the list, then click the Favorites folder.
Your newly saved clip art picture should appear in the folder. Other images may be in this folder as well.

12. Close [X] the Clip Organizer window. Click No when you are asked if you wish to keep pictures that are currently on the clipboard.
Since you have already pasted the picture you need, there is no need to keep it on the clipboard.

13. Click on one of the paper bag pictures and tap the DELETE key.
Now there should be just one paper bag picture on your document.

14. Save the document.

Scaling Pictures

Once you place a picture on a document, you can scale it to larger and smaller sizes. One especially easy way to scale a picture is to drag on its handles. Sizing a picture by its handles allows you to preview exactly how large it will be and adjust its size accordingly.

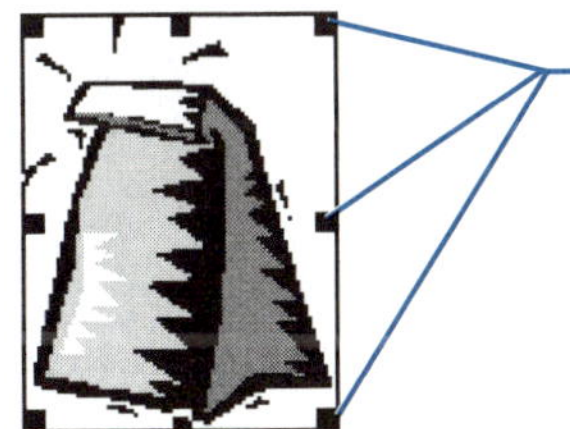

The small squares around the edge of an image are handles.

To scale an image proportionally, drag on its corner handles.

Scaling and Proportions

Most of the time, you will want to change the size of an image proportionally. That is, if you reduce the height, you will want the width to change by the same factor. If you don't scale an image proportionally, it will appear "scrunched" on the page.

The original image.

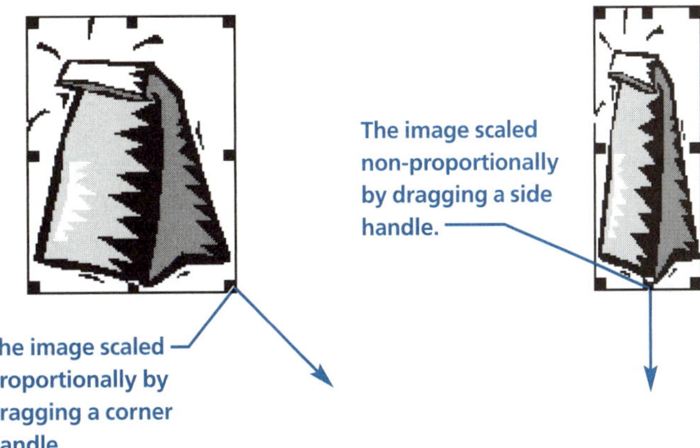

Hands-On 6.5 Scale a Picture

In this exercise, you will practice scaling a picture larger and smaller.

1. Click anywhere on the picture of the paper bag to display its handles.
2. Follow these steps to scale the picture larger and smaller:

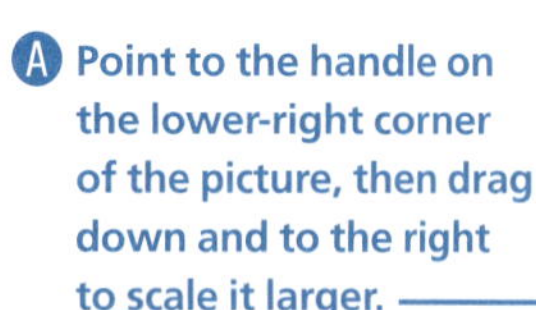

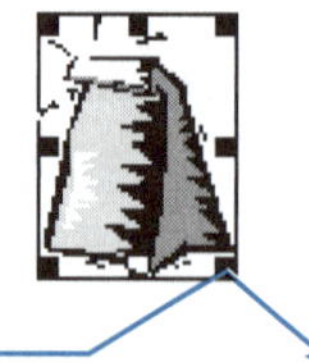

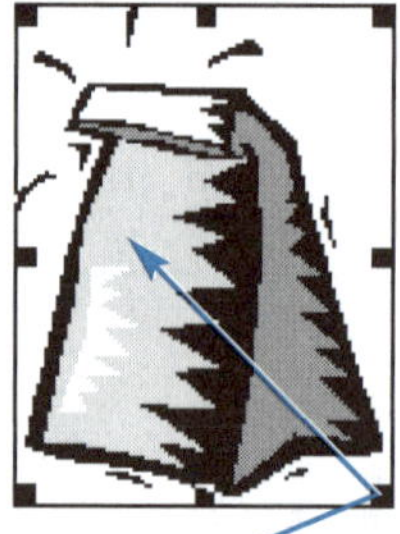

Notice how the picture is distorted by your last scale command. Since you dragged on a side-handle, the picture's proportions changed. Fortunately, it's easy to undo this if it was unintentional.

3. Click Undo on Word's toolbar to undo your last scaling command.
4. Drag up and to the right on the upper-right handle until the picture is about one-third as tall as the size of the page.
There's no need to be exact about the picture size on this last step. If the picture turns out to be too large or too small, you can always scale it again later.
5. Click the Align Right button on the Word toolbar.
This places the picture on the right side of the page. Sometimes a picture is more effective when it appears in a spot where the reader does not expect it.
6. Tap the END key, then tap ENTER to start a new line.
7. Click the Align Left button on the Word toolbar to resume the normal horizontal alignment.

The Paragraph Space Setting

Thus far, when you have needed extra space between lines, you have simply tapped ENTER one or more times to create a double-space. While this technique is simple and effective, it often creates more space than you need. A more precise and elegant way to create extra space between paragraphs is the paragraph space setting. This allows you to pad the space between paragraphs with a precise amount of space (usually measured in points—see page 151.)

Paragraph Space Compared to Line Spacing

You create a new paragraph every time you tap the ENTER key. As your typing reaches the right margin, Word automatically creates a new line for you within the paragraph. The space between lines within a paragraph is set by the line space setting. The figures below illustrate the difference between the two settings.

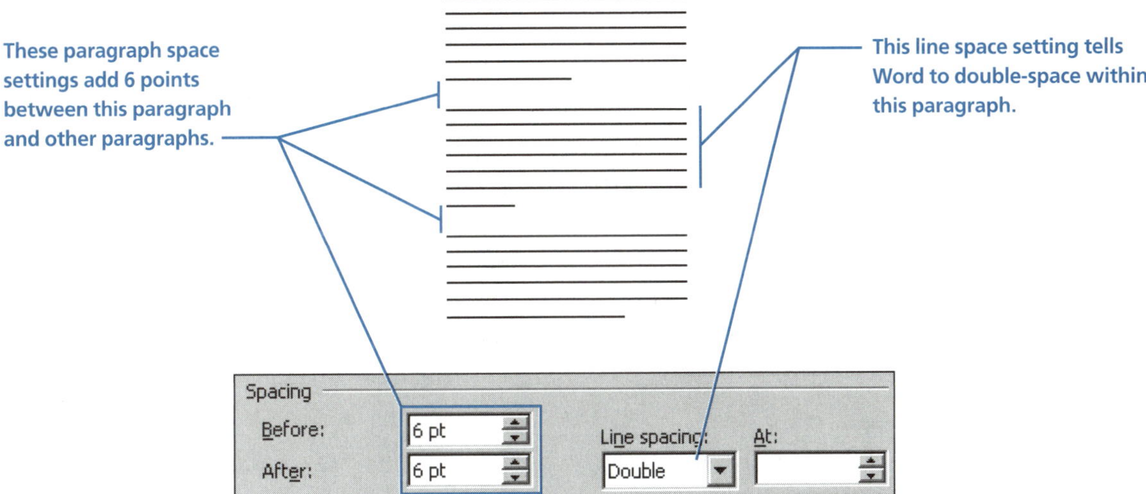

QUICK REFERENCE: SETTING PARAGRAPH SPACE

Task	Procedure
Set paragraph space for text that has already been typed	■ Select the paragraph(s) to be formatted. ■ Choose Format→Paragraph from the menu bar. ■ Click the spinner bar buttons on the Before and After boxes in the Spacing section as desired (to adjust the spacing in 6 point increments), or manually type the desired space setting.

Hands-On 6.6 Set Paragraph Spacing

In this exercise, you will enter text for the flyer, then use paragraph spacing to adjust the space between many of the lines.

Enter Text for the Flyer

1. Set the font to Comic Sans MS.
2. Type **Brown bag discussion** on the line below the picture, then tap ENTER.
3. Set the font size to 28 pt, then type **The Ergonomically Challenged Office**, then tap ENTER.

(Continued on the next page)

4. Set the font size to 18 pt, then click the Bullets button on the toolbar and type the following bulleted text items:

   - **`How the setup of your office equipment can affect your productivity and health.`**
   - **`Questions and answers about your computer workstation.`**

Add Paragraph Space

5. Select the two bulleted item paragraphs you just typed, then choose Format→Paragraph from the menu bar.
6. Follow these steps to adjust the paragraph spacing:

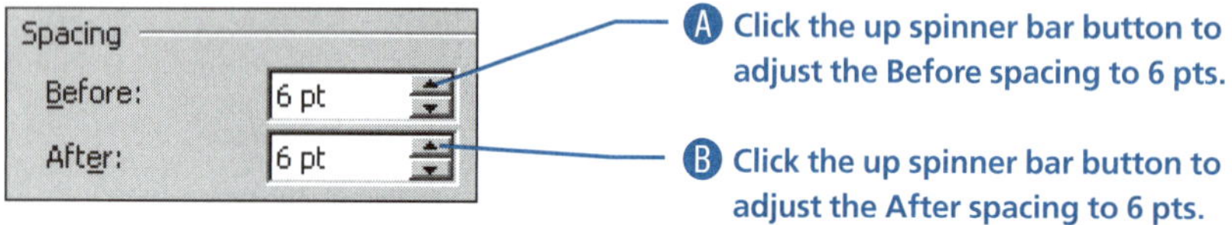

   Each click on the spinner bar increases the space setting by six points. You can also manually type a new setting directly into the box.

7. Click OK.
   There should now be additional space above and below each of the bulleted items. Next, you will add some additional space between the first bullet and the title.
8. Click anywhere on the title of the flyer, then choose Format→Paragraph from the menu bar.
   You do not have to select the entire paragraph when you make a paragraph-level format setting.
9. Manually enter **`25 pt`** as the spacing After the paragraph as shown at right, and click OK.
   Now there is a significant amount of space between the title and the first bullet. You could also have added to the Before space setting of the first bullet rather than adding to the space After setting of the title.

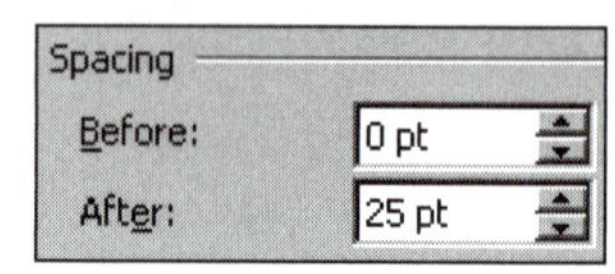

10. Click at the end of the last bulleted item and tap ENTER to start a new paragraph.
11. Click the Bullets button on the toolbar to switch off the bulleted list.

Finish Typing the Flyer

12. Make a left tab setting at the 1.25 inch point on the ruler.
13. Type the remaining text for the flyer as shown below. Apply Bold font formatting to Where and When on the next two lines.

    `Where: The Bakery Cafe`

    `When: Wednesday, September 27th at 12 Noon`

    `A catered lunch will be provided.`

14. Follow the steps below to scale the picture smaller if any of your text flows onto a new page. Otherwise, continue with the next step.
    - Scroll back up to page 1.
    - Click on the picture to make its handles appear.
    - Drag on a corner handle to scale the picture smaller, until all of your text appears on page 1 again.
15. Save the document.

Special Font Formatting

Along with bold and italics, Word features other special font formatting you can apply to text in your documents. These help make the document look or read better. Some examples of special font formatting are:

Strikethrough	~~This text should be eliminated from the final document.~~
Small Caps	THIS HELPS EMPHASIZE A TITLE
All caps	THIS LINE WAS TYPED IN LOWERCASE LETTERS
Shadow	Shadow should be used sparingly
Superscript	Text with a ^{superscript}
Subscript	Text with a $_{\text{subscript}}$

Animated Font Formatting

In addition to special font formatting, Word also allows you to apply several different animated font formats to your text. These formats are visible whenever the text is viewed in the Word program window.

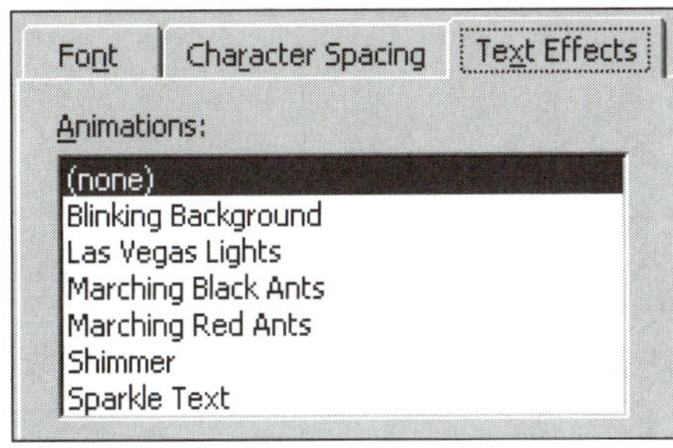

The Text Effects tab in the Font dialog box allows you to apply several types of animations to text characters.

QUICK REFERENCE: ADDING SPECIAL FONT FORMATTING

Task	Procedure
Apply a special font format to text.	■ Select the characters to be formatted. ■ Choose Format→Font from the menu bar, then choose the Font tab. ■ Click the checkbox(s) for the desired special font format(s) and click OK.
Apply an animation effect to text.	■ Select the characters to be formatted. ■ Choose Format→Font from the menu bar, then choose the Text Effects tab. ■ Choose the desired Animation effect from the list and click OK.

Hands-On 6.7 Work with Special Font Formats

In this exercise, you will change the date for the discussion and use strikethrough to indicate that the original date was changed. You will also apply an animation effect to highlight the words catered lunch.

Apply Special Font Formatting

1. Select T*he Bakery Cafe* on the Where line.
2. Choose Format→Font from the menu bar, then make sure that the Font tab is chosen.
3. Place a checkmark in the Small Caps box in the Effects section, then click OK.

The lowercase letters in the name convert to uppercase style shapes. However, they are also smaller in size compared to normal uppercase letters. This format effect is often useful to give additional emphasis to names and titles.

4. Change Wednesday to **Tuesday** on the When line.
   Next, you will change the date and add a superscript after the number.
5. Click to place the insertion point just to the right of the h in 27th, then tap the BACKSPACE key three times.

September 27th at

6. Type the numeral **6** to set a new date.
7. Choose Format→Font from the menu bar, then place a checkmark in the Superscript box and click OK.

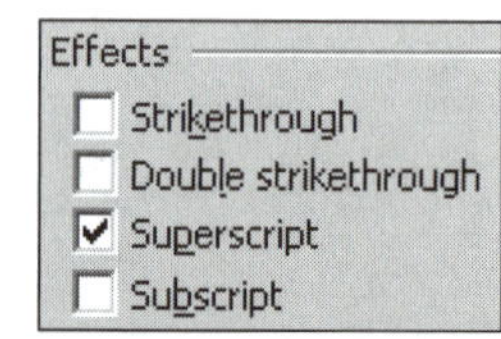

8. Type **th** after the 6.
   Notice that the superscript setting not only makes these letters higher, it also makes them significantly smaller.

9. Choose Format→Font from the menu bar, then remove the checkmark in the Superscript box and click OK.
   Since you are finished using this special font format, you should switch it off so that it does not affect any further typing on this line.

Apply Animated Font Formatting

To make the catered lunch item stand out, you will apply an animation effect to it.

10. Select the words *catered lunch* on the last line of the flyer.
11. Right-click (don't left-click) on the selection, then choose Font from the pop-up menu and choose the Text Effects tab.
12. Choose the Blinking Background animation effect, then click OK.
13. Click at the end of the line to dismiss the selection and view the animation effect.
    This animation effect creates a blinking black background on the selected text.
14. Select *catered lunch* again, then choose Format→Font from the menu bar.
15. Choose the Sparkle Text effect, click OK, then click at the end of the line to dismiss the selection.
    This animation will only be visible when the document is viewed in Word.
16. Compare your flyer to the one shown on page 147 at the start of this lesson. It should appear quite similar to the illustration.
17. Save the document, then close it.

Concepts Review

True/False Questions

1.	Landscape indicates tall (rather than wide) page orientation.	TRUE	FALSE
2.	Word is limited to a specific selection of allowable paper sizes.	TRUE	FALSE
3.	You can instruct Word to align all of the contents of a page.	TRUE	FALSE
4.	Most of the clip art available with Word is stored on your hard drive.	TRUE	FALSE
5.	Clip art includes sound and animations.	TRUE	FALSE
6.	Every clip art picture is associated with one or more key words.	TRUE	FALSE
7.	You can change the size of a clip art picture.	TRUE	FALSE
8.	The paragraph space setting sets the distance between each line of text with in a paragraph.	TRUE	FALSE
9.	Bold and italic are examples of special font format settings.	TRUE	FALSE
10.	The Clip Organizer can store online images on your hard drive.	TRUE	FALSE

Multiple Choice Questions

1. Which method below will ensure that you will scale a picture proportionally so it will not appear distorted?
   a. Drag on any handle
   b. Drag on any handle while holding down the SHIFT key
   c. Drag on any corner handle
   d. None of the above

2. The figure at right displays a window from the

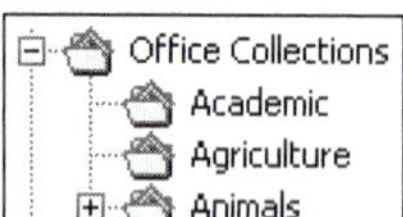

   a. Clip Organizer
   b. Insert Clip Art task pane
   c. Both the above
   d. None of the above

3. Which of the lines below does not contain an example of a special font format?
   a. This is an EXAMPLE.
   b. This is an ~~example~~.
   c. This is an ^{example}.
   d. This is an **example**.
   e. All of the above contain a special font format.

4. In the figure below, which letter points to an example of paragraph spacing?
   a. x
   b. y
   c. z
   d. Both y and z

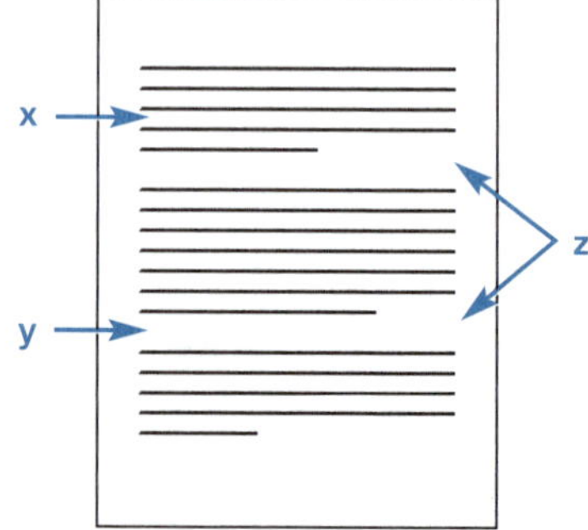

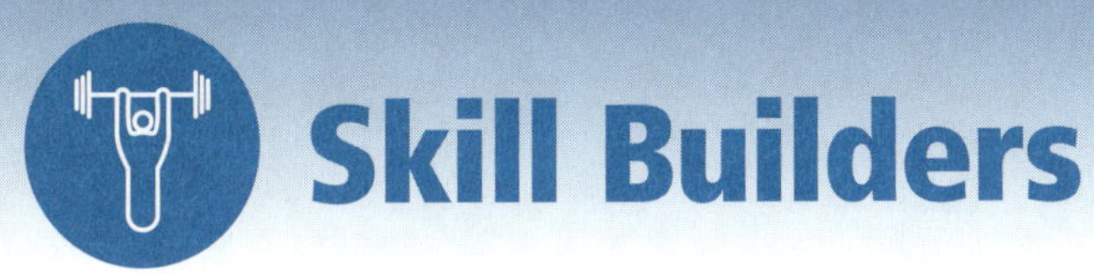

Skill Builders

Skill Builder 6.1 Insert Clip Art from the Task Pane

In this exercise, you will practice searching for and inserting clip art related to a variety of key words.

1. Start Word and create a new document. Save the document to your exercise diskette as **`Skill Builder 6.1`**.

Search in the Task Pane

2. Choose Insert→Picture→Clip Art from the menu bar. Click Later if an Add Clips to Organizer dialog box appears.
3. Follow these steps to search for clip art in the entire collection:

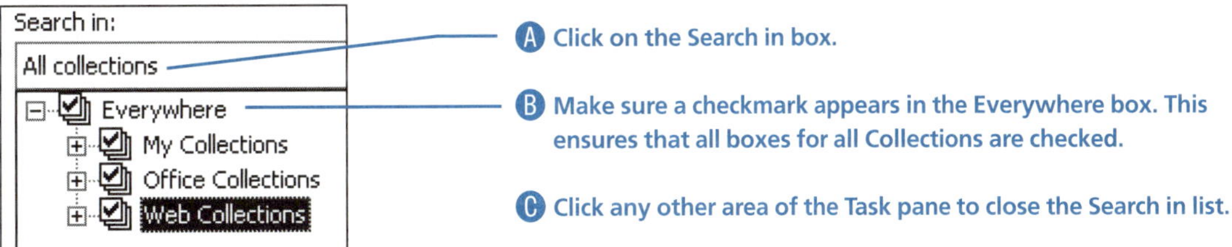

4. Enter **`Office Furniture`** in the Search text box, then tap ENTER.
   The pictures on your hard drive will appear right away. After a pause, the pictures available in the Web Collection will start to appear as well.
5. Scroll down the list until you find a picture that looks attractive. Type a caption for the picture in your Word document, then click the picture in the Task pane to enter it into your document beside the caption. Your caption and picture should be similar to the figure at right.

A File Drawer 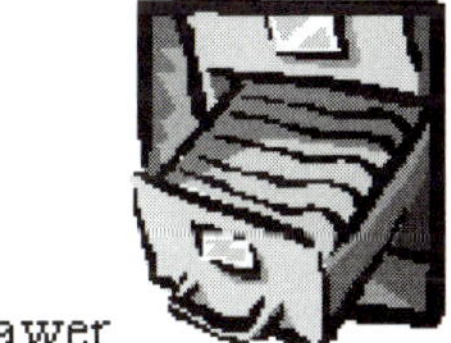

6. Click on the picture, then drag on its handles to scale it larger or smaller. (You will want to fit a total of five pictures on this page.) When you are finished scaling the picture, tap the END key, then tap ENTER to start a new line.
7. Click the Modify button near the bottom of the Task pane, then follow these steps:

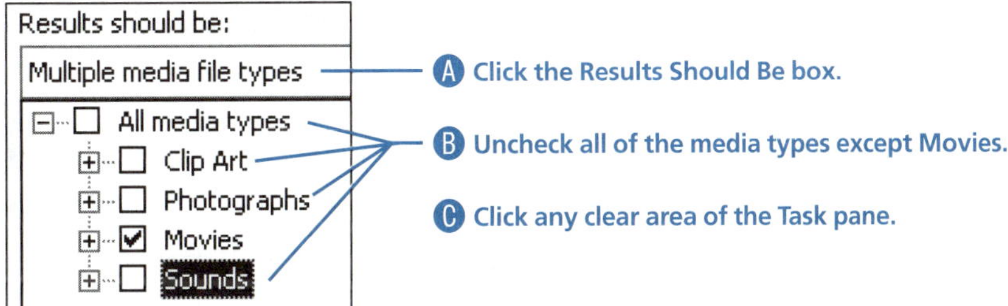

(Continued on the next page)

8. Click the Search button.
   Now a much smaller number of pictures appear. Notice the small animation symbol at the lower-right corner of each picture.
9. Click any picture to insert it onto your document.
   Although all of these pictures are "movies," this picture doesn't do anything in the Word document view. To see the animation, you must view this page as it would appear in a Web browser.
10. Choose File→Web Page Preview from the menu bar.
    Word converts your brief document to Web page format and launches Internet Explorer to display it. The picture is now animated! (The picture would also be animated if it were used in a PowerPoint presentation.)
11. Close the Internet Explorer window, then delete the movie image.
12. Click the Modify button, then click on the Results Should Be box. Place a checkmark on the All Media Types box.
    Now your searches will once again include all available media.

Search for More Pictures in the Task Pane

13. Enter a new search word from the list below. When you find an image you like, type a caption for it and insert it onto your document—as you did in Steps 4 to 6. Continue until you have found a picture related to the four topics listed below. Scale each picture larger or smaller so that all of the pictures fit on a single page.
    - National holiday
    - A group in a business meeting
    - Flying to a travel destination for a travel brochure
    - Washing cars for a neighborhood fundraising event
14. When you finish, Save the document and then close it.

Skill Builder 6.2 Use the Clip Organizer

In this exercise, you will search for clip art using the Clip Organizer.

1. Create a new document and save it as **Skill Builder 6.2**.
2. Choose Insert→Picture→Clip Art on the menu bar then click the Clip Organizer link at the bottom of the task pane. Click Later if an Add Clips to Organizer dialog box appears.
3. Click the plus sign beside the Office Collections folder, then click the plus sign beside the Communication folder.

4. Click on the Communication folder and its three subfolders to view the pictures available in this category.
The Office Collections folder displays pictures available on the hard drive. Notice that the selection of pictures is quite limited.

5. Click the minus sign beside the Office Collections folder to collapse the display of its subfolders.

6. Click the plus sign beside the Web Collections and Design Gallery Live folders, then click on the Communications folder.
There will be a pause as the thumbnail images for this folder download to your computer over your Internet connection. As you can see, a much larger selection of pictures is included in the Web Collection. Notice also that some of the items are sounds rather than pictures. Sounds would probably be more useful with a presentation program such as PowerPoint.

Insert a Picture from the Clip Organizer

7. Select any picture in the Communications folder, then click the Copy button on the Clip Organizer toolbar. Pause until the hourglass icon disappears before you proceed to the next step.
Depending on the size of the picture and the speed of your Internet connection, several seconds or more may pass before the picture is downloaded to your computer.

8. At the end of your Word document, type a caption for the picture on a new line.

9. Click the Paste button on the Word (not the Clip Organizer) toolbar.

10. Click on the newly pasted image, then drag on its handles to scale it larger or smaller.

11. Search in the Web Collections for at least two more clip art pictures. You can choose from any category you find interesting. Enter a new line and a caption for each picture you insert. Scale the pictures so that they all fit on a single page.

Save a Picture to Favorites

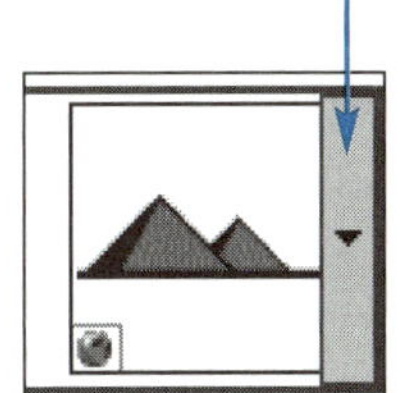

12. Select any picture in the Clip Organizer, then click on its drop-down list button and choose Copy to Collection from the drop-down menu. Choose Favorites as the folder into which the picture is copied and click OK.
The picture is copied from the collection into the Favorites folder on your hard drive.

13. Scroll to the very top of the folder list on the left side of the Clip Organizer window, then click the Favorites folder.
The newly copied picture should be visible in this folder. Additional pictures, added to this folder by other students, may also be included.

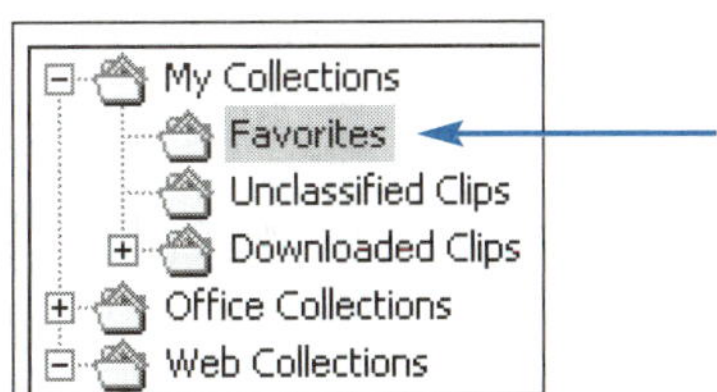

14. Close the Clip Organizer window.

15. Save the document and close it.

Skill Builder 6.3 Use Special Character Formatting

In this exercise, you will use special character formatting to create a fraction, and to indicate an edit in text.

Create a Fraction

1. Create a new Word document and save it as **`Skill Builder 6.3`**.
2. Set the Zoom level to 200%, then type the line below:

   `The doorway measures 19 and 15/16 inches.`

3. Select the 15 in the line you just typed, then choose Format→Font from the menu bar.
4. Make sure that the Font tab is chosen, then place a checkmark in the Superscript box and click OK.
5. Select 16 in the line you just typed and set the font formatting to Subscript.
   The fraction should now match the example at right.

   $^{15}/_{16}$

Indicate a Trademark

6. Choose Format→Paragraph from the menu bar.

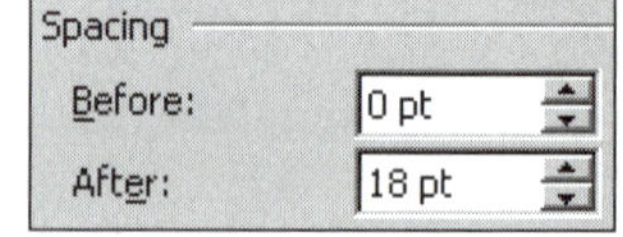

7. Set the Paragraph Space After to 18 pts. You can use the spinner bar to make this setting, or manually type it in the After box.
   You won't see any change yet. This setting will create plenty of space after this line when you tap ENTER *in the next step.*
8. Tap the END key, tap ENTER, then type the line below:

   `Microsoft Office XP is a software suite.`

9. Place the insertion point just to the right of the P in XP, then choose Format→Font from the menu bar, set the font format to Superscript, and click OK.
10. Type **`TM`** in uppercase letters.
    These should appear small and elevated, to indicate a trademark.

Use Strikethrough and Animation

11. Tap the END key, tap ENTER, then type the line below.

    `The meeting will take place on Tuesday at 10:00 A.M.`

    Notice that your previous paragraph space setting continues to function on each new paragraph you create.

12. Select the word *Tuesday* in the line you just typed, then set the font format for this word to Strikethrough.
13. Type **`Wednesday`** after the word Tuesday. You will have to turn off the Strikethrough setting if it appears as you type the new word.

14. Select *10:00 A.M.* at the end of the line, then choose Format→Font from the menu bar. Choose the Text Effects tab, then select any animation effect to apply to the time and click OK. Click outside the selection to deselect the text.

15. Select the time again and apply another animation effect to it.

16. Save the document and close it.

Skill Builder 6.4 Create a Flyer

In this exercise, you will create a new flyer on a topic of your choice, with clip art, a page border, and other refinements.

1. Decide on a topic for your flyer, such as one of the suggestions below:
   - An announcement of a job or school activity
   - Publicity for a community group you in which you participate
   - The opening of a new movie, or an upcoming concert
   - Make up a fictional event

Set Up the Page

2. Create a new Word document, then save it as **Skill Builder 6.4**.

TIP!

You might want to try using an art border. Review the options in the Art drop-down list in the Page Border dialog box.

3. Choose File→Page Setup from the menu bar, then make the settings indicated below and click OK.
   - Set the Page Orientation to Landscape.
   - Set the Page Margins to 1 inch on all sides.
   - Choose a Vertical Alignment for the page, such as Centered, Top, or Bottom.

4. Choose Format→Borders and Shading, then choose the Page Border tab. Add a page border in any color and line type you wish.

Note: If you attempt to choose Art for the page border, Word may tell you that this feature is not installed. Click No if you receive this prompt and choose a line border instead.

5. Save the document.
   It's always a good habit to save your document when you complete a stage of work.

(Continued on the next page)

Design the Flyer

6. Choose a clip art picture to appear on the flyer. Scale the picture as you see fit.
7. Type the text for the flyer. Include information items such as the ones below:
   - A title for the flyer
   - The date and time of the event
   - Where the event will take place
   - What the event is about
   - Other details as appropriate
8. Click on the Title line and apply paragraph space after it to separate the body of the flyer from its title.
9. Select the paragraphs below the flyer title and add paragraph space above and/or below to make each paragraph easy to read. Experiment with different space settings until you like the appearance of the body paragraphs.
   Giving more space between paragraphs can give the flyer a more "open" appearance that will be more attractive to readers. Cramped information is often difficult to read.
10. Save the document, then print it.
    Just prior to printing is another excellent stage to save your document.
11. Proofread the flyer: make corrections as appropriate and then print the final version.

Assessments

Assessment 6.1 Find Clip Art

In this assessment, you will find clip art related to a specific topic. You will search both on the hard drive and online.

NOTE!

You may search both the Office Collection and Web Collection clip art.

1. Create a new document named **Assessment 6.1**.
2. Using either the Task pane, Clip Organizer, or both, locate clip art pictures related to the following topics. Place each picture on a line, preceded by a caption describing the picture.
   - A picture for use in a document describing emergency first aid procedures.
   - A picture for use with a contest with an ocean voyage as the grand prize.
   - A picture for use on a flyer promoting an election.
3. Searching only the Office (and excluding the Web) Collection, locate a picture of a telephone. Place the picture and caption as you did for the items in Step 2.
4. Expand your search to include all collections (including the Web Collection), then find a photograph (not a clip art image) of a house. Place a caption and the image on a new line of your document.
5. Save the document and close it.

Assessment 6.2 Use Special Character Formatting

In this exercise, you will use special character formatting on text.

1. Create a new document named **Assessment 6.2**.
2. Type the line below:

   Use 1 2/3 cups of flour.

3. Convert 2/3 to a properly formatted fraction.
4. Tap the END key, then tap ENTER once and type the lines below:

   This monument is one of the most beautiful in the country, and is a short bus ride from the capital.

5. Add 21 pts of space between these lines and the previous line. (Do not tap ENTER again.)
6. After the period, add text that appears like the example at right: capital. See Note 1
7. Add an animated text effect to the word *monument*.
8. Save the document, and then close it.

Assessment 6.3 Create a Flyer

In this exercise, you will design a flyer to match the example below.

Take Note

Staff Meeting: 9:00^{AM} to 10:30^{AM} Thursday Morning

1. Create a new document named **Assessment 6.3**.
2. Set up the page according to the following specifications:
   - Page orientation = landscape.
   - Page Margins = 1 inch on all sides.
   - Page vertical alignment = bottom.
3. Add a shadow-style page border.
4. Search for and insert a clip art picture similar (but not necessarily identical) to the one shown in the example.

TIP!

Search with keywords that reflect the features of or the intended use of the picture.

5. Add the lines of text shown below the clip art picture using the guidelines given below.
   - Use Comic Sans MS as the font.
   - Be sure to match the font setting for AM used in the meeting times. For example: 9:00^{AM}.
6. Scale the picture so that it fills up about 75% of the height of the page, but is not so large that the text below it is pushed down to the next page.
7. Apply a font animation effect to the Take Note flyer title.
8. Save and print the flyer.
9. Proofread your flyer and, if necessary, perform a final printout.

Critical Thinking

Critical Thinking 6.1 On Your Own—Create a Flyer Announcing a Class

Create a flyer that announces the next offering of any class you are attending now. It should indicate the subject matter of the class and use visual imagery to get the reader's attention.

Flyer Title: [The Class Name]

Main Message: The skills that enrollees in the class can expect to learn.

Create a new Word document and save it as **`Critical Thinking 6.1`**, then begin creating a flyer based on the title and main message notes above.

Your flyer should:

- have a title indicating the class name and number.
- use landscape orientation and 1 inch page margins.
- contain one or more relevant pictures from the clip art collections.
- have a page border with any line style and/or color you prefer.
- indicate the date, time, and location of the next offering of your class (this could be for a section later this term, or one taking place the following term).
- indicate where to enroll in the course.
- usc font formatting to help the main message of the flyer stand out.

Critical Thinking 6.2 On Your Own—Create a Flyer on a Topic of Your Choice

Come up with an idea for a flyer about an event or an idea. It could be an advertisement promoting a service, a performance event (music, dance, drama, or film), or convey some other distinct message. This flyer should be about a real event, organization, or service—not a made up one. Use the space below to record the title and a brief (2 lines maximum) description of the flyer's main message.

Flyer Title: ____

Main Message: ____

____

Create a new Word document and save it as **`Critical Thinking 6.2`**, then begin creating a flyer based on the title and main message notes above.

Your flyer should:

- have a title.
- use either portrait or landscape orientation, as you prefer.
- contain one or more relevant pictures from the clip art collections.
- have a page border with any line style and/or color you prefer.
- indicate the date, time, and location of the event.

Some additional tips:

- Use font formatting as appropriate to make various parts of the message stand out. However, avoid the use of too much bold type. When everything's bold, nothing's bold.
- Be selective and discriminating about the clip art you use for this flyer. Make sure each picture relates to and helps to communicate the main message.
- While big, bold images get attention, sometimes less is more. Don't allow any image to totally dominate the flyer, unless this serves a distinct purpose.
- Some clip art pictures are small, and will become jagged if you scale them too large. If this proves to be the case, look for another image or scale the picture smaller.
- Don't forget to allow some white space. Give your message room to "breathe" and give the reader's eyes a place to settle and focus. If every part of the flyer is shouting for attention, readers may feel distracted and miss your main message.

Critical Thinking 6.3 As a Group—Quick Flash Flyer Exercise

After you and other group members create flyers according to Critical Thinking Exercise 6.2, test their effectiveness as a group with the steps below.

- Each person should flash his or her flyer into view for exactly 1 second, then have members of the group write down what they think is its main message.
- Have each group member read his or her impression of the main message. As a group, score each member's impression as:
  - **Strong (3 points)**—the group member's impression matches the flyer's main message exactly.
  - **Moderate (2 points)**—the group member's impression partially matches flyer's main message.
  - **Weak (1 point)**—the group member's impression hardly relates to the flyer's main message.
  - **Missed (0 points)**—the group member's impression misses the flyer's main message completely.
- Look over the three flyers that had the highest scores. Discuss the following ideas, with one group member taking notes to share later:
  - What visual features do these flyer's have in common?
  - How did the clip art selected add to their effectiveness?
  - How did the use of fonts and type add to their effectiveness?
- Look over the three flyers that had the lowest scores. Discuss the following ideas, with one group member taking notes to share later:
  - What visual features do these flyer's have in common?
  - Did the clip art selected detract from their effectiveness?
  - Did the use of fonts and type detract from to their effectiveness?
- Type up the discussion notes and print copies of the documents for all of the group members. Save this document as **`Critical Thinking 6.3`**.

Critical Thinking 6.4 As a Group—Revise and Compare Flyers

- Each group member should revise their flyer based on the group discussion of the highest- and lowest-rated flyers.
- Take turns displaying and reviewing the original and revised versions of each group member's flyer. As each flyer is displayed, discuss the following questions, with one group member taking notes to share later:
  - What is the most significant visual difference between the two flyers?
  - What is the most effective change made between the original and revised versions?
  - What is the least effective change (if any) made between the original and revised versions?
  - Is this flyer ready for prime time?
- Type up the discussion notes and print copies of the document for all of the group members. Save this document as **`Critical Thinking 6.4`**.

Critical Thinking 6.5 Web Research—Find Other Clip Art Resources

The Web features numerous sites devoted to clip art. Some of these are free, while others charge a monthly or annual subscription fee. Use your favorite search engine to locate several clip art resources and compare the samples they display for quality and variety.

Create a Word document named **`Critical Thinking 6.5`**.

Complete the following:

- Give the names and URL's of at least three different clip art Web sites.
- Describe any difference you observe between "free" sites and those that charge a subscription fee.
- Describe how the variety of images available from the Web sites compare to the clip art available on Word?
- Describe how the image quality of the Web sites compares to the clip art available with Word. Do you consider it to be poorer, equal, or better? If possible, include one or two examples from a Web site to justify your description.

Critical Thinking 6.6 Web Research—Considering Copyright

Many computer users believe that if they can copy or download an image, then it is theirs to use as they please. However, this attitude ignores the reality of copyright and copyright law. The advent of the Internet has added a great deal of complexity to copyright issues. For the first time in history, an individual can steal a work of art without the artist being aware of it. Not only that, but the piece of art (if it's digital art) is exactly like the original.

Create a Word document named **`Critical Thinking 6.6`**.

Answer the following question for the three Web sites you wrote about in Critical Thinking exercise 6.5:

- What is the copyright (or usage) policy for clip art available from each Web site?

  You should see a prominent link on the home page or search pages that direct you to the copyright policy for artwork downloaded from that Web site. These links will have labels such as copyright or usage guidelines.

The ArtToday.com Web site has a Usage Guidelines link on its Home page. This page explains the uses to which subscribers can and cannot apply to art downloaded from the Web site.

Navigate to the Web page, then give the command Edit→Find (on this page) from the browser's menu bar. Search for a word such as use, usage, terms, copyright, etc. This search will work best if you just search for one word at a time.

After you have described the copyright/usage policies of the three Web sites, compare them.

- Are some policies more liberal than others? For example, do some Web sites prohibit commercial use of images and others allow such use?
- Do the three Web sites have any common restrictions?

LESSON 7

Working with Tables

Tables are one of Word's most useful tools for organizing and formatting text, numbers, and graphics. Tables are powerful, flexible, and easy to use. Word provides a variety of tools that let you set up, modify, and format tables. In this lesson, you will use tables to create resumes and other documents. You will also learn important techniques for creating effective resumes.

IN THIS LESSON

Word 2002 Core MOUS Objectives Covered in this Lesson

MOUS Objective Number	MOUS Objective Description	Concept Page References	Exercise Page References
W2002-3-4	Create and modify tables	190, 193, 205	191, 194–195, 205–206

See the Lesson 7 Web Page at: labpub.com/learn/bc/word1/lesson7

Case Study

Gladys Kline is employed as an Administrative Assistant at Renquist Communications. Recently, Gladys decided to search for other career opportunities. Although she enjoys working at Renquist, Gladys wants new challenges and opportunities for advancement. She begins her job search by preparing a resume. No serious job search can be conducted without one. There are a variety of resume formats from which Gladys can choose. However, she chooses the chronological format to emphasize her substantial employment history. Using Word 2002's powerful tables capabilities, Gladys produces a resume that is certain to impress any prospective employer.

Gladys Kline
845 Maple Street El Cerrito, CA 94803 (510) 215-6902

OBJECTIVE:	To obtain an Administrative Assistant position where I can apply my computer skills and extensive work experience.
EXPERIENCE: March 1995—Present	ADMINISTRATIVE ASSISTANT FOR DIRECTOR OF MARKETING, Renquist Communications, Fulton, CA • Compose letters, memorandums, and other business correspondence. • Maintain the Director of Marketing's schedule. • Manage multiple projects assigned by the Director of Marketing.
January 1992— February 1995	WORD PROCESSING SPECIALIST, Smart Paging Systems, Berkeley, CA • Composed documents as required by supervisor, using Microsoft Word for Windows. • Used Microsoft Excel to create worksheets.
January 1991— December 1992	STUDENT ASSISTANT, Contra Costa College, Pinole, CA • Assisted students with questions regarding financial aid. • Answered incoming telephone calls, filled out forms, and mailed literature.
EDUCATION:	Certificate of Completion, 2001, Bay Area R.O.P., Hayward, CA • Received extensive training in Microsoft Office applications, office procedures, and keyboarding. A. S. Business Administration, Contra Costa College, 1992, Pinole, CA • Worked as a student intern for the Vice President of Sales at Chevron Corporation. • Extra-curricular activities included participation in student body government, athletics, and tutoring of disadvantaged youths.
COMPUTER SKILLS:	Word 2002, Excel 2002, PowerPoint 2002, Outlook 2002, Windows XP, and Adobe Acrobat.

Resumes for the New Millennium

A resume is the most important tool in the job search process. When creating a resume, always keep the purpose of the resume in mind: to get an interview with a person who has the authority to hire you! Also keep in mind that a resume is just one of many tools that you will use in the job search process. The following general guidelines will help you develop effective resumes.

- Always send a cover letter with your resume. The cover letter should provide a general overview of why you are interested in and qualified for the position.
- Resumes should be short and to the point. In general, you should limit your resume to two pages at most. It is even better if you can condense your resume to a single page. Few employers have the time to review resumes that are longer than two pages. Once again, the purpose of the resume is to get the interview.
- Resumes should be visually attractive and error-free. Your resume is a direct reflection of you. You should also print your resume on high-quality paper using a laser printer.
- Hand-deliver resumes whenever possible. Personal contact is the most effective way to connect with employers. If hand-delivering a resume is impractical, then make sure you follow-up with a telephone call after the potential employer has had adequate time to review the resume.

Types of Resumes

There are three primary types of resumes that you can use depending upon your experience, skills, education, and the type of employment opportunity you are pursuing. If you are serious about finding employment, then you should develop all three types of resumes so that you have "a resume for every occasion." A brief overview of the three types follows. A more detailed discussion and examples of the various types appear on the following pages.

- **Chronological Resume—**A chronological resume is most effective when you have a history of employment and a track record of success. The chronological resume emphasizes your work experience by providing an overview of your experience in reverse chronological order.
- **Functional Resume—**A functional resume is useful when you want to de-emphasize paid work experience and emphasize skills. The functional resume emphasizes the functions or skills that you can contribute to the job.
- **Entry-level Resume or Skills Sheet—**This type of resume is useful for students who have little paid work experience or for individuals who are new to the job market. It emphasizes educational achievement and any type of skills the applicant may have.

Scannable Resumes

Technology has introduced dramatic changes in the methods employers use to screen potential applicants. Many large employers now scan resumes into an electronic database. Potential candidates are identified by querying the database for "key words" in the resumes. If you know an employer is scanning resumes, then use the following guidelines to create one that can be easily and accurately scanned.

- Use plain white paper and print with a laser printer. Scanners may have difficulty identifying characters if you use colored paper or an ink jet printer.
- Don't fold or bend the resume in any way.
- Don't use bold, italics, underlining, or shading.
- Use a 12-point font size and fonts that are easy to read. Appropriate fonts include Arial and Times New Roman.
- Include keywords somewhere in the resume that will be picked up by the OCR (Optical Character Recognition) software. For example, employers often program OCR software to search for specific application names such as Word, Excel, and Outlook.

What to Include and Not to Include in a Resume

- Do include phrases or statements that demonstrate positive personal qualities, such as team player, excellent organizational skills, creative, and customer-oriented.
- Do not refer to your age, gender, marital status, height, weight, or other personal details unless they will help you get the job for which you are applying. Also, never list your social security number!
- Do not list references on a resume. References can be supplied on a separate reference sheet, or in person at the interview.
- Do not mention salary requirements or the amount of income you earned in previous occupations.
- Do not mention gaps in your employment history or the reasons for leaving previous positions. However, be prepared to address these issues at the interview.

Chronological Resume

Use a chronological resume when you have a significant amount of work experience that is applicable to the job for which you are applying. The most recent experience should appear first (reverse chronological order), as shown in the following example.

All resumes should have a clearly stated employment objective as the first substantive item. You can tailor the objective to the job for which you are applying.

Work experience appears directly below the objective because the chronological style emphasizes work experience. The most recent experience should appear first. Always include the dates of employment, job title, company name, location, and a clear and concise description of your responsibilities.

The chronological resume should include educational achievements and may include optional categories, such as computer skills and community service.

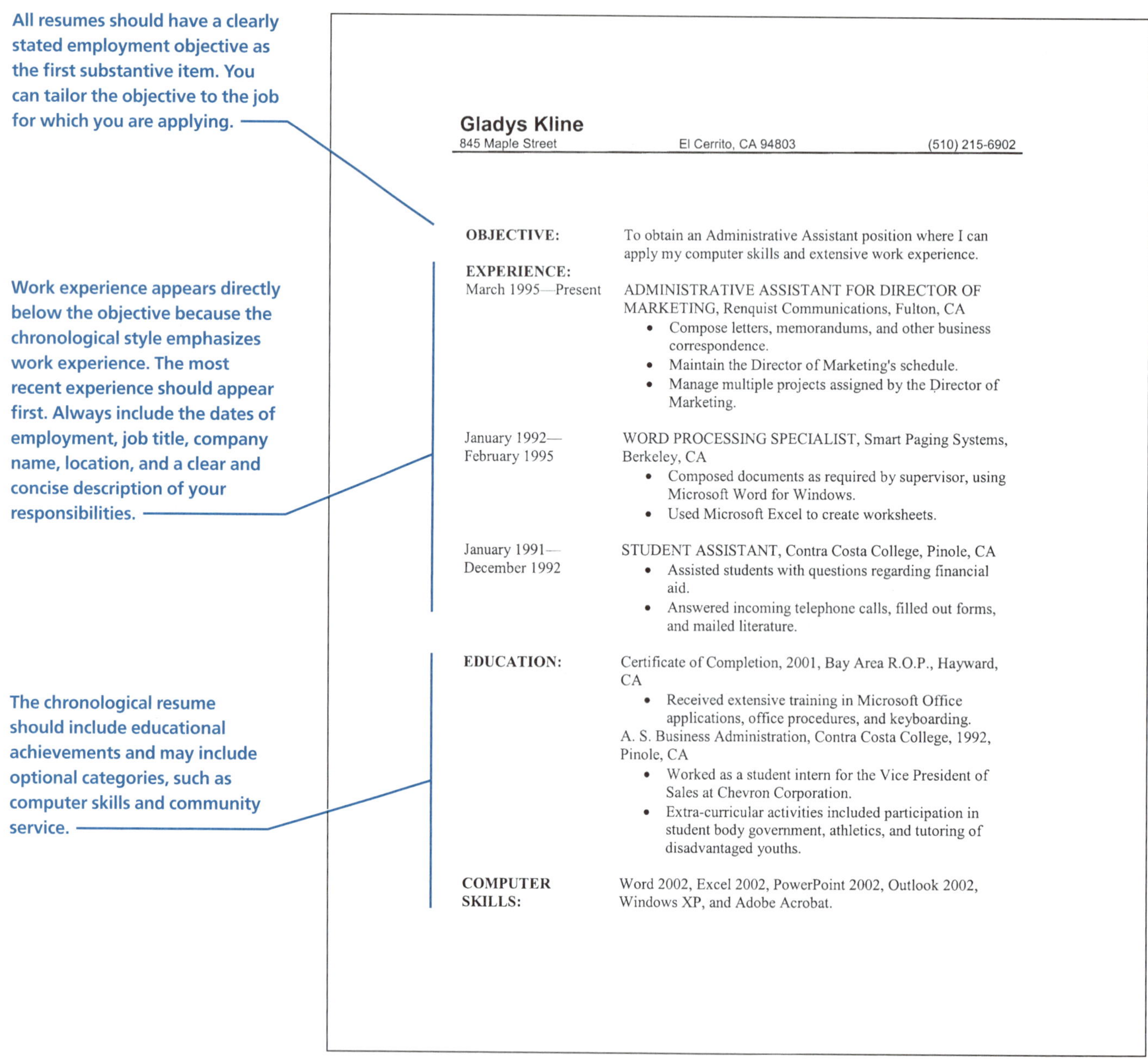

Gladys Kline

845 Maple Street | El Cerrito, CA 94803 | (510) 215-6902

OBJECTIVE: To obtain an Administrative Assistant position where I can apply my computer skills and extensive work experience.

EXPERIENCE:

March 1995—Present
ADMINISTRATIVE ASSISTANT FOR DIRECTOR OF MARKETING, Renquist Communications, Fulton, CA
- Compose letters, memorandums, and other business correspondence.
- Maintain the Director of Marketing's schedule.
- Manage multiple projects assigned by the Director of Marketing.

January 1992—February 1995
WORD PROCESSING SPECIALIST, Smart Paging Systems, Berkeley, CA
- Composed documents as required by supervisor, using Microsoft Word for Windows.
- Used Microsoft Excel to create worksheets.

January 1991—December 1992
STUDENT ASSISTANT, Contra Costa College, Pinole, CA
- Assisted students with questions regarding financial aid.
- Answered incoming telephone calls, filled out forms, and mailed literature.

EDUCATION:

Certificate of Completion, 2001, Bay Area R.O.P., Hayward, CA
- Received extensive training in Microsoft Office applications, office procedures, and keyboarding.

A. S. Business Administration, Contra Costa College, 1992, Pinole, CA
- Worked as a student intern for the Vice President of Sales at Chevron Corporation.
- Extra-curricular activities included participation in student body government, athletics, and tutoring of disadvantaged youths.

COMPUTER SKILLS: Word 2002, Excel 2002, PowerPoint 2002, Outlook 2002, Windows XP, and Adobe Acrobat.

Functional Resume

Use a functional resume when you want to de-emphasize paid work experience, and emphasize skills. List skills that are applicable to the job for which you are applying.

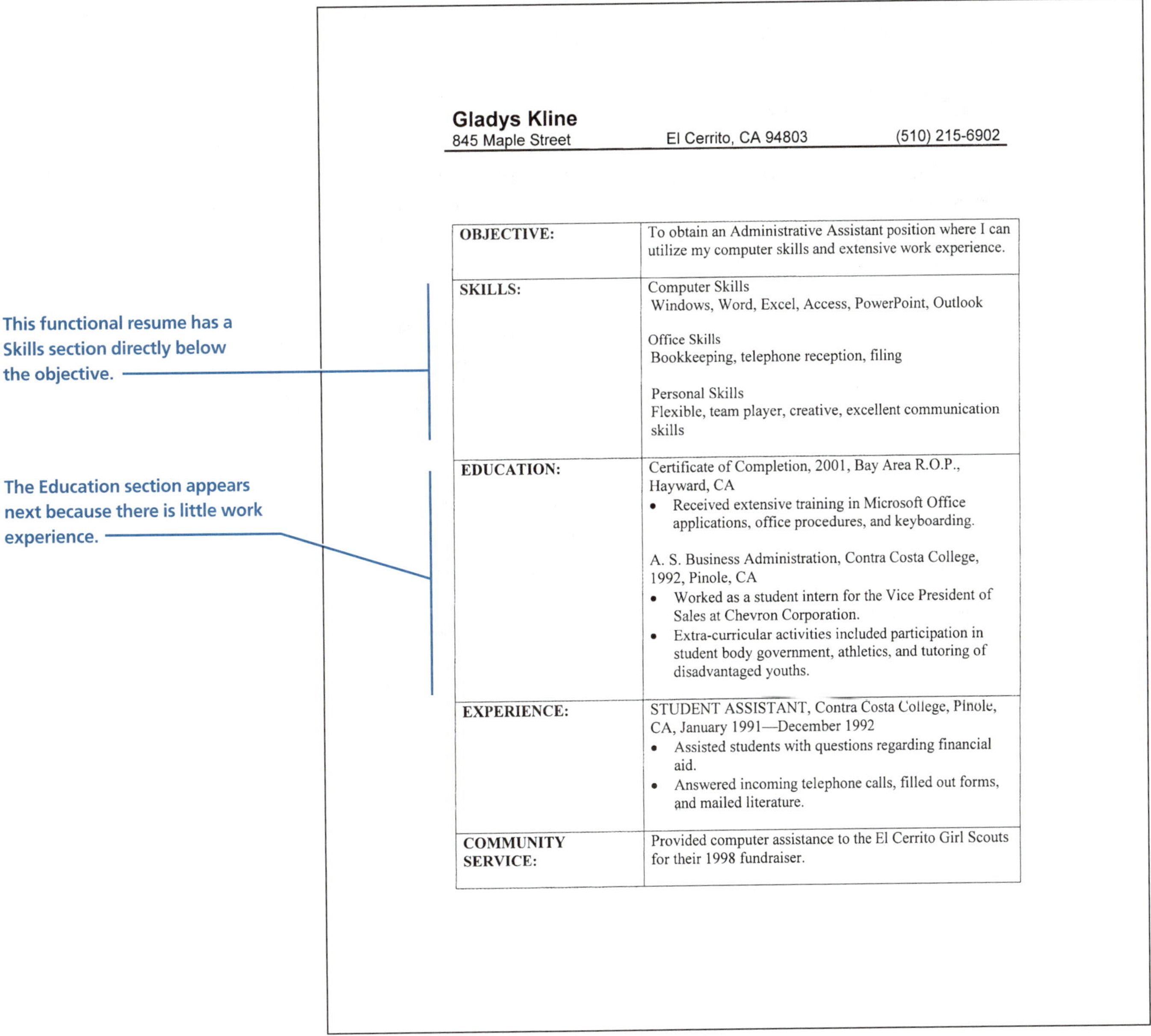

This functional resume has a Skills section directly below the objective.

The Education section appears next because there is little work experience.

Gladys Kline
845 Maple Street El Cerrito, CA 94803 (510) 215-6902

OBJECTIVE:	To obtain an Administrative Assistant position where I can utilize my computer skills and extensive work experience.
SKILLS:	Computer Skills Windows, Word, Excel, Access, PowerPoint, Outlook Office Skills Bookkeeping, telephone reception, filing Personal Skills Flexible, team player, creative, excellent communication skills
EDUCATION:	Certificate of Completion, 2001, Bay Area R.O.P., Hayward, CA • Received extensive training in Microsoft Office applications, office procedures, and keyboarding. A. S. Business Administration, Contra Costa College, 1992, Pinole, CA • Worked as a student intern for the Vice President of Sales at Chevron Corporation. • Extra-curricular activities included participation in student body government, athletics, and tutoring of disadvantaged youths.
EXPERIENCE:	STUDENT ASSISTANT, Contra Costa College, Pinole, CA, January 1991—December 1992 • Assisted students with questions regarding financial aid. • Answered incoming telephone calls, filled out forms, and mailed literature.
COMMUNITY SERVICE:	Provided computer assistance to the El Cerrito Girl Scouts for their 1998 fundraiser.

Inserting Tables

Tables are one of Word's most useful tools for organizing text, numbers, and graphics. Tables are composed of cells organized in vertical columns and horizontal rows. Word lets you insert, edit, align, and format text within cells just as you would in a normal document. You can also change line spacing, apply bullets, and use virtually any other text or paragraph formats within cells.

Insert Methods

You can use the Insert Table button on the Standard toolbar to insert a new table. The Insert Table button displays a grid. You specify the number of rows and columns for the new table by dragging in the grid. The table is inserted at the insertion point and all columns are of equal width. You can also insert a table with the Table→Insert→Table command. This method displays a dialog box where you can specify the number of rows and columns and several options.

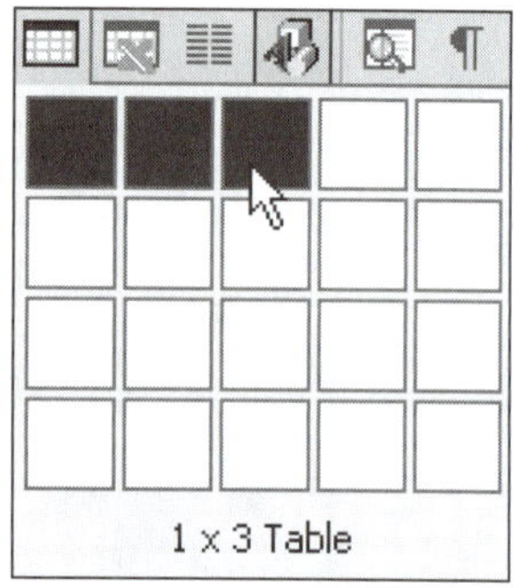

Using the Insert Table button

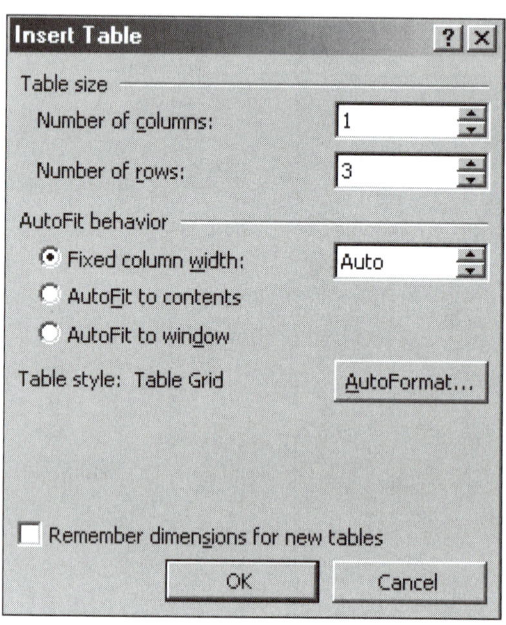

The Insert Table dialog box

Before You Insert

You should take the time to visualize your completed table prior to inserting it. You may even want to sketch it out on a piece of paper. Word lets you modify tables after they have been inserted; however, it is easier if you insert a table correctly in the first place. In particular, try to determine the correct number of rows and columns before inserting. It is very easy to adjust column widths and row heights in a table. However, inserting new columns and rows into an existing table can be cumbersome.

Hands-On 7.1 Insert a Table

In this exercise, you will use the Insert Table button to insert a table with one row and three columns. The table will contain the name, address, and telephone number at the top of the resume.

1. Start Word to display a new document window.
2. Follow these steps to insert a table.

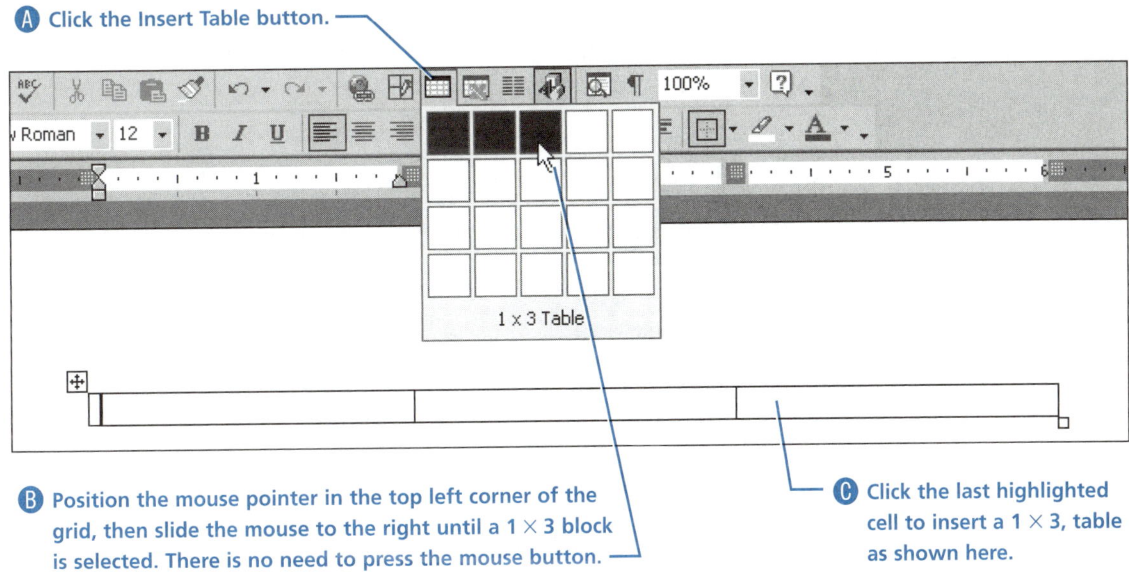

Notice that all columns are of equal width. The Insert Table button always inserts tables with equal column widths.

3. Save the document as **Hands-On Lesson 7**.
   You will continue to develop the resume throughout this lesson.

Working with Table Entries

You can type text and numbers and insert pictures in table cells. When typing text, Word will wrap the text when it reaches the right edge of a cell. The cell height will also expand to accommodate the wrapped text. You can also use ENTER to insert blank lines in a cell and expand the cell height.

Navigating in Tables

You can position the insertion point in a cell by clicking in the desired cell. However, it is often more efficient to use the keyboard to move between cells. You use the TAB key to move forward one cell and SHIFT+TAB to move back one cell. If the insertion point is in the last cell of the table, then the TAB key adds a new row to the bottom of the table.

Aligning Entries

The Align Left, Center, and Align Right buttons align entries horizontally within table cells. In addition, you can use nearly all paragraph formatting commands within table cells, including line spacing, spacing before and after, and indents. Text entries can be formatted using the same techniques that are used in other parts of a document.

Hands-On 7.2 Enter the Personal Information

1. Make sure the insertion point is positioned in the first table cell. If necessary, click in the first cell to position the insertion point there.
2. Type the name **`Gladys Kline`**, and tap ENTER once.
   Notice that the row height increases for all three cells.
3. Type **`845 Maple Street`** on the second line of the first cell.
4. Tap the TAB key to move the insertion point to the second cell.
5. Click the Center button, and type **`El Cerrito, CA 94803`**.
6. Tap the TAB key to move the insertion point to the third cell.
7. Click the Align Right button, and type **`(510) 215-6902`**.
   As you can see, tables are useful for mixing alignments on a single line.
8. Tap the TAB key again; Word will add a new row to the table.
   A new row is always added when the insertion point is in the last table cell and TAB is tapped.
9. Click Undo to remove the new row.
10. Save the changes, and continue with the next topic.

Table Selection Techniques

There are several methods you can use to select table text and table elements such as cells, rows, and columns. The following Quick Reference table describes the various table selection techniques.

QUICK REFERENCE: TABLE SELECTION TECHNIQUES

Item to Select	Technique
Text within a cell	Drag over the desired text. You can select a single word by double-clicking the word.
All text within a cell	Click in the left cell margin. The left cell margin is the area between the text and left cell edge. You can also choose Table→Select→Cell from the menu bar.
A row	Click in the left margin next to the row. You can also choose Table→Select→Row from the menu bar. You can select multiple rows by dragging down in the left margin.
A column	Click the top of the column. You can also choose Table→Select→Column from the menu bar. You can select multiple columns by dragging across the tops of the desired columns.
A group of cells	Drag the mouse over the desired cells.
An entire table	Choose Table→Select→Table from the menu bar.

Hands-On 7.3 Format the Table Text

1. Make sure the insertion point is in the table, and choose Table→Select→Table from the menu bar.
   The insertion point must be positioned within a table cell before you can use this command.
2. Set the font to Arial and the size to 10.
3. Click anywhere below the table to deselect it.
4. Drag the mouse over the name Gladys Kline to select only the name.
5. Increase the size to 16, and apply bold formatting to the text.
6. Click anywhere below the table to deselect the table.

The Tables and Borders Toolbar

The Tables and Borders button on the Standard toolbar displays the Tables and Borders toolbar. The Tables and Borders toolbar lets you apply borders and shading to table cells. You can also use the Tables and Borders toolbar to adjust the alignment of text within table cells and to set other options.

You can also use the Tables and Borders toolbar to apply borders and shading to paragraphs within a document.

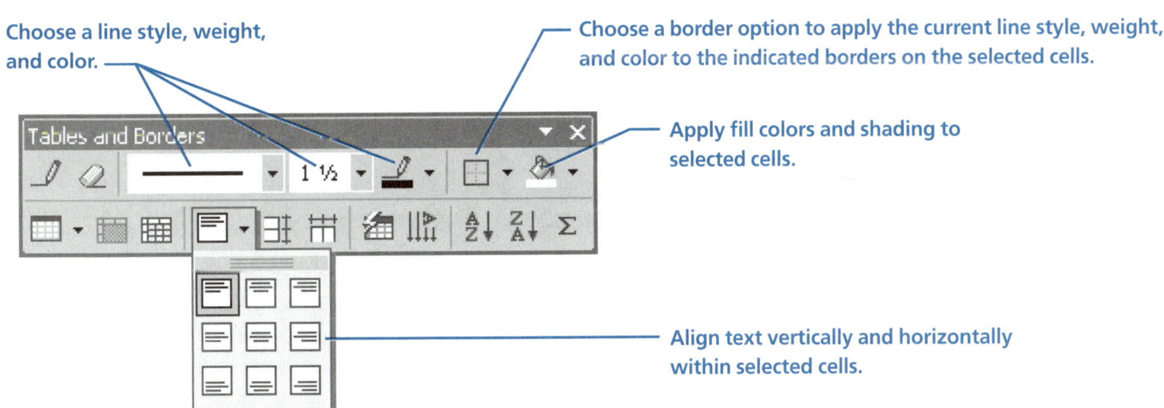

Gridlines

When you insert a new table, Word formats the table by applying borders to all edges of all cells. If you remove the borders, then it is difficult to see the cell boundaries. For this reason, Word provides the gridline option. Gridlines are dotted lines that surround each cell. Gridlines are not printed, and you can display or hide them at your convenience. You use the Table→Show Gridlines and Table→Hide Gridlines commands to display and hide gridlines.

Hands-On 7.4 Change the Vertical Alignment, and Remove Borders

Use Print Preview

1. Click the Print Preview button on the Standard toolbar.
2. Zoom in by clicking the mouse pointer anywhere on the document.
   Notice that the table borders are visible in Print Preview. Later in this exercise, you will remove the borders and turn on gridlines. Gridlines look like borders; however, they are not printed and will not be visible in Print Preview.
3. Zoom out by clicking on the document.
4. Click the Close button on the Print Preview toolbar to exit from Print Preview.

Remove All Borders, and Apply a Thick Bottom Border

5. Locate the Tables and Borders button on the Standard toolbar.
6. If necessary, click the Tables and Borders button to display the Tables and Borders toolbar.
   If you just displayed the Tables and Borders toolbar, then your mouse pointer may take on the shape of a pencil. The pencil tool is used to draw new cells. You will use the pencil tool in the next exercise.
7. If the Pencil icon is displayed, then click the Draw Table button on the Tables and Borders toolbar to turn it off.
8. Click in the table and use the Table→Select→Table command to select the table.
9. Follow these steps to remove all borders.

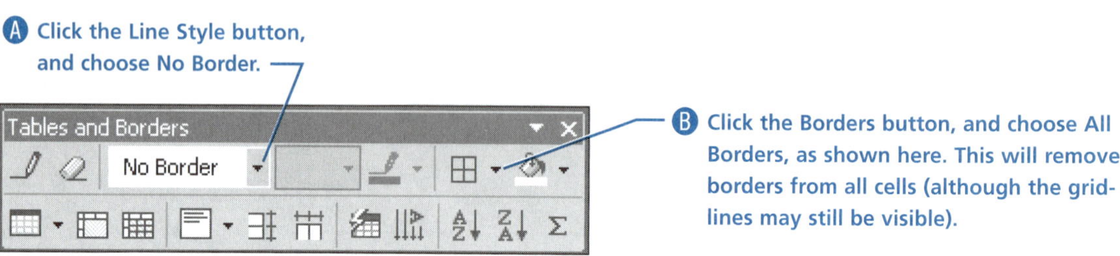

10. Follow these steps to apply a 1½-point border to the bottom edge of each cell.

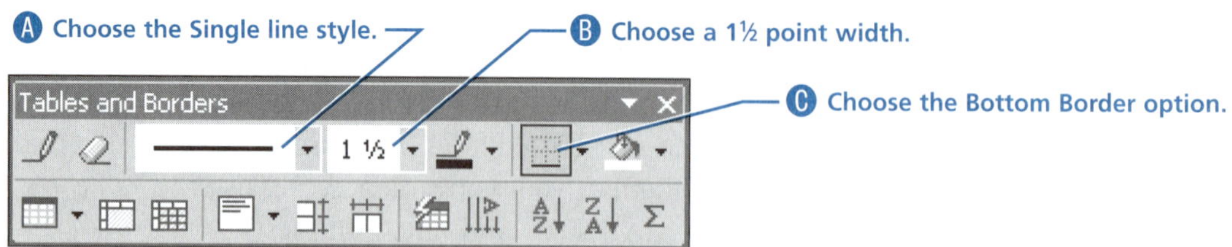

Set the Vertical Alignment

11. Follow these steps to set the vertical alignment of the text within the cells.

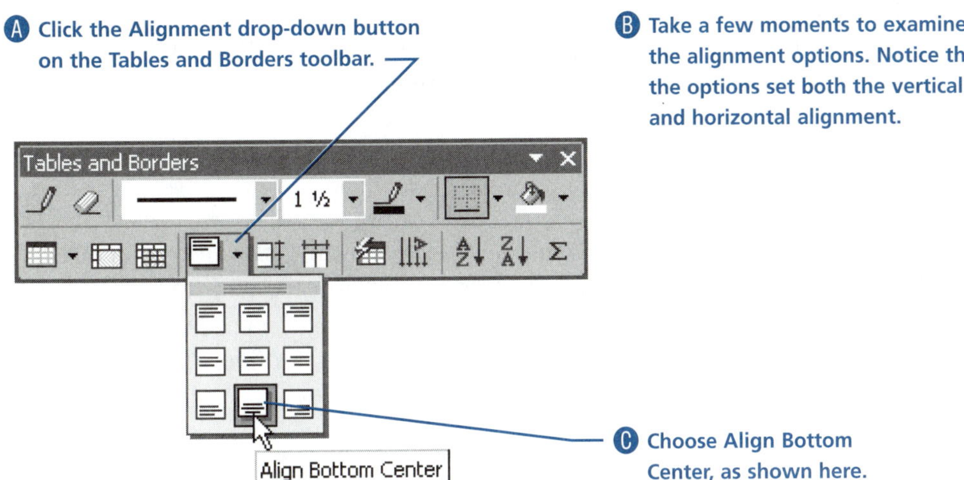

The cell entries should now be aligned with the bottom edge of each cell and centered horizontally. Unfortunately, this is not the proper horizontal alignment for the first and last cells.

12. Click in the first cell, and click the Alignment drop-down button.
13. Choose Align Bottom Left from the alignment list.
14. Apply the Align Bottom Right setting to the third table cell.
15. Click below the table, and a border should be visible at the bottom of each cell.
16. If necessary, choose Table→Show Gridlines to turn on table gridlines. The Table→Show Gridlines command will not be available if gridlines are already displayed.
    Gridlines are light lines that appear on the cell borders.
17. Click the Print Preview button.
    Notice that the gridlines are not displayed, but that the bottom border is displayed. Gridlines are not printed when the document is printed. They are only visible in the document window to assist you in seeing the cell borders.
18. Close the Print Preview window.
19. Choose Table→Hide Gridlines to hide the gridlines.
20. Choose Table→Show Gridlines to redisplay the gridlines.
21. Save the changes to your document, and continue with the next topic.

Drawing Tables

The Draw Table button displays a Pencil pointer that you can use to draw tables. This can be convenient if you want to create a table with a precise size and location within the document. To use the Draw Table tool, simply click the Draw Table button, and draw the outside border of the desired table in the document. After drawing the outside border, you can draw the desired rows and columns.

The Eraser Tool

The Eraser tool can be used to erase borders from tables. You can erase borders from tables created with the Draw Table tool and from tables inserted with the Insert Table button. If you erase an outside border, then you are simply removing the border style. If you erase an interior border, then you are erasing an actual row or column gridline. This will cause cells within the table to merge together to form larger cells.

Hands-On 7.5 Draw a Table, and Erase a Line

In this exercise, you will draw a table that will be used for the body of the resume.

1. Click below the existing table, and tap ENTER four times to insert blank lines.
2. Use the Line Weight 1 ½ button on the Tables and Borders toolbar to set the line weight to ½.
   This will cause all lines to appear with a weight of ½ as you draw the table.
3. If necessary, click the Draw Table button to display the Pencil pointer.
4. Follow these steps to draw the outside border.

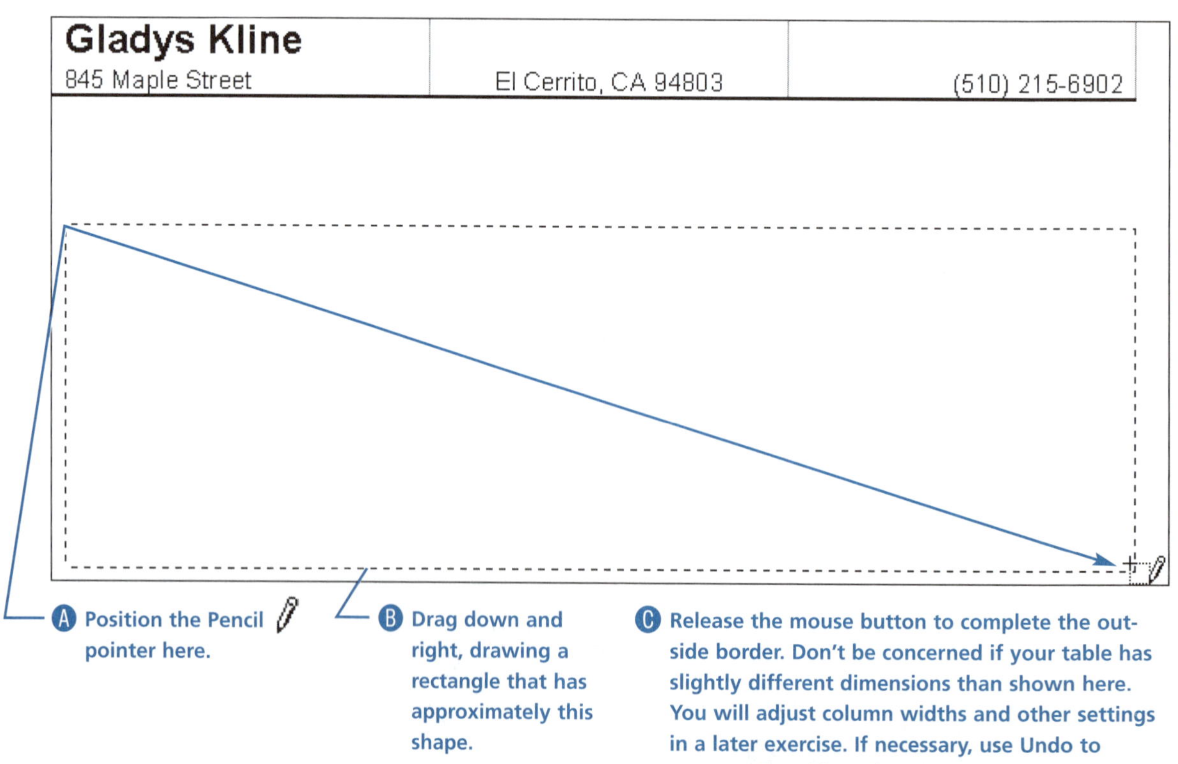

5. Follow these steps to draw horizontal gridlines and vertical column gridlines.

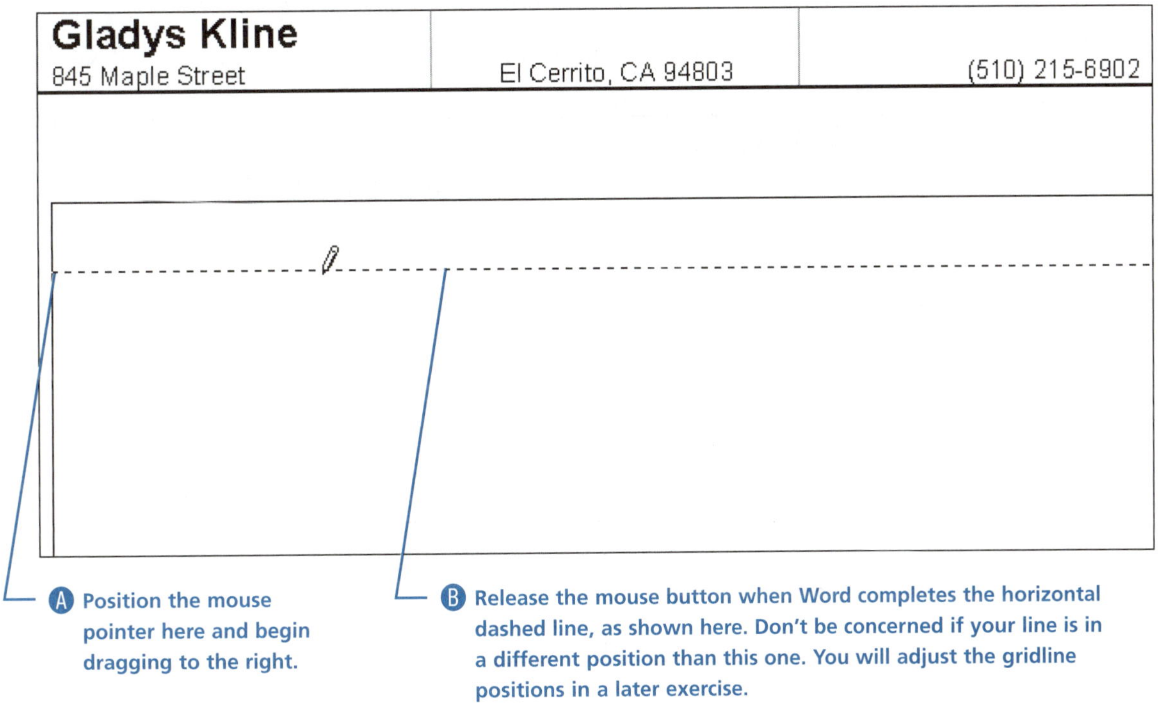

Gladys Kline 845 Maple Street	El Cerrito, CA 94803	(510) 215-6902

Ⓐ Position the mouse pointer here and begin dragging to the right.

Ⓑ Release the mouse button when Word completes the horizontal dashed line, as shown here. Don't be concerned if your line is in a different position than this one. You will adjust the gridline positions in a later exercise.

6. Draw three more horizontal gridlines and two vertical gridlines to complete a five-row by three-column table, as shown below. Once again, don't be concerned if your gridlines are in different positions than shown here.

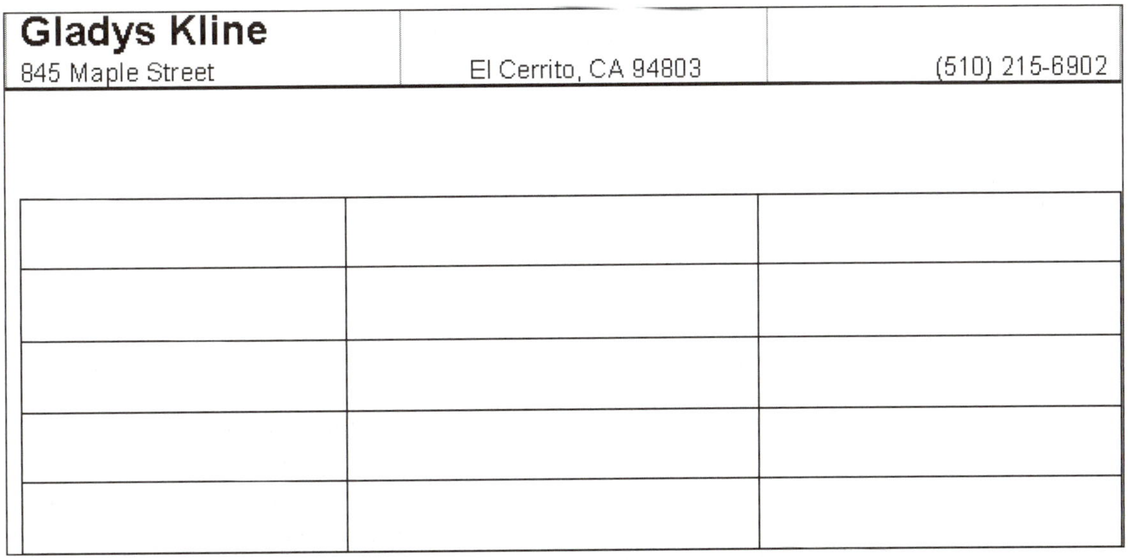

Gladys Kline 845 Maple Street	El Cerrito, CA 94803	(510) 215-6902

(Continued on the next page)

Erase a Line

7. Click the Eraser tool on the Tables and Borders toolbar.
8. Follow these steps to erase the second vertical gridline.

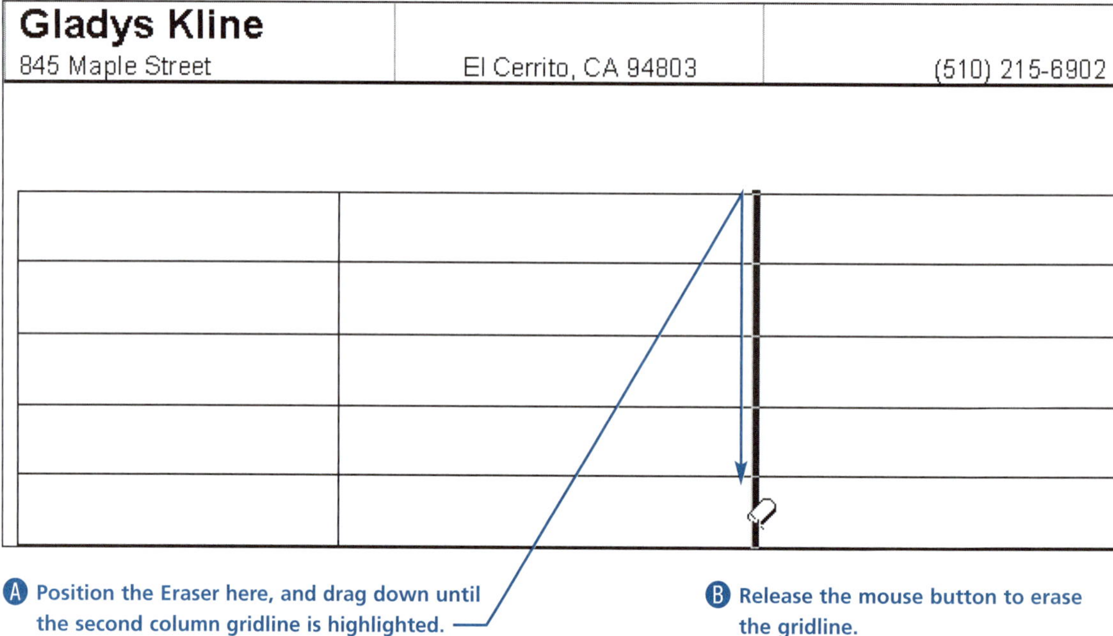

Ⓐ Position the Eraser here, and drag down until the second column gridline is highlighted.

Ⓑ Release the mouse button to erase the gridline.

You should now have a five-row by two-column table. At this point, the row heights may be inconsistent, and the column widths will be unequal.

9. Click the Eraser button to turn off the eraser.

Sizing Rows and Columns

Word 2002 provides a variety of techniques for sizing rows and columns. Many of these techniques were made available in Word 2000; others were available in previous versions of Word.

Distributing Rows and Columns

The Distribute Rows Evenly and Distribute Columns Evenly buttons on the Tables and Borders toolbar let you allocate the space in a table equally among the rows and columns. For example, if a table is six inches wide and has three columns, then the Distribute Columns Evenly command would adjust the width of each column to two inches. You can also issue these commands by choosing Table→AutoFit from the menu bar and choosing the desired command.

Hands-On 7.6 Distribute the Space Evenly

1. Make sure the insertion point is somewhere within the large table.
2. Click the Distribute Columns Evenly button on the Tables and Borders toolbar.
   Both columns should now be the same width.
3. Click the Distribute Rows Evenly button to make all rows the same height.
4. Click in the first cell, and type **OBJECTIVE:**.
5. Tap the TAB key, and type the text shown below in the second table cell.

OBJECTIVE:	To obtain an Administrative Assistant position where I can apply my computer skills and extensive work experience.

Adjusting Row Heights and Column Widths by Dragging

FROM THE KEYBOARD

Press ALT while dragging to display column measurements on the ruler.

The adjust pointer appears whenever you position the mouse pointer on a row or column gridline. You can adjust column widths and row heights by dragging the gridline when the pointer appears. When you drag a column gridline, the width of the column to the left of the gridline is adjusted. When you drag a row gridline, the height of the row above the gridline is adjusted.

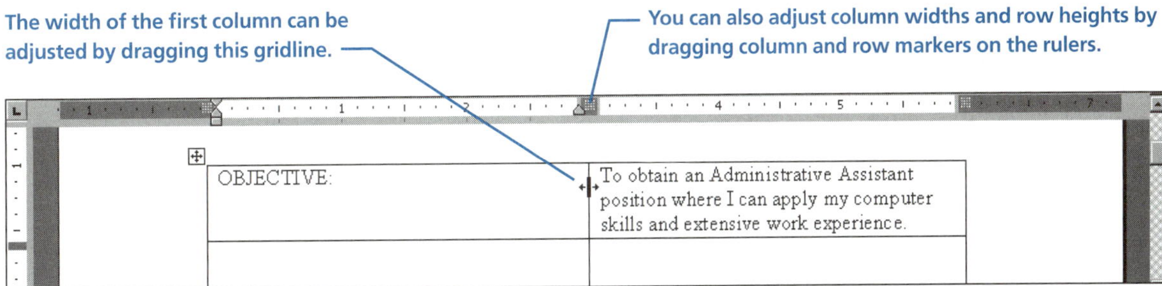

Hands-On 7.7 Adjust Column Widths

1. Position the mouse pointer on the column gridline as shown in the preceding illustration, and drag to the left and right.
   Both column widths will change as you drag. When you adjust the width of a column, the width of the column or columns to the right also changes.
2. Follow these steps to adjust the column widths by using the column marker on the ruler.

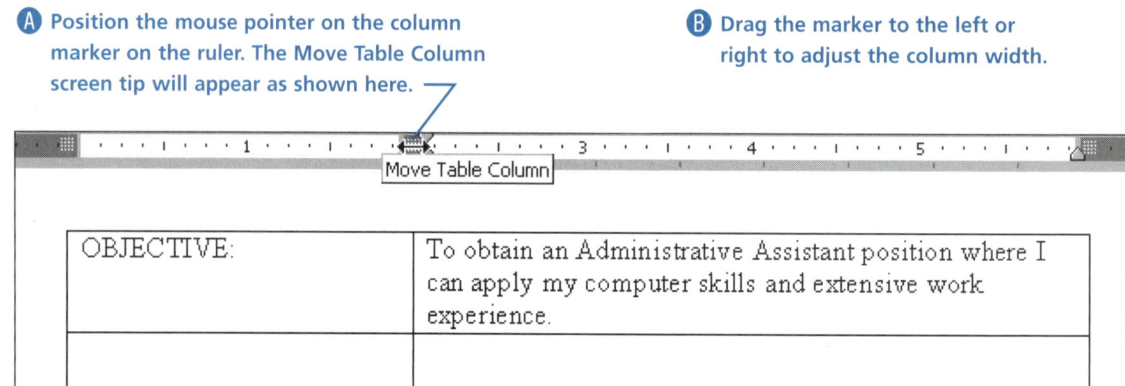

3. Adjust the column widths using either technique until the paragraph in the second cell occupies just two lines.
4. Save the changes to your resume, and continue with the next topic.

AutoFit Options

You can easily AutoFit a column to fit the widest entry in the column by double-clicking a column gridline. For example, the widest entry (and only entry) in the first column of your table is the word OBJECTIVE:. If you double-click the gridline between the columns, then the column width will be reduced to fit the OBJECTIVE: heading. You can also use this technique to AutoFit row heights. However, AutoFit has limitations, especially when table cells have paragraphs that wrap or when there are a large number of columns. AutoFit works best for adjusting column widths when cells have single-line entries.

AutoFit Options on the Table Menu

There are three AutoFit options available on the Table→AutoFit menu. You can use these options to AutoFit entire tables. The following table describes these options.

AutoFit Option	Description
AutoFit to Contents	AutoFits the widths of all table columns.
AutoFit to Window	Automatically resizes a table to fit within the text area (area between the margins). This feature is useful when tables are used on Web pages. The table size will automatically adjust to fit within the Web browser window.
Fixed Column Width	Sets each column to a fixed width using the current column widths.

Hands-On 7.8 AutoFit Columns and Add Data

AutoFit Columns

1. Follow these steps to AutoFit the first column.

Ⓐ Position the mouse pointer on this gridline, and double-click when the adjust pointer appears. The column width will narrow, as shown here.

Ⓑ Notice that the overall table width has been reduced. The table no longer fills the space between the margins.

OBJECTIVE:	To obtain an Administrative Assistant position where I can apply my computer skills and extensive work experience.

2. Choose Table→AutoFit→AutoFit To Contents from the menu bar.
Word will AutoFit the first column and expand the second column to the right margin. This command always expands or contracts the table to occupy the space between the margins.

Add Data

3. Click in the cell below the heading OBJECTIVE:, and type **EXPERIENCE:**. Make sure you type in all caps, and include the colon after the word.
The column will automatically widen to accommodate the heading. Columns widen automatically when a single word is entered that is wider than the column.

4. Click in the cell below the heading EXPERIENCE:, and type **March 1995-Present**.
The text will wrap within the narrow column because it is composed of several words.

(Continued on the next page)

5. Now follow these guidelines to enter the data shown below into the table.
    - Type the text using all caps and bullets where necessary.
    - Tap ENTER after the last bulleted paragraph in each list, and turn off bullets. This will insert blank lines between the table rows. Also, use ENTER to insert a hard return after the large paragraph in the first row. This will create a blank line between the first and second table rows.
    - Let word automatically wrap any lines that appear wrapped in the example below. The first column will automatically widen as you type text in certain cells.

OBJECTIVE:	To obtain an Administrative Assistant position where I can apply my computer skills and extensive work experience.
EXPERIENCE:	
March 1995—Present	ADMINISTRATIVE ASSISTANT FOR DIRECTOR OF MARKETING, Renquist Communications, Fulton, CA • Compose letters, memorandums, and other business correspondence. • Maintain the Director of Marketing's schedule. • Manage multiple projects assigned by the Director of Marketing.
January 1992—February 1995	WORD PROCESSING SPECIALIST, Smart Paging Systems, Berkeley, CA • Composed documents as required by supervisor, using Microsoft Word for Windows • Used Microsoft Excel to create worksheets
COMPUTER SKILLS:	Word 2002, Excel 2002, PowerPoint 2002, Outlook 2002, Windows XP, and Adobe Acrobat.

Table Properties

The Table→Table Properties command displays the Table Properties dialog box. The Table Properties dialog box lets you set various properties for tables, columns, rows, and cells. For example, you can adjust the position of an entire table horizontally on the page. You can also use table properties to specify precise settings for column widths and row heights.

Column Properties

The Column tab of the Table Properties dialog box lets you specify preferred column widths. For example, you can set the width of a column to a specific number of inches or a specified percentage of the total table width.

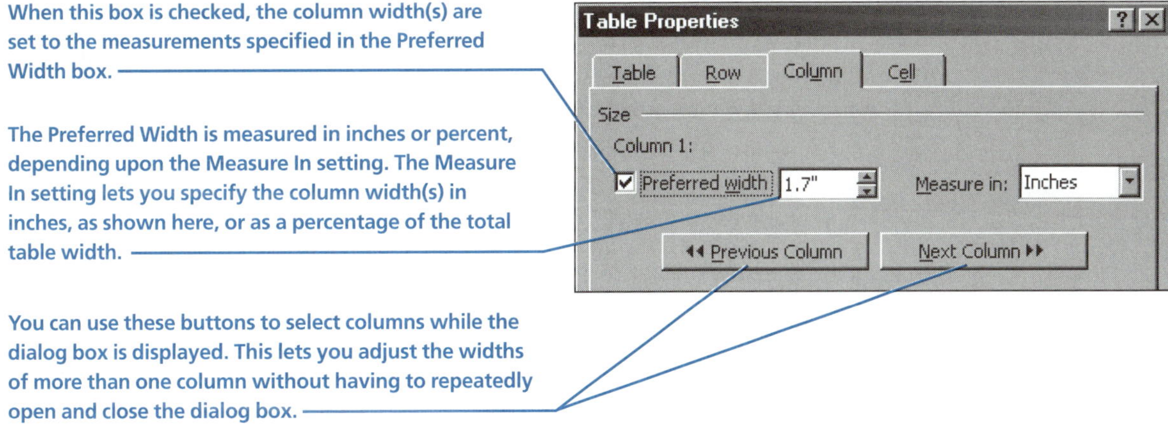

Row Properties

The Row tab of the Table Properties dialog box lets you specify row heights and other row options.

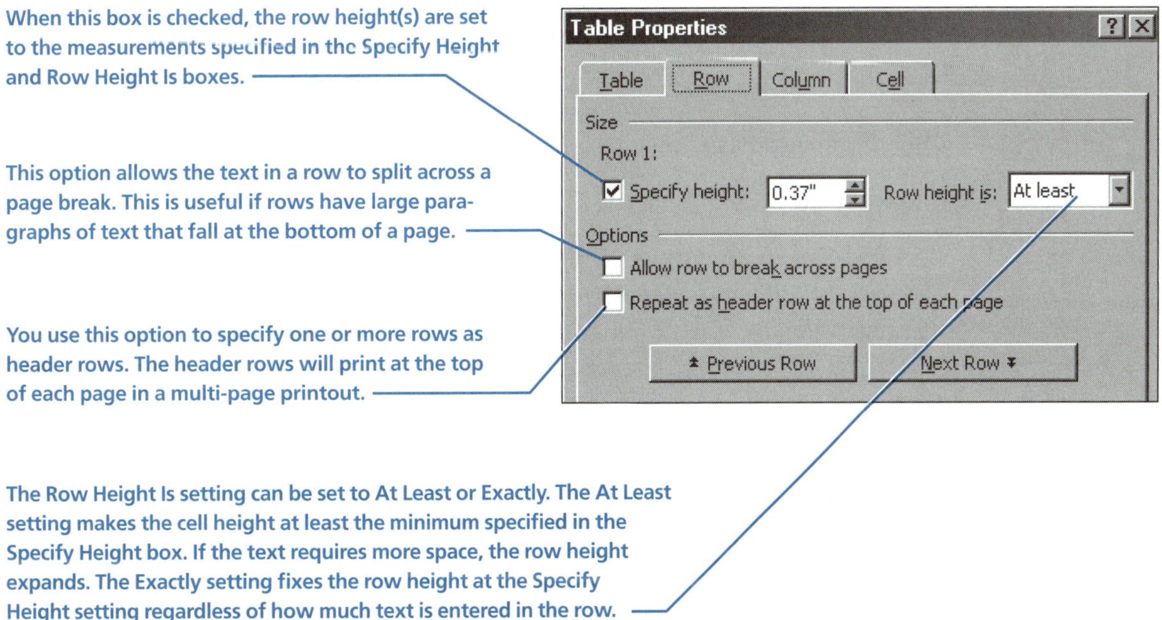

Hands-On 7.9 Adjust Column Widths and Row Heights

Set the Column Width

1. Click in the cell with the EXPERIENCE heading.
2. Choose Table→Table Properties from the menu bar.
3. Click the Column tab.
4. Click the Preferred Width check box, make sure the Measure In setting is set to inches.
5. Set the Preferred width to **1.7″** as shown to the right, and click OK.
   You probably won't see much of a change in the column width. However, this setting will ensure that the column is just wide enough to display the March 1995–Present heading without it wrapping.

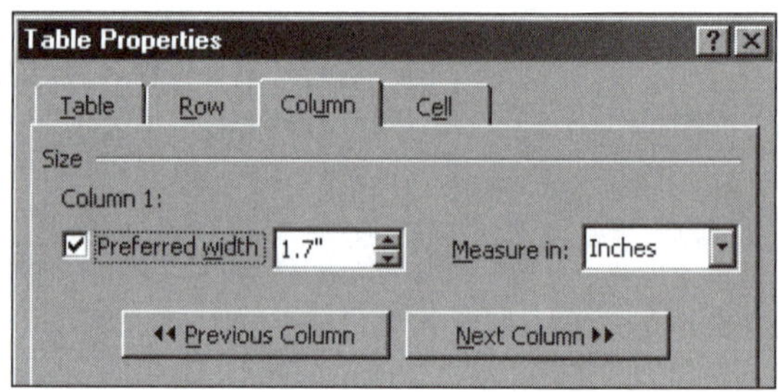

Adjust the Height of One Row

6. Make sure the insertion point is in the EXPERIENCE cell, and choose Table→Table Properties.
7. Click the Row tab.
   Notice that the Specify Height box is checked and the height is set to an At Least measurement in inches. When you first create a table, the Specify Height check box is unchecked for all rows in the table. This allows the row height to expand and contract depending upon the amount of text entered in the rows. The row heights in your table were changed to the At Least setting when you used the Distribute Rows Evenly command in Hands-On Exercise 7.6.
8. Uncheck the box, and click OK.
   The row should now be just high enough to display the EXPERIENCE heading.

Adjust the Heights of All Rows

9. Choose Table→Select Table to select the entire table.
10. Choose Table→Table Properties from the menu bar.
11. Click the Specify Height check box once or twice until it is unchecked, and click OK.
    The heights of all rows will now automatically adjust to fit the text within the rows. However, some of your rows will have a blank line at the bottom because you inserted hard carriage returns in the previous exercise. You can always adjust all row heights and column widths in a table by first selecting the entire table.
12. Save the changes to your resume, and continue with the next topic.

Inserting and Deleting Rows and Columns

You can insert new rows and columns after a table has been created. Word 2002's Table menu contains commands that let you insert rows above or below existing rows, and new columns to the right or left of existing columns. If you wish to insert more than one row or column, then you must first select the same number of rows or columns that you wish to insert. The following Quick Reference table describes techniques for inserting rows and columns.

QUICK REFERENCE: INSERTING AND DELETING ROWS AND COLUMNS

Task	Procedure
Insert rows.	■ Click in the desired row, or select the same number of rows that you wish to insert. ■ Choose Table→Insert→Rows Above or Table→Insert→Rows Below.
Insert columns.	■ Click in the desired column, or select the same number of columns that you wish to insert. ■ Choose Table→Insert→Columns to the Left or Table→Insert→Columns to the Right.
Delete rows or columns.	■ Select the desired rows or columns. ■ Choose Table→Delete→Rows or Table→Delete→Columns.

Hands-On 7.10 Insert and Delete Rows, and Add Text

1. Click anywhere in the last table row.
2. Choose Table→Insert→Rows Above to insert a row above the row with the insertion point.
3. Select the new row and the last row by dragging the mouse pointer in the left margin.
   The last two rows should be selected.
4. Choose Table→Insert→Rows Below to add two new rows to the end of the table.

(Continued on the next page)

5. Enter the text shown below into the new table rows. Notice that you are entering text in the row above the row with the COMPUTER SKILLS heading and in the two new rows below that row. Also, make sure you use ENTER to add hard returns and a blank line to the end of each bulleted list. The top portion of the table is not shown in this illustration.

January 1991— December 1992	STUDENT ASSISTANT, Contra Costa College, Pinole, CA • Assisted students with questions regarding financial aid. • Answered incoming telephone calls, filled out forms, and mailed literature.
COMPUTER SKILLS:	Word 2002, Excel 2002, PowerPoint 2002, Outlook 2002, Windows XP, and Adobe Acrobat.
EDUCATION:	Certificate of Completion, 2001, Bay Area R.O.P., Hayward, CA • Received extensive training in Microsoft Office applications, office procedures, and keyboarding.
	A. S. Business Administration, Contra Costa College, 1992, Pinole, CA • Worked as a student intern for the Vice President of Sales at Chevron Corporation. • Extra-curricular activities included participation in student body government, athletics, and tutoring of disadvantaged youths.

6. Save the changes to your resume, and continue with the next topic.

Moving and Copying Text, Rows, and Columns

IMPORTANT!

The contents of destination cells are erased when you move or copy to those cells.

You can move or copy text from a source cell to a destination cell with the Cut, Copy, and Paste buttons, or with drag and drop. If you move or copy a block of cells, then the cells are pasted as a block when the move or copy is completed. The moved or copied block will overwrite any text or graphics in the destination cells.

You can also move and copy entire rows and columns. To do this, simply select the rows or columns, and then use Cut, Copy, and Paste, or drag and drop. Word will restructure the table to accommodate the moved or copied rows or columns.

Hands-On 7.11 Move Text and a Row

In this exercise, you will use drag and drop to move text and a row. Use Undo if you make a mistake at any point in this exercise.

1. Follow these steps to move the text from the last cell to the cell above.

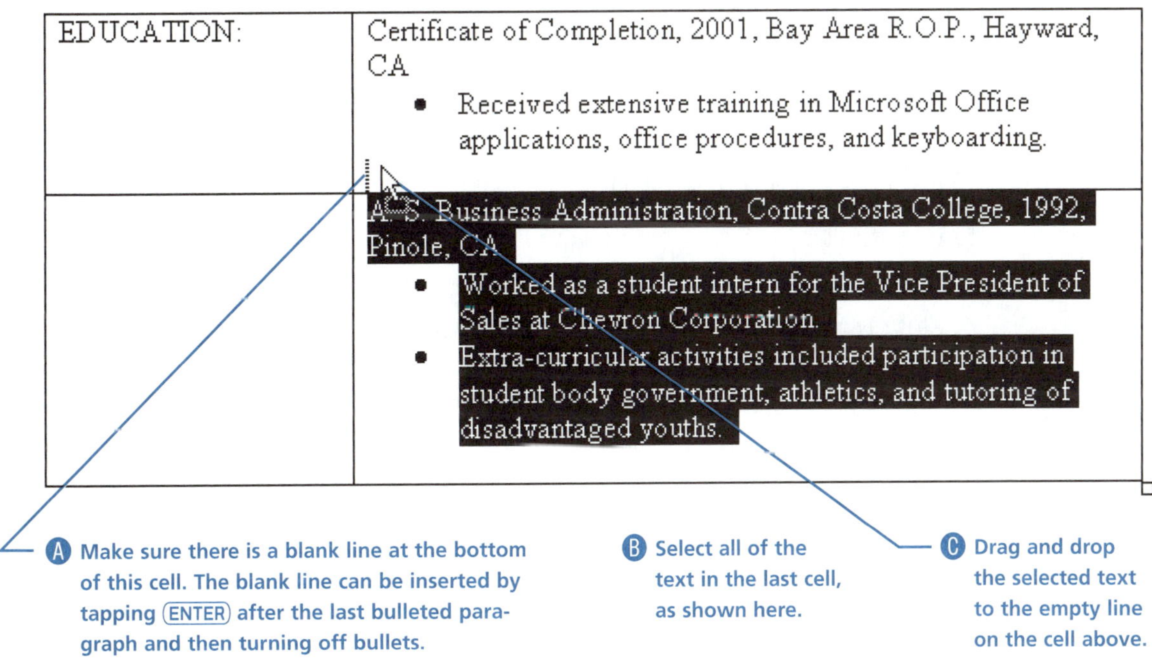

A Make sure there is a blank line at the bottom of this cell. The blank line can be inserted by tapping (ENTER) after the last bulleted paragraph and then turning off bullets.

B Select all of the text in the last cell, as shown here.

C Drag and drop the selected text to the empty line on the cell above.

You should now have an empty row at the bottom of the table.

2. Click anywhere in the empty row, and choose Table→Delete→Rows to remove the row.
In a properly structured chronological resume, the education section should be above the skills section. In the next step, you will restructure the resume with drag and drop.

(Continued on the next page)

3. Follow these steps to move the education section above the computer skills section.

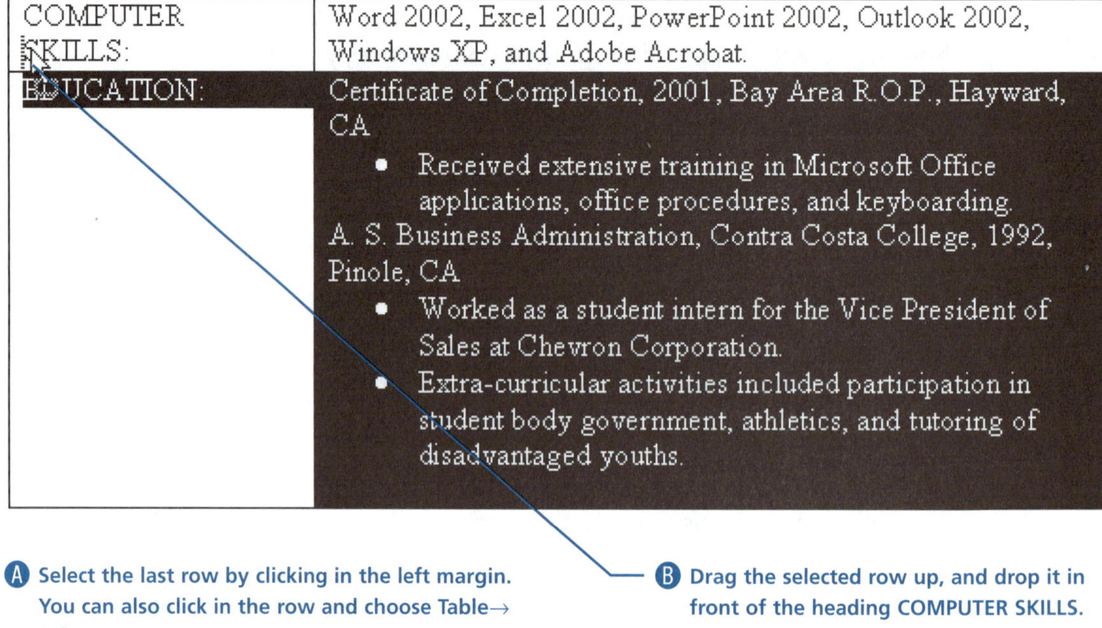
COMPUTER SKILLS:	Word 2002, Excel 2002, PowerPoint 2002, Outlook 2002, Windows XP, and Adobe Acrobat.
EDUCATION:	Certificate of Completion, 2001, Bay Area R.O.P., Hayward, CA • Received extensive training in Microsoft Office applications, office procedures, and keyboarding. A. S. Business Administration, Contra Costa College, 1992, Pinole, CA • Worked as a student intern for the Vice President of Sales at Chevron Corporation. • Extra-curricular activities included participation in student body government, athletics, and tutoring of disadvantaged youths.

A **Select the last row by clicking in the left margin. You can also click in the row and choose Table→Select→Rows.**

B **Drag the selected row up, and drop it in front of the heading COMPUTER SKILLS. The rows should now be interchanged.**

4. Now select the entire table, and remove all borders. Do not remove the border from the single row table at the top of the page.

5. Use Print Preview to examine your completed resume.
   At this point, your resume should match the one shown in the case study at the start of the lesson.

6. Close Print Preview, save the changes to your resume, and then close the document.

Concepts Review

True/False Questions

1.	A chronological resume emphasizes skills and education.	TRUE	FALSE
2.	The Insert Tables button inserts tables with unequal column widths.	TRUE	FALSE
3.	Table gridlines are printed when the document is printed.	TRUE	FALSE
4.	Table row heights are fixed to an exact height when a table is first inserted.	TRUE	FALSE
5.	A new row is added to the bottom of a table whenever the TAB key is tapped.	TRUE	FALSE
6.	Tables can be drawn using the Draw button on the Tables and Borders toolbar.	TRUE	FALSE
7.	When you double-click a column gridline, the column to the right of the gridline is AutoFit.	TRUE	FALSE
8.	Rows can be inserted above or below the row with the insertion point.	TRUE	FALSE

Multiple-Choice Questions

1. Which statement most accurately describes the way the row height functions in a new table?
   a. The row height automatically increases as text is typed.
   b. The row height is fixed at 12 point.
   c. The row height depends upon the number of columns in the table.
   d. None of the above

2. Where does the insertion point move to when it is in a table and SHIFT+TAB is used?
   a. Back one cell
   b. Forward one cell
   c. Above the table
   d. Below the table

3. Which keystroke adds a row to a table when the insertion point is in the last table cell?
   a. TAB
   b. SHIFT+TAB
   c. ENTER
   d. CTRL+ENTER

4. How many rows should be selected if you want to insert two rows?
   a. 1
   b. 2
   c. 3
   d. 0

Skill Builder 7.1 Create and Format a Table

In this exercise, you will create the table shown below. The amount of space allocated to the last column will be maximized. The space allocated to the first three columns will be minimized.

1. Start a new document, and use the Insert Table button to insert a table with seven rows and four columns.
2. Enter the data shown in the table below.
   At this point, don't be concerned with the alignment, text wrapping, or formats.
3. Select the entire table, and choose Format→Paragraph from the menu bar.
4. Set the Spacing Before to **6**, and click OK.
   This will create extra white space above each paragraph.
5. Select the first row, and set the Font to Arial 11 Bold.
6. Select the second column by clicking just above the top border, and center-align the text.
7. Select the third column and right-align the text.
8. Use the Table→AutoFit→AutoFit to Contents command to AutoFit the table.
   Examine the first column; the phrase Oil Pump may be wrapping within the cell.
9. Double-click the border between the first and second columns to AutoFit the first column.
   All text entries should now occupy just one line within the column.
10. If necessary, use the Tables and Borders button to display the Tables and Borders toolbar.
11. Select the first row, and use the Shading Color button on the Tables and Borders toolbar to apply a gray shade or color of your choice to the row.
12. Save the document as **`Skill Builder 7.1`**, and then close the document.

Item	Quantity	Cost	Description
Oil Pump	20	$78.20	Lubricates the engine by pumping motor oil.
Oil Filter	20	4.95	Cleans the oil as it circulates through the engine.
Battery	10	45.00	Provides electric current to start the engine.
Starter	10	150.00	Receives energy from the battery, and turns the crankshaft to start the engine.
Muffler	30	79.00	Muffles the sound produced by the engine.
Radiator	5	230.00	Holds and cools the antifreeze.

Skill Builder 7.2 Restructure a Table

In this exercise, you will open a document on your exercise diskette that contains a table. You will format the table, and you will use drag and drop to arrange the rows in alphabetical order.

1. Open the document named Skill Builder 7.2.
2. If necessary, use the Table→Show Gridlines command to turn on gridlines.
3. Select the fourth row (the row that begins with Allan).
   The Allan row should be the first row in alphabetical order.
4. Drag the row up and drop it in front of/above the Weinstein row.
5. Continue arranging the rows until they are in alphabetical order, as shown in the table on the following page.
   In the next few steps, you will reorder the columns.
6. Select the third column (the column labeled Q1) by clicking the top of the column.
   This column should be the second column.
7. Drag the column to the left, and drop it in front of the Q4 column.
8. Continue arranging the columns until they are in the order Q1, Q2, Q3, and Q4.
9. Select Columns 2–5, and right-align the text.
10. Select the entire table, and set the paragraph spacing before to **6**.
11. Use the Tables and Borders toolbar to choose a single-line style with a 1.5-point weight.
12. Apply the 1.5-point weight single line to the Outside Border.
13. Select only the first row, and use the Bottom Border button to apply the 1.5-point single line to the bottom border of the row.
14. Apply a 10% gray shade to the first row.

(Continued on the next page)

15. Format the text in the first row as Arial 12 Bold.

16. Hide the table gridlines, and the table should match the example below.

17. Save the changes to the document, and then close the document.

Sales Rep	Q1	Q2	Q3	Q4
Allan	3,000	5,000	6,000	9,000
Bolson	7,000	1,000	6,000	2,000
Colden	4,000	4,000	8,000	2,000
Davis	6,000	2,000	4,000	7,000
Johnson	5,000	3,000	2,000	5,000
Oliver	1,000	7,000	2,000	3,000
Smith	2,000	6,000	4,000	6,000
Weinstein	1,000	8,000	2,220	2,200
Ziegfried	2,000	5,000	1,000	9,000

Skill Builder 7.3 Use a Table in a Flyer

1. Follow these guidelines to create the document shown below.
   - Center the page vertically.
   - Place the bulleted lists in a one-row by two-column table. Remove all borders from the table.
   - Use Times New Roman and Arial fonts. Use your best judgment when determining font sizes, alignment, and other settings.
2. Save the completed document as **`Skill Builder 7.3`**, and then close the document.

ARGS

Anne's Reliable Gift Service

My goal is to provide a wide variety of quality giftware, jewelry, home décor, and electronic items at reasonable prices.

We Have

Gifts From

Around The World

• Shop at home catalog • Fund raising program available for churches, schools, and groups • The latest products	• Income opportunities • Gift, premium, and incentive program for businesses and offices • Volume discounts

For more information or to place an order call…

(510) 236-1864

Satisfaction Guaranteed!

50% deposit required on all orders

Skill Builder 7.4 Create a Sign-In Sheet

In this Skill Builder, you will use a table to create a sign-in sheet.

1. Start a new document, and set the top, bottom, left, and right margins to **.75″**.
2. Center align the title **Sign-in Sheet** at the top of the document, and tap (ENTER) twice to create two blank lines below the title.
3. Format the Sign-in Sheet title with an Arial 20 Bold font.
4. Position the insertion point on the second blank line below the title, and set the alignment to left.
5. Insert a table with 17 rows and 4 columns.
6. Use the Table Properties box to specify precise column widths as follows:

   Column 1—**1.45″**

   Column 2—**2.25″**

   Column 3—**1.3″**

   Column 4—**2.15″**
7. Use the Table Properties box to set the height of Row 1 to exactly **0.3″**.
8. Enter the headings **Name**, **Address**, **Phone**, and **Comments** in the cells in Row 1, and format the headings as Arial 12 Bold.
9. Use the Align Bottom Left option on the Tables and Borders toolbar to align the headings in Row 1 with the bottom left edges of the cells.
10. Set the height of all other rows to exactly **0.5″**.
11. Apply a 2¼-point border to the outside of the table and to the bottom of Row 1. Leave all other borders as they are.
12. Apply a 10% gray shade to the cells in Row 1.
13. Center the page vertically.
14. Save the document as **Skill Builder 7.4**, and then close the document.

Skill Builder 7.5 Create Your Own Scannable Functional Resume

In this exercise, you will create a functional resume for yourself. Functional resumes emphasize skills, accomplishments, and achievements. You will format the resume so that it can easily be scanned into an electronic database. You may want to review the sample resumes at the start of this lesson before continuing.

1. Start a new document, and insert a table with one row and two columns.
2. Click in the right cell and use the Align Bottom Right option on the Tables and Borders toolbar to set the alignment to bottom right.
3. Use the Tables and Borders toolbar to remove all borders.
4. Apply a single ¾-point line to the bottom edge of both cells.
5. Enter your name, address, email address, and telephone number as shown below.

Your Name Your Street Address Your City, State Zip	Your Email Address Your Telephone Number

6. Position the insertion point below the table, and tap ENTER four times.
7. Insert a table with five rows and two columns.
8. Remove all lines from the table. Make sure table gridlines are turned on.
9. Use the Table Properties dialog box to set the width of the first column to **1.5"** and the width of the second column to **4.6"**.
10. Enter your own personal information using the resume on the following page as an example. As you can see, this functional resume emphasizes skills and education. You should place your work experience before education if you have extensive work experience. Also notice that the resume lacks any type of character formatting. This is because it is designed for scanning into an electronic database. You should use keywords in the Office Skills section that are relevant to your skills and that will give your resume a high probability of being chosen by a potential employer's OCR software.

(Continued on the next page)

11. When you have finished, save your resume using a descriptive name such as Functional - Scannable Resume, and then close the document. You may want to use a separate Job Search diskette for all of your resumes, cover letters, and job search correspondence. Make sure you have a backup copy of your resume on another diskette, or in some other safe location.

Your Name
Your Street Address
Your City, State Zip

Your Email Address
Your Telephone Number

OBJECTIVE:	State your objective here
SKILLS:	Computer Skills Windows 95, Word, Excel, Access, PowerPoint Office Skills Bookkeeping, telephone reception, filing Personal Qualities Flexible, team player, creative, excellent communication skills
EDUCATION:	Degree, graduation date, school, location List any honors, accomplishments, or extra curricular activities that are relevant.
EXPERIENCE:	List job responsibilities, skills acquired, company, and date of employment.
OTHER:	You may include a community service section or some other section that details information relevant to the job for which you are applying.

Skill Builder 7.6 Enhance Your Functional Resume

In this exercise, you will enhance the appearance of the resume that you created in the previous exercise. The enhanced resume will be used as a functional resume but will not be designed specifically for scanning. However, you do not want to "go overboard" on formatting in case a potential employer unexpectedly scans the resume.

1. Open the resume that you created in the previous exercise.
2. Use File→Save As to save the resume with a new name, such as Functional Resume.
3. Enhance the appearance of the resume by formatting your name, the headings, and any other elements that you feel are necessary. You can use larger point sizes, bold, and other typefaces.
4. Save the changes to the resume, and then close it.

Skills Builder 7.7 Create Your Own Chronological Resume

In this exercise, you will open the resume that you developed in the Hands-On exercises. You will personalize the resume for your own use. This resume uses a chronological style that emphasizes paid work experience.

1. Open the Hands-On Lesson 7 document.
2. Change all information in the resume to your own personal information. Try to maintain the formatting by selecting a phrase or word, and typing a new phrase or word in its place.
3. Use the File→Save As command to save the completed resume to your job search diskette with a descriptive name, such as Chronological Resume.
4. Leave the resume open; you will continue to use it.

Skill Builder 7.8 Create Your Own Scannable Chronological Resume

In this exercise, you will convert the chronological resume into a scannable chronological resume.

1. Use the File→Save As command to save the resume to your job search diskette with a descriptive name, such as Chronological - Scannable Resume.
2. Select the entire document, and remove all text formats by setting the font to Times New Roman 12. You will need to turn off bold and any other text formats that may be present. The paragraphs should remain properly aligned because you used tables, indenting, bullets, and other alignment features.
3. Browse through the resume and try to insert key words in any locations where they may be important. For example, use words such as Word and Excel in a job description if you used those software applications as part of your job.
4. Save the changes, and then close the document.

Assessments

Assessment 7.1 Create and Format a Table

1. Start a new document, and follow these guidelines to create the table shown below.
   - Insert a table with six rows and five columns.
   - Set the width of the first four columns to one inch and set the width of the last column to two inches.
   - Use the paragraph Spacing Before option to add six points of spacing before each paragraph.
   - Center align the text in the second and third columns and right align the text in the fourth column.
   - Remove all borders from the table, and then apply a 1½-point border to the outside of the table and to the bottom border of Row 1.
   - Apply a 10% gray shade to Row 1, and format the text in Row 1 with bold.
2. Save the document as **`Assessment 7.1`**, and then close it.

Item	**Status**	**Quantity**	**Value**	**Customer Name**
A423	S	9	$100.90	Harold Johnson
A321	S	23	$45.87	Alexander Robertson
S345	I	7	$43.23	Bruce Pique
E567	H	6	$78.90	Al Chess
S230	I	5	$23.45	Roberta Brown

Assessment 7.2 Use a Table in a Business Letter

1. Follow these guidelines to create the document shown on the following page.
   - Start a new document, and type today's date on the first line of the document.
   - Create the block style letter shown on the following page.
   - Place the company, Word version, and contact person information in a six-row by three-column table. Leave the column widths set to the default widths that are used when the table is first inserted.
   - Remove all borders from the table.
   - Center-align the text in the middle column, and right-align the text in the third column.
   - Apply bold formatting as shown.
   - Center the completed letter vertically using the Vertical alignment option on the Page Setup dialog box.
2. Save the document as **`Assessment 7.2`**, and then close it.

(Continued on the next page)

Today's Date

Ms. Wanda Sample
HiTech Temps
1744 Lexington Avenue, Suite B
El Cerrito, CA 94530

Dear Ms. Sample:

Thank you for taking the time to speak with me yesterday. Per your request, I am providing you with the Word version and contact at each company where I have used Word.

Company	**Word Version**	**Contact**
BPI	6.0 for DOS	Dan Johnson
Exxon	6.0 for DOS	Maria Velasquez
City of Oakland	Word 97	Mary Smith
Centron	Word 2000	Ralph Watson
Constructo	Word 2002	Ben Johnson

Ms. Sample, please contact me as soon as you have had the opportunity to review my application and check my references. I am eager to begin working with HiTech Temps and applying my excellent computer skills.

Sincerely yours,

Donna Benson

Critical Thinking

Critical Thinking 7.1 On Your Own

Christy Chan is the Human Resources Manager for Vectron, Inc. Christy requires all managers at Vectron to give new employees 30-, 60-, and 90-day reviews. In order to achieve consistency and help eliminate discrimination in the review process, Christy has asked you to set up a standardized form for evaluating employees. Christy has given you the following evaluation criteria and rating system.

Evaluation Criteria—Tardiness, job knowledge, communication skills, problem solving ability, team-oriented

Rating system—Poor, fair, good, excellent

Set up a Word document that can be used as an evaluation form. Include a table with the evaluation criteria and rating system. The user of the form should be able to check the appropriate box in the table to specify the evaluation criteria and rating. Use paragraph spacing before to increase the height of the table rows. Apply borders and shading as you deem appropriate. Also, include a title at the top of the form and a place where the employee's name, the date, and the type of review (30-, 60-, or 90-day) can be entered. Save your completed document as **Critical Thinking 7.1**. Close the document when you have finished.

Critical Thinking 7.2 On Your Own

After using the employee evaluation form for some time, Christy Chan has decided to make several changes to it. Open the Critical Thinking 7.1 document, and save it as **Critical Thinking 7.2**. Add the following two new evaluation criteria to the table: "Self-starter" and "Computer skills." Add a rating of "Very good" to the table. You may need to insert a column or row to accomplish this. Adjust all column widths as necessary to allow the table to fit within the margins. Rearrange the rows until they are in alphabetical order. Save the completed document, and then close it.

Critical Thinking 7.3 Web Research

Alexia Williams is the Information Systems Manager of Bellmont Health Care. Bellmont is a rapidly growing health care concern with over one billion dollars in FY 2002 revenues. Alexia has mandated that beginning in FY 2003 at least 50% of Bellmont's technology purchases will be made using online purchasing systems. Alexia believes this strategy will reduce costs and increase the efficiency of the procurement process. As a student intern working under the direction of Alexia, you have been assigned the task of locating five vendors that allow personal computers and accessories to be purchased online. Alexia has asked you to construct a Word document with a table that includes the vendor's name, Web site URL, and their customer service telephone number. Use Internet Explorer and a search engine of your choice to conduct your research. Record your results in a Word table, and save the document as **Critical Thinking 7.3**.

Critical Thinking 7.4 With a Group

You and your classmate have decided to prepare a customer survey form to be distributed by Health-e-Meals.com's drivers. Normally, you encourage customers to fill out survey forms online, but thus far the response has been small. For this reason, you want the drivers to hand out the forms when they deliver meals. Work with your classmate to determine the eight most important survey questions you can ask of your customers. The questions should be oriented towards helping you improve your product and service.

Prepare a Word document that includes a table with the customer survey questions and Yes and No columns so that customers can simply check yes or no to each question. The survey form should also include a location for the customer's name, mailing address, and telephone number. Incorporate the name, address, and telephone information into a table. Use the right column of the table to create lines where the customers can write their name, address, and telephone number. You can accomplish this by removing all lines from the table except for the horizontal lines where the name, address, and telephone number are to be placed. Save the completed document as **`Critical Thinking 7.4`**.

Index

Check out: File New

If word doesn't decide the margin automatically, so must delete

(can also store ~~in~~ A DRIVE in a floppy)

Folder in C DRIVE

(use up one level)

C:\

↳ STUDENT

↳ WORD CLASS file

To Put A TAB in a TABLE, use control TAB